EAST OF THE GABILANS

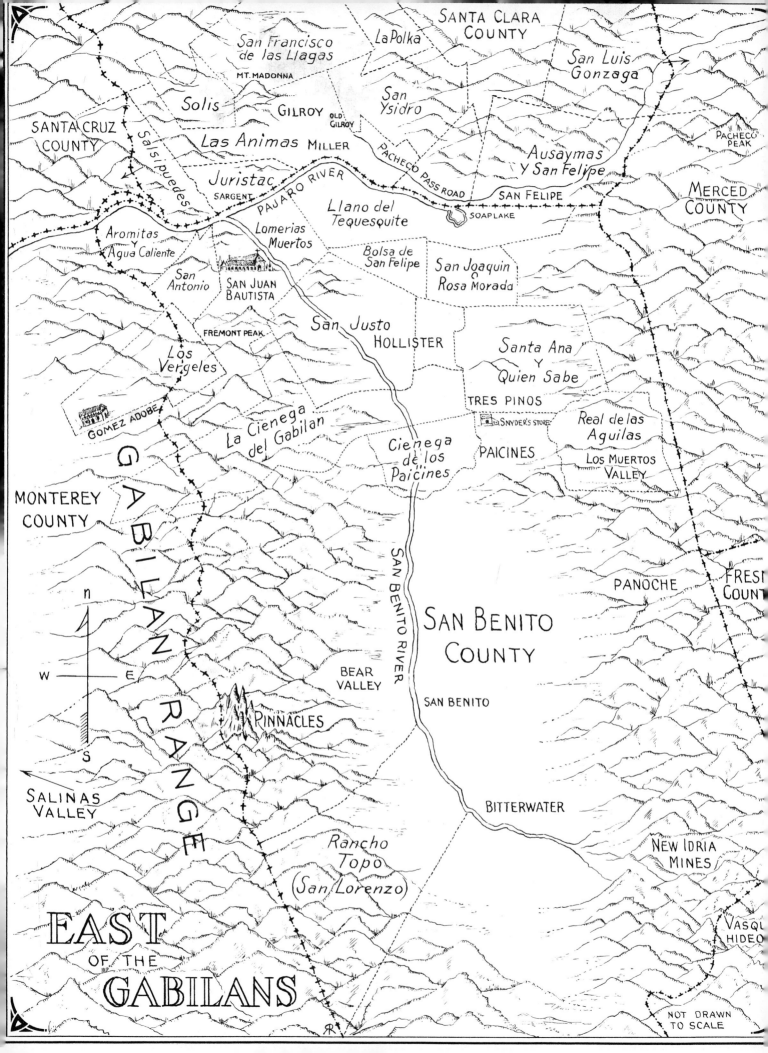

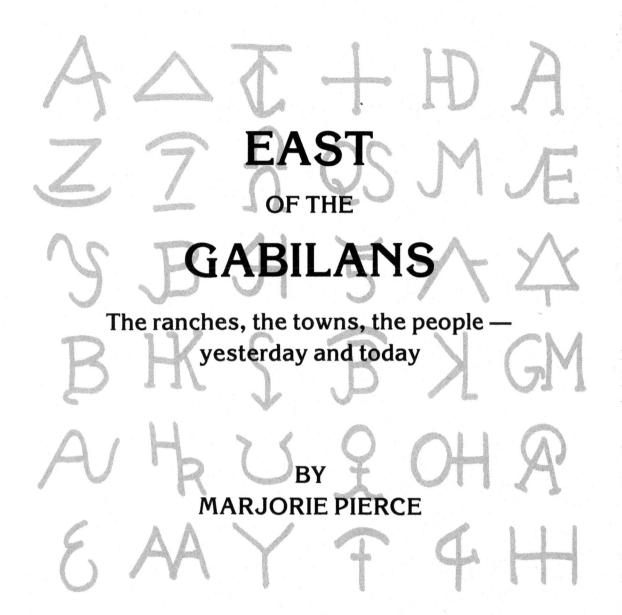

EAST
OF THE
GABILANS

The ranches, the towns, the people —
yesterday and today

BY
MARJORIE PIERCE

FOREWORD AND COVER ART BY BARNABY CONRAD

FRESNO   *Valley Publishers*   1977

Library of Congress No. 76-56566

International Standard Book No. 0-913548-39-1

First Edition

Manufactured in the United States of America

Dedication

For
Bob and Mark,
who were with me
all the way

Acknowledgements

The writing of *East of the Gabilans* has taken me on an arduous but never dull journey. There were countless hours spent in libraries and museums; time spent sifting through old family scrapbooks, diaries and photograph albums.

A special bonus was visiting the ranches and talking to the people: wonderful people, many of whose families have been on the same land for generations. It's been a journey I wouldn't have missed.

To try to name all those who have helped along the way would be an impossibility, but here is a partial list:

Joseph B. Ridder; Carmencita Baker Cardoza; Martin Penn; Dr. Albert Shumate; Mary Prien; Marjorie Flint and her sister, the late Dorothy Flint; Juanita Joseph and the San Benito County Cowbelles; Roberta Hughan; the late Marilyn Fahey; Francis C. Thomas; J. Vincent Gallagher; Aline Ramona Ortega; Kenneth Castro; Ernestine Carpenter; Sally Nickel Mein; Betty and Harry Farrell; Carroll and Martha Hayes; Arch Hayes; Marian O'Connell; Richard Gularte; Frances and Theron Fox; Monsignor Armancio Rodriguez, pastor of Mission San Juan Bautista; Sister Suzanne Wilson, R.S.C.J.; Adele Morrison; Judy Abuhamdeh; and Phil Pereira, Bob Pierce and Fred Matthes who did photography for the book;

Also the *San Jose Mercury-News* for permission to use the photographs which ran with my column, "Socially Yours," and Ralph Rambo for his map of the ranchos.

I want to thank the following organizations for their cooperation in allowing me to use their photographs: San Juan Bautista Historical Society, San Benito Historical Society, Gilroy Museum, the Bancroft Library, and San Juan Historical Publisher.

Marjorie Pierce

Table of Contents

Foreword

"On one side of the river the golden foothill slopes curve up to the strong and rocky Gabilan Mountains..."
—John Steinbeck, *Of Mice and Men*, 1937

If for no other reason, I am delighted that Marjorie Pierce has written this book so that my children, fourth generation Californians, can learn about this segment of their state's fascinating rural history. It is a book that has long needed writing, and it is one that Mrs. Pierce is eminently qualified to write.

Christened Marjorie Elizabeth Upstill at Riverside Mission, she moved with her family to Los Angeles when she was four years old. Her first job was as a movie extra during the depression years.

Subsequently she worked in the offices of 20th Century Fox Studios as a secretary to writers and directors, a reader in the story department, and, finally, in the Production Office at Fox she was classified as an assistant director.

Along the way she also worked in the Spanish Department at Fox and because of her love of the language and all things Spanish, she translated scripts written by such playwrights as Gregorio Martinez Sierra and Jose Lopez Rubio.

In 1945 she took a job in Sao Paolo, Brazil, in a program that the United States government sponsored with with the Brazilian Air Ministry. She taught Gregg shorthand in Portuguese at the Escola Tecnica da Aviacao.

"Never having seen a Portuguese Gregg Shorthand book before, this was an experience," she says, "but somehow ⌐ managed to keep one step ahead of the students."

While in Sao Paolo she met and married Robert Pierce, a businessman; subsequently they returned to the United States and settled down to raise a family in San Jose. The itch to write came back to her and she took a job as a society columnist on the *San Jose Mercury*. Some five years ago she wrote a story about the Castro-Breen adobe in San Juan Bautista and the Breen family who still ranch there. The reader response was so great that she wrote other pieces on the Spanish and Mexican land grants and the ranches that were carved out of them.

Finally so many people clamored for a book on this facet of California history that she gave in—"little knowing the work involved."

Many natives, including this writer, will be eternally grateful that Marjorie Pierce persisted in her great love affair with early California history, and she herself feels the effort has been well worth it.

"Visiting these lovely old ranches with their weathered barns, lichen covered picket fences, oak covered hillsides and open spaces—and most of all, the people—has been a great experience!"

So, come—let us visit the ranches under Marjorie Pierce's sure and loving and knowledgeable guidance!

—Barnaby Conrad

Introduction

A visit to the cattle ranches of today located east of the Gabilan Mountains with a backward look into their history was the theme for a series of columns written for the *San Jose Mercury and News* and was the inspiration for this book.

The "Gabilans" in the title refers to the range of mountains that formed one of the geographic boundaries when Monterey County was divided in 1874. The land east of the Gabilans became the new San Benito County.

In most cases these ranches were carved out of Mexican land grants (only a very few were Spanish) which had in turn been carved out of the San Juan Bautista Mission ranches after the secularization of the missions by Mexico in 1834.

Looking backward still further, the stock for the first missions had been brought up with the first settlers from Northern Mexico by the De Anza party in 1775. As the mission herds grew in size the padres shared them with the new missions. When Mission San Juan Bautista was founded in 1797, for example, the padres received gifts of cattle, horses, sheep and chickens from neighboring Mission San Carlos Borromeo and Mission Santa Clara.

The history of the Mexican longhorn cattle dates back to the year 1521. By the time of the arrival of the Americans in the middle of the last century, they had multiplied to such an extent that they were running wild over most of the state. Cortez had completed his famous conquest of Mexico, and the beef cattle were brought over from Santo Domingo. In 1540, Coronado, in search of the Seven Cities of Cibola, brought the longhorns to Northern Mexico and Arizona, Many were abandoned along the way in Sinaloa.

With the coming of the Americans and the entrance of California into the Union, life changed drastically for the Californians of Mexican descent. The Americans were businessmen. The Californians were a carefree people whose hospitality knew no limits. The traveler was always invited to spend the night and to share his table. Fiestas were given at the drop of a sombrero. A musical people, there were always those who could play the violin, strum the guitar and click the castanets for the *jota,* the *fandango* and the *jarabe.*

In legal matters the spoken word and a shake of the hand was the law. The boundaries of a piece of property might be designated by a willow tree, an arroyo, or maybe a pile of rocks. A handful of grass was thrown into the air and the deal was made. The Californians didn't understand the patents, which were written in an unfamiliar language, and many couldn't afford to wait years to receive the title.

The Mission San Juan Bautista was an important place to the rancheros. Here their children were baptized and married, their elderly buried. On Sundays they would come in their *carretas,* primitive wooden carts with wooden wheels, put together with wooden pegs and pulled by oxen, for mass. They also came for the fiestas in the plaza square, the bull and bear fights, and the barbecues.

By the 1860s and 70s, the Americans had made their impact, and the little mission town of San Juan Bautista was a bustling community. It was a crossroads for travel by stagecoach from the San Joaquin Valley, via the Pacheco Pass, San Jose, Monterey and the New Idria Mines. Travelers from the north and south often stopped over in San Juan. However, the railroads bypassed the town in the 1870s, and cattle and grain buyers no longer came and the once important business town reached a standstill. As someone once put it, the town that might have become a city "like Rip Van Winkle, was locked in perpetual sleep." It is hard to imagine that San Juan Bautista once had 17 bars and four newspapers, that there was a willow tree on the Alameda known as the hanging tree, where men were hung without trial, that the noted bandit Tiburcio Vasquez once had a shoot-out on the main street, that General Fremont was in and out of town with his men during the Mexican War, and that here General Jose Castro plotted two revolutions against the Mexican governors.

Now the tourists come to see the newly restored mission church, with its long colonnade of arches facing the plaza, and its neighbors, the Plaza Hotel, the Castro-Breen Adobe, the stables and the Zanetta House. With the exception of the mission, the Plaza is a part of the California State Parks. The locust trees still grow around the Plaza and a part of El Camino Real can be seen below the church, as can the San Andreas Fault next to the Rodeo Grounds.

For the newcomer or visitor to California the Spanish names are often confusing. "Gabilan" is the name of a hawk, a rather pretty one with bright red feathers which is seen in these mountains. San Benito was the name given to the river that runs through the county by Captain Pedro Fages and party, who camped on its banks in 1772 and, as Padre Crespi wrote in his diary, named it for St. Benedict whose birthday it was. The Indians had beaten a path across the Gabilans which was used by the explorers and became part of El Camino Real, the King's Royal Highway, which extended from Guatemala to Sonoma and was a link between the 21 missions in California.

On a previous trip inland with Gaspar de Portola, Padre Crespi had recorded the naming of the Pajaro River which was to become the northern boundary of San Benito County. In his diary he wrote, "We saw in this place a bird which the heathen had killed and stuffed with straw. To some of our party it looked like a royal eagle. For this reason some of the soldiers called the stream 'Rio del Pajaro' and I added 'La Senora Santa Ana del Rio del Pajaro.' "

Cattle raising and agriculture still dominate San Benito County and southern Santa Clara County. There is a camaraderie and life style among these ranching families that is uniquely their own. They help each other at roundups and brandings, and many times afterwards there is a barbecue. Their children grow up riding horseback, take part in their own Bolado Park Horse Show, go off to Cal Poly to school, and usually return to work on the ranch.

Pertinent Dates
In California History

A brief resume of important dates in California
history leading up to admission as a state in 1850.

1542 JUAN RODRIGUEZ CABRILLO, a Portuguese pilot under orders of Viceroy Mendoza during the reign of Charles V of Spain, sails from Navidad, Mexico, to the port of San Diego, where he goes ashore. He then continues up the coast stopping at Santa Catalina Island, past Point Pinos as far as Point Mendocino.

1579 SIR FRANCIS DRAKE sails up the California coast on the *Golden Hind* to what is presumed to be Drake's Bay north of San Francisco.

1602 SEBASTIAN VIZCAINO, who had sailed the Spanish galleons along this coast from Manila to Acapulco, departs from Acapulco with 200 men, including a cartographer and three Carmelite friars. Vizcaino names all of the places where he stops along the coast such as Monterey for the Conde de Monterey, Rio del Carmelo for the Carmelite fathers, and the Santa Lucia Mountains for the saint whose birthday it was when he first saw them. Many of the places are named for Saint's Days.

1769 DON GASPAR DE PORTOLA, Governor of Lower California, and PADRE JUNIPERO SERRA, Presidente of the Franciscan Missions, are sent on an expedition to Alta California. Padre Serra stays in San Diego to start a settlement while Portola heads north to occupy Monterey. He and his men miss Monterey but Golden Gate is discovered by his scout, JOSE FRANCISCO ORTEGA.

1770 Second expedition of PORTOLA overland and SERRA by sea to establish New Spain in Monterey. Successful this time in finding Monterey, Portola takes possession in name of Charles III.

1770-1772 CAPTAIN PEDRO FAGES, accompanied by PADRE CRESPI, makes exploratory trip inland from Monterey.

1775-1776 JUAN BAUTISTA DE ANZA EXPEDITION. Colonists with livestock and supplies come overland from Sonora, Mexico, by way of Gila River into the Colorado Desert to San Gabriel and then up to Monterey. Opens inland supply route.

1797 MISSION SAN JUAN BAUTISTA established.

1822 SPANISH RULE ENDS — replaced by Mexico.

1833-1834 SECULARIZATION OF MISSIONS. Mexico confiscates Church lands.

1847 END OF MEXICAN WAR with States. ANDRES PICO makes agreement with JOHN C. FREMONT to accept sovereignty of United States.

1848 TREATY OF GUADULUPE Y HIDALGO. Formal transfer of the territory to the United States. The U.S. agrees to honor Mexican land grants.

1850 CALIFORNIA admitted into the Union.

Mission and town of San Juan Bautista. Drawing by Henry Miller, 1853. (Courtesy Bancroft Library)

Mission San Juan Bautista. At this time, it still had the New England style steeple added by Father Rubio in 1865 during modernization of the church. The steeple succumbed to the elements in 1915.

Mission San Juan Buatista after restoration, 1976.

CHAPTER I

Mission San Juan Bautista

The village of San Juan Bautista is a monument to the rich culture of California's Spanish and Mexican heritage and a treasure-trove for those who savor that culture. Fifteenth and largest in the chain of 21 missions built in New Spain by the Franciscan Friars, Mission San Juan Bautista was part of the plan by Spain to colonize the country as a protection against invasion by England, France or Russia, who were making more frequent appearances along the coast, and to Christianize the pagans.

As part of the master plan of Fray Junipero Serra to locate the missions a day's walking distance apart, the padres received permission in 1795 from Mexico City to establish a mission between the San Carlos Borromeo de Carmel and Santa Clara Missions which were separated by a distance of 26 leagues. Ensign Hermangildo Sal and Fray Danti were sent to find a location. They chose a site not far from the San Benito River, called Popeloutchom by the Indians, and raised a cross there. It was not far from the place where Captain Pedro Fages and his party had camped on an inland exploration trip. Father Crespi wrote in his journal that it was March 21, 1771, St. Benedict's Day, and they named the river in honor of this saint.

There was plenty of timber growing nearby, such as willow, poplar and alder trees; the soldiers had told them about the redwood at the Chittenden Pass; there were tules for roofing and there was limestone at one league. Most important to the padres, there were *rancherias* or Indian villages in the area, and for them that was what it was all about—Christianizing the heathens. Overlooking the lush San Juan Valley, where herds of antelope could be seen crossing, the site offered endless possibilities for fruit orchards, for growing grapes for altar wine, for raising grain, and for cattle grazing lands.

On June 24, 1797, in the presence of Padre Presidente Fermin Francisco de Lasuen and Padre Magin de Catala from Mission Santa Clara, accompanied by a guard of soldiers, the dedication of the new mission, named for St. John the Baptist, took place. The ceremonies were described on the title page of the baptismal register of the mission:

First Book of Baptisms of Mission San Juan Bautista, Precursor of Jesus Christ, founded at the expense of the Catholic King of Spain Carlos IV (God keep him), and by order of his Excellent Lord, the Marquis de Branciforte, Viceroy of New Spain on the spot called Popeloutchom by the natives but by our own people from the first discovery, San Benito.

Named as the first missionaries for the new church were Father Joseph Manuel de Martiarena and Father Pedro Adriano Martinez.

With the allotment of the customary one thousand dollars from the Pious Fund, which came from rich Spaniards of Mexico, supplies such as field implements, tools, church goods, and gifts of beads and trinkets for the Indians began to arrive by mule pack, along with skilled workmen from Mexico. Work began immediately, and by the end of the year it was reported that a *capilla* (chapel) fifteen *varas* long and six *varas* wide had been built of adobes. The roof was probably of tules. Cattle, sheep, horses and chickens were sent from neighboring San Carlos Borromeo and Santa Clara Missions which, by this time, had ample. Living quarters for the missionaries were built, as well as a granary, a kitchen, guardhouse, and housing for the soldiers.

The garrison was where the Plaza Hotel was later built on the plaza. Opposite from the church was the *monjerio* where the single women were housed. (The adobe bricks from this building were later used in the construction of the Zanetta house.) The

Mission Bells. One on left bears inscription "Ave Maria Purisima - San Fernando - Ruelas me Fese 1809." Translation: "Hail Mary Most Pure - San Fernando - Ruelas cast me in 1809." San Fernando was the headquarters of the Franciscan Order in Mexico City. The last of the original nine bells, they are hanging in the new bell tower.

single women worked in the shops during the day and could visit their relatives after work. This institution was deemed "an indispensable necessity due to the carnal propensities of the Indians, and as a protection against either white or Indian Libertines." When a young man wanted a wife he would apply to the mission father and tell him the name of his intended. If the girl agreed, plans were made for a wedding in the church, and the couple was assigned a house of their own in the village.

Unaware that they were on what has come to be known as the San Andreas Fault, although severe shocks had done damage to the chapel in 1800, the padres built the present mission on the same site. On December 31, 1812, the blessing of the new church was celebrated by the Very Reverend Father Esteban Tapis, Presidente of Missions, and the Reverend Fathers Felipe Arroyo de la Cuesta and Roman Fernandez Ullibarri, assisted by the missionary fathers of Santa Clara and San Jose.

Father Tapis returned to San Juan later that year after completing his duty as presidente. A man of great intelligence, he had not only learned the Indian dialects but was talented musically. He taught the children to sing the Gregorian chant by use of square musical notes in colors. Some of this music is still on display in the mission museum. At his death in 1825 Father Tapis was buried in the sanctuary by the communion rail.

Probably the most scholarly of the mission priests was Father de la Cuesta who became head of the San Juan Bautista Mission operation in 1808. Whether by whimsy or because of his intellectual bent, he called the Indian children by such names as Plato, Cicero, Alexander and Caesar. He made a record of the Mutsen Indian language.

The new church, considered one of the most beautiful of the missions, was the only mission church with three naves. The walls were four feet thick and one of its most distinctive features was the long arched corridor across the front. The doors off this opened into the monastery rooms. Besides the quarters for the padres, there were rooms for weaving, spinning and crafts. Many prominent visitors were overnight guests here on their way to and from Monterey, including writer Alfred Robinson. On an inland trip Dr. William Maxwell Wood, naval surgeon, and a group of officers were guests of Padre Anzar, the last Franciscan Padre assigned to San Juan Bautista, and his brother, Don Juan Anzar, a prominent citizen and wealthy landowner. Padre Anzar stayed on at the mission for 20 years after secularization by Mexico and assisted many of the Californians who did not speak English in getting United States patents to their ranches.

Distinctive features of the mission church which can still be seen include the baptismal font, which was hand carved of limestone from a nearby quarry and was used to baptize thousands of Indian babies and is still in use; the large square tiles of the flooring bearing the imprint left before they were dry by animals such as bear, mountain lion and coyote; the wooden carved statue of St. John the Baptist, finely done as to every detail, which was brought to the church in 1809; the sun dial in the garden used by the padres to tell the time to ring the mission bells which, when a rawhide attached to the bell tongue was pulled, could be heard for miles; and the reredos on the altar painted by a Boston sailor named Thomas Doak, a carpenter with artistic ability who was passing through in about 1819.

Doak and a friend named Bob had skipped ship in Monterey. Both were baptized Catholic. Doak took the name Felipe Santiago, and Bob the name Juan Cristobal. With his new name Bob wandered up north, but Doak remained to marry Maria Castro, daughter of Mariano Castro, and to live happily ever after on the Rancho Las Animas.

The wars between Mexico and Spain made changes for the missionaries. After 1810 the *memorias,* a $400 per year stipend, could no longer be sent to California. With this money the padres had purchased merchandise for the kitchen, shops and field, church goods, gifts for the Indian children, or maybe an occasional new robe. They now found themselves in the position of having to be completely self-supportive. The mission herds had multiplied rapidly and with the great abundance of cattle, the padres found a new source of income. They would ship the hides and large *arrobas* of tallow to Monterey by ox-drawn carretas (wooden two-wheel carts) to be exchanged for merchandise from the Yankee trading ships that were making regular stops at Monterey. According to Richard Henry Dana in his widely read book *Two Years Before the Mast,* these ships were floating department stores. People would come out by boat and go aboard to make their exchanges.

The procuring of these hides, which were worth a dollar or two in exchange for merchandise, was part of the rodeo, a source of great excitement for the Indians as well as the Californians. However, before 1818 it was not legal for Indians to ride horseback—it was feared they might become warriors like the Apaches. This was according to the Law of the Indies, under which the missions were ruled. After the Indian's designation as a *vaquero* by the Viceroy, he could then take part. In the rodeo the *matanza,* the killing of the animals by the *nuqueadores,* was followed by the work of the skinners and butchers who saved the best of the meat for drying. The choice tallow, which was called *manteca,* was used for cooking or sent to Monterey for trade. Feasting and partying followed the butchering.

The Indians would eat until they could eat no more, which resulted in indigestion. During the rest of the week they ate *pozole,* made of a mixture of wheat, beans, peas and other vegetables. In one of his *respuestas* to his superiors, Father de la Cuesta reported, "They will not let a chance pass to catch rats, squirrels, moles, rabbits and other animals which they are wont to eat." Referring to their pagan life, he said, "They would get drunk on lime and wild tobacco juice mixed with a little water...[they] adore the sun or the moon..."

Writing about the *gente de razon* or colonists, de la Cuesta said they were from Sonora, Sinaloa, and other parts of Mexico, soldiers and their families who live in the mission and maintain themselves with "the wages paid by the King, Our Lord," that the men wore trousers, stockings, shoes and hats, adding that the pagans did not understand the use of dress—"the most they have is a cape of rabbit skin." Later he wrote that a blanket or breechcloth served to cover them decently, that the women wore an overall of cotton manufactured at the mission.

The Indians were very fond of music and song and retained some of their pagan tunes, some sad

Sundial in mission garden, used by padres to tell time to ring mission bells, which could be heard for miles.

and some cheerful, depending on the circumstances. They had their own musical instruments for non-church occasions, such as sticks on a hollow ball containing small pebbles, and whistles made of goose or deer bones. They would sometimes deck themselves out in feathers and paint their bodies, and, as they cavorted about in circles, would give out shouts and yells.

In 1829 Father de la Cuesta reported the addition of a three cylinder barrel organ. In her book, *California Missions and Their Romances,* Mrs. Fremont Older told about Father Tapis playing the organ to frighten off invading Indians—a good story but hardly likely. One of the tunes to come out of the organ, enjoyed by the Indians and not recognized by the padres until years later, was "The Siren's Waltz."

During a much later period, circa 1860, the Indians liked to sing at mass, but aware of their weakness for alcoholic liquor they would ask Father Mora to lock them up on Saturday night so they would be able to sing with the choir on Sunday.

In 1823 the mission population reached its peak. There were 641 male and 607 female Indians, and 22 dwellings of adobe and tile to accommodate the neophyte families. Three years later in response to an inquiry from Mexican Governor Jose Echeandia, the padres reported their cattle on two plains to be 6,500, 502 mares pastured, with 250 tamed and broken horses and 37 mules, that to the east was a

Footprint of wild animal in tile floor of mission. Animals that roamed the area left imprints before tiles were dry.

Indian cemetery on north side of mission church, above original El Camino Real and San Andreas Fault, where 4,000 Indians are buried. Olive trees were planted by the first padres.

Pear orchard believed to be the father of all pear orchards in California. All the early travelers commented on the succulence of the fruit. Orchard was originally surrounded by a moat to keep out wild animals. Only one of the original trees remains.

Original baptismal font, carved of limestone from nearby quarry. It was used to baptize thousands of Indian babies and is still in use.

Wood statue of St. John the Baptist, brought to the church in 1809. The wood carving is outstanding—veins and muscles are delicately detailed. The colors are still vivid.

ranch for sheep, another to the northeast. The report told about the springs in the Gavilan from which ran a *zanja* of water which passed by the mission and served to irrigate the garden, vineyard, and a small corn field.

A few years later, in 1834, with the secularization of the missions in California, all the land was to be taken from the missions, which were divided into large grants to Californians. In 1858, however, 58 acres were returned to the church at San Juan Bautista, which was the only mission of the 21 never to be without a pastor in residence.

When the Americans started coming through San Juan Bautista, they invariably commented in their writings on the pears in the orchard, which is supposed to be the parent of all pear orchards in the state. It was surrounded by a moat to keep the cattle out. Bayard Taylor, traveling on foot to Monterey in 1849 to attend the constitutional convention, described in his book *El Dorado* the succulence of the pears he was given at the mission. In telling of his experiences he said he had spent the previous night at the Martin Murphy Rancho (Las Llagas) and on his way from there had dinner at the Castro *milpas* (Rancho El Solis).

"By sunset I emerged from the mountains, waded the Rio Pajaro, and entered on the valley of San Juan which stretched for leagues before me as broad and beautiful as that I had left." Taylor described the road across the valley as seeming endless as he looked for the mission. Finally he met an Indian vaquero who pointed the direction to him. "Soon afterwards the sound of a bell chiming vespers broke on the silence, but I was still more weary before I reached the walls where it swung."

After William Tecumseh Sherman, who was later to become famous as a general in the Civil War, visited San Juan Bautista in 1846 he wrote:

The mission was in a beautiful valley—very level and bounded on all sides by hills. The plain was covered by wild grasses and mustard. Cattle and horses were seen in all directions, and it was manifest that the priests who first occupied the country were good judges of land.

It was Sunday and all the people had come to church from the country "round and about." The Mission of San Juan Bautista bore all marks of high prosperity at a former period and had a good pear orchard under the plateau where stood the church.

Still another visitor to San Juan, Edwin Bryant, who became alcalde of San Francisco in 1849, in his book *What I Saw In California* told of a trip from Sacramento with a force of 25 under Captain Charles Weber (founder of Stockton). At Weber's

Barrel organ brought to mission in 1829, duly reported by Father de la Cuesta. It had come to Monterey by whaling ship. One of the tunes enjoyed by the Indians but not recognized by the padres until later years was "The Siren's Waltz."

These musical notes were written in color by Father Tapis to teach Indians the Gregorian Chant.

rancho (Canada de San Felipe y Las Animas) they captured 200 to 300 public horses and delivered them to Fremont. He told of passing Gilroy's rancho and reaching Mission San Juan just before dark, and wrote:

This has been one of the most extensive of these mission establishments. The principal buildings are more durably constructed than those of other missions I have visited and are in better condition.

The valley was watered by a large arroyo and highly fertile. Gardens and other lands were enclosed by elevated willow hedges, and there were hills or mountains beyond this valley to the east and west [the Gabilans and the Diablo Range].

Large herds of cattle are scattered over the valley greedily cropping the fresh green herbage which now carpets the mountain and plains.

Another prominent visitor to the mission who wrote about it in her book *Glimpses of California and the Missions* and in an article for *Century* magazine, was Helen Hunt Jackson. Author of the novel *Ramona,* Miss Jackson described the church interior:

In the sacristy are oak chests full of gorgeous vestments of brocades with silver and gold laces...the mission

The Matanza — the killing of the animals for hides by the nuqueadores. Before 1818 Indians were not allowed to ride horseback.

Rev. Valentine Closa, who came to the mission in 1874 and stayed for over 40 years, until his death. He was much loved by Protestants as well as Catholics. He planted the olive trees within the mission garden, and both Helen Hunt Jackson and Mrs. Fremont Older wrote about him and his gardens.

church is well preserved which fact is mainly due to the deep interest of its present pastor, the Rev. Valentine Closa. Its grounds are enclosed and cared for; in its garden are still blooming roses and vines, in the shelter of palms, and with the old stone sun dial to tell time.

She wrote about the locust-walled plaza and of the orphan girls' school kept by the Sisters of the Sacred Heart:

At 6 o'clock every morning the bells of the church ring for Mass, as they used to ring when over a thousand Indians flocked to the summons. Today, at the sound there comes a procession of little girls and young maidens, the black-robed sisters walking before them with crossed hands and placid faces....It was barely dawn in the church as the shrill yet sweet childish voices lifted up the strains of the Kyrie Eleison.

Padre Jose Antonio Anzar was the last of the Franciscans at Mission San Juan Bautista. He came in 1833 and remained as pastor until 1854 when he returned to his home at Colima, Mexico.

The orphanage was damaged by an earthquake in the 1890s, and the children were moved.

Fiestas

San Juan always seemed to have a talent for staging a fiesta or pageant. For the 110th anniversary of the founding of the mission, a committee of non-Catholics collected money to erect a large 30-foot cross made of redwood from Santa Cruz Mountains on the Mt. Holy Cross to replace the one it was said a Mormon had chopped down 50 years before to use for fencing. Early in the morning of June 24, 1907, St. John's Day, a committee, including Mr. and Mrs. George Moore (he always gave the address for the flag raising ceremony at

Orphanage founded by Sisters of Charity. It was badly damaged by an earthquake in the 1890s and the children were moved to Los Angeles.

The altar and colorful reredos were painted by Thomas Doak, a carpenter who was passing through in 1816, after skipping ship at Monterey. When he was baptized he took the name Felipe Santiago. He married Maria Castro and lived on Rancho Las Animas.

Fremont Peak), George Abbe, and Harry Breen, went up for the ceremony and then hurried back to town for the parade.

There were also horse events that day—the quarter mile saddle horse race was won by Joe Ayer of the Sargent Ranch, with John Anzar, grandson of Don Juan Anzar, second; and the most graceful equestrienne award was given to Domie Indart. The Honorable M. T. Dooling of Hollister was the orator of the day, a maypole dance was given in the plaza by 30 young ladies, and there was a grand ball in the evening at Plaza Hall with music by an orchestra from Gilroy. Festivities closed with the illumination of the giant cross.

The following year there was another fiesta, this one instigated by Mrs. Fremont Older, who wrote about it in her book *California Missions and Their Romances.* She and her husband, the editor of *San Francisco Call-Bulletin,* had been in San Juan the previous year, enroute to Monterey, when their car broke down. Spending some time at the mission with Father Valentine Closa and seeing the damage from the earthquake of 1906 of the previous year, Mrs. Older decided to help raise funds for its restoration.

It must have been quite a sight June 24, 1908 as the Olders arrived from San Francisco in their white Stanley Steamer, followed by a fleet of white cars. The day started as usual with a mass, after which there was a grand barbecue in the olive or-

chard. Two steers were roasted to feed the hungry throng and sporting events were held in the large corral set up in the plaza. Thirty cowboys and cowgirls appeared in procession. The vaquero sports were followed by girls performing the Virginia Reel on horseback, among them such names as Indart, Murphy, Perry, Valledoa, French, and Ward. Among the men participating were Breen, Duarte, Crowley, Machado (Avilla), Indart, Etcheverry, Bryan, and Butts. The day grossed $18,000.

Starting in the 1930s, during the pastorship of Rev. Francis Caffrey, M.M., the fiestas were revived. Pageants were the big thing. Fenton McKenna, who was director of drama at Santa Clara University and later San Francisco State University, used to direct, as did Arthur Kenny, now of Vallejo. The late Federal Judge Edward Murphy of San Francisco, who was a professor of drama at Santa Clara for awhile, was one of the leading actors, and James Baccigalupe of Hillsborough was among the Santa Clara students who played leading roles.

The protagonists would come up from the El Camino on horseback and in costume, by the side of the mission. The front of the mission was the stage while the audience watched from bleachers set up in the plaza for the event.

Judge Murphy became quite attached to the town of San Juan and was a frequent visitor, as was actor

A portion of El Camino Real can be seen below mission wall.

Mission wall before restoration in 1976. Shows thickness of walls.

A scene from the Fiesta which was staged in the plaza in 1908 to raise funds for the restoration of the mission.

Leo Carrillo, descendant of one of the first California families, who used to stay with Jack Welch on his ranch.

The *San Jose Mercury* of June 22, 1930 reported that the San Juan Pageant, as written by Grace Therese Mitchell, would depict the life of the mission, woven around the life of saintly Padre Estevan Tapis, "music master of the mission," and that his original music would be played during the production. Each year a different episode in the mission's history would be portrayed. In keeping with the tradition, there would be a barbecue and a dance.

In recalling the fiestas, Father Caffrey, now at the Maryknoll House in Mountain View, said that a Policeman's Band and Mayor Rossi would come from San Francisco, and many Hollywood people also came. Jane Withers, child star, came up in 1937 to present the Bing Crosby Radio Trophy prize; Sally Blaine, actress and sister of Loretta Young, and her husband, Norman Foster, a movie director, attended the pageant; Jimmy and Lucille Gleason used to drive up every year. "One time Jimmy brought up a group of his friends from Hollywood to play polo down where the rodeo grounds are," Father Caffrey said. "I prayed that

one of those horses wouldn't get his hoof in a squirrel hole."

He also talked about Brother Louis Reinhardt, who had been a Shakespearean actor, and of his contribution not only to the pageant but to the mission. The gardens were never so beautiful. Midnight Mass at Christmas was so spectacular—the mission church all candlelight and flowers—that people would come from all over.

Harry Carr, famous columnist of the *Los Angeles Times,* came up with his artist one time to spend a day. He stayed for a week, writing stories, and became friends with Father Caffrey, When he died, Father Caffrey was asked to deliver the eulogy at his funeral.

San Juan still has its fiestas. They are no longer on St. John's Day, however, because that date was taken by another horse show—rodeo at Bolado Park. Now held in July, the day of the fiesta starts with a parade and the big event is the rodeo held just below the plaza.

CHAPTER II

The Town of
San Juan Bautista

"At San Juan there lingers more of the atmosphere of the olden time than is to be found in any other place in California," wrote Helen Hunt Jackson, who is said to have started writing her famous novel *Ramona* during her stay in San Juan Bautista in 1883. She added, "San Juan has a charm of sun, valley, hill, seaward off-look, unsurpassed in all California."

Describing her meeting with 85-year-old Dona Pilar, whose husband had been one of the soldiers of the old Mission Guard, Miss Jackson said that the woman told her about the thousands of Indians in the old days, that the Indians were good and the padres were always kind, that every eight days 50 oxen were killed and everybody had all they wanted to eat. Dona Pilar was one of those who had seen three flags fly over San Juan. First there was the crimson and gold flag of Spain when the mission was established. In 1822 it was lowered and the red, green and white flag of Mexico, with eagle and snake design, was raised. Undoubtedly Dona Pilar was in the crowd that gathered in the plaza to hear the proclamation by the governor that Mexico had declared its independence from Spain. She must also have been in the plaza when John C. Fremont raised the stars and stripes of the United States.

Except for the influx of tourists, San Juan is much the way Dona Pilar knew it. Most of the old adobes are still standing as are the early frame buildings built after the arrival of the Americans. A sawmill was started in the Hecker Pass area by a man named Bodfish, and the lumber was hauled to San Juan in a wagon drawn by four yoke of oxen.

The old mission church still faces the plaza, which is still bordered with locust trees. At a right angle to it is the Plaza Hotel. Many prominent visitors were guests here—H. C. Ralston, San Francisco banker and financier, Henry Miller, cattle and land baron, General William Tecumseh Sher-

man, who became famous during the Civil War for his "march to the sea," and writer Richard Walton Tully, who used the mission garden where the sundial is as a model for one of his sets in his play, "Rose of the Rancho," which opened in San Francisco in 1906. Bessie Barriscale, the actress who created the role, also frequently stayed at the hotel.

Next door to it is the Castro-Breen adobe, considered one of the finest examples of Monterey colonial architecture in the state. General Jose Castro, who had always been too busy fighting in the Mexican war except for the time he was here plotting two revolutions against the Mexican governors, to spend much time there, sold to Patrick Breen who, with his family, had crossed the Sierras in the winter of 1846–47 with the tragedy-ridden Donner Party.

On the opposite side of the square from the mission are the plaza stables built in the 1860s by Angelo Zanetta and his partner, John Comfort, to accommodate the horses of the Coast Line Stage and for livery stables. Zanetta also built a home for himself and his family next door.

Upstairs was Zanetta Hall, a town meeting place. The dances which were the center of San Juan's social life were also held there. This room had the first spring maple dance floor in California and a piano inlaid with mother-of-pearl. The faces of old timers in San Juan light up as they describe that dance floor.

Zanetta was originally from New Orleans and a master at the art of French cooking. The hotel became noted for the excellence of its cuisine. In the Plaza Hotel bar today can be seen the announcement of its opening, stating that he, the former owner of the Sebastopol Hotel, would be receiving and entertaining the traveling public at his new hotel situated on the Plaza after 20 December 1859, that C. McLaughlin and Company's line

One of the original maps of San Juan. Note streets, names in Spanish: Calle Primera (First Street), Calle Segunda (Second), and so on.

Artist Henry Miller made this sketch of San Juan around 1853. On the right is the convent for Indian women (monjerio) across from the mission church. In the center is the Castro Adobe and next to it the adobes of Jose Maria Sanchez and Juan Anzar, which were converted into the Plaza Hotel. On the other side is the Crane House. The building with the cupola is the Sebastopol Hotel (not correctly located). To its right is the rooftop of the adobe known as "La Pulguita," recently restored; then the Tuccoletta Hall. Further down Third Street is the St. John's Hotel. The first hotel built in San Juan, it was destroyed by fire in 1867.

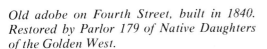

Old adobe on Fourth Street, built in 1840. Restored by Parlor 179 of Native Daughters of the Golden West.

Tuccoletta Hall, built in the early 1800s. Adolph Vache had his bakery in this building.

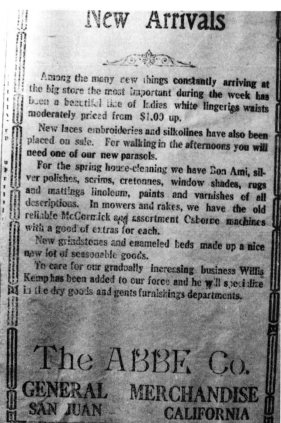

New Arrivals

Among the many new things constantly arriving at the big store the most important during the week has been a beautiful line of ladies white lingerie waists moderately priced from $1.00 up.

New laces embroideries and silkolines have also been placed on sale. For walking in the afternoons you will need one of our new parasols.

For the spring house-cleaning we have Bon Ami, silver polishes, scrims, cretonnes, window shades, rugs and mattings linoleum, paints and varnishes of all descriptions. In mowers and rakes, we have the old reliable McCormick and assortment Osborne machines with a good of extras for each.

New grindstones and enameled beds made up a nice new lot of seasonable goods.

To care for our gradually increasing business Willis Kemp has been added to our force and he will specialize in the dry goods and gents furnishings departments.

The ABBE Co.

GENERAL MERCHANDISE
SAN JUAN — CALIFORNIA

One of the advertisements of the Abbe Co., which had the store for over 50 years. Among new items just arrived were grindstones and enamel beds.

Stephen Lavagnino, proprietor of the Plaza Market, originally the Vache adobe. His wife, Maria, and daughter, Mamie Avilla, are at left.

Right: The general merchandise store of the Abbe family. Felipe Gardella built this building in the 1860s. It is said that he had a trained parrot that watched the store for him. If it saw anyone picking up something, it would scream, "Felipe, te roban!" ("Felipe, they are robbing you!").

11

Sandstone buildings constructed after the fire of 1867 were owned by Antoine Taix, whose son is seated in the buggy in the center of the picture. Photo was taken in 1894.

The National Hotel, built in 1858 by John Geaster. During the Civil War enlisted men were housed here. The Masonic Lodge held meetings in an upstairs room until their building on Second Street was completed.

of U.S. Mail stages to and from San Jose, Monterey, Santa Cruz, and Watsonville would arrive and depart from this hotel every day of the week, and that he was offering "unexceptional" rooms by the week or month. He also stated that he had excellent stable accommodations connected with the hotel.

The opening of the hotel must have been a grand occasion, with the dons and their senoras coming from their ranchos in their colorful dress, a band playing on the upstairs veranda, and a bullfight in the plaza.

This was the beginning of an era of great prosperity for San Juan. Businessmen would come to buy and trade in sheep, horses, hogs and grain, especially for San Francisco and San Jose. The cattle purchased would then be driven overland to their destination. Many of the cattle and mining businessmen would take a room at the Plaza Hotel, hire a horse and buggy, visit their customers in Watsonville, Salinas and other points and return to the hotel at night for Zanetta's fine food.

When the stages came into town the guests would dine in San Juan, usually at the Plaza Hotel, while their baggage was being transferred to another stage.

In those halcyon days of San Juan Bautista it was a crossroads for travel between San Francisco and Los Angeles, San Jose, Watsonville, Salinas and Monterey. In 1866 William E. Lovett submitted the lowest bid for the Coast Line Stage from San Jose to Los Angeles which began in July of 1866. Two years later he sold to Flint-Bixby Company.

In his book *Early Days at the Mission San Juan Bautista* Isaac Mylar gave a vivid description of these stages. He remembered as a boy seeing the stages start south over the Old Stage Road, the original El Camino Real, through the San Juan Pass to the Salinas Valley. In the winter when the weather was dark and stormy, there were only two lights, and dim ones at that, on either side of the driver's seat. Under the seat was the U.S. mail and the express box. Over it was a leather apron which the driver and the passengers sitting up front with him would pull up over themselves for protection against the cold.

Instead of springs, the body of the coach rested on several thicknesses of leather. They were easy to ride on, but on those unpaved roads they would sway and rock back and forth. When they got to a place where the grade became too steep, the gentlemen would be requested to get out and walk. As a protection against the dust, which at times was almost smothering, both men and women wore long linen dusters tightly buttoned up and drawn closely around the neck.

The first financial boon to San Juan was the opening in 1854 of the New Idria Quicksilver Mines which became one of the three largest in the world. Bret Harte wrote about it in *Story of a Mine*. The

Old San Juan School as it appeared in the 1870s, on First Street. It was moved in 1907 to Third and Polk Streets and is now owned by the I.O.O.F. Lodge. Built in 1868.

Texas Masonic Lodge building on Second Street. Library and Mary Poole's Antiques are downstairs. San Juan has one of the oldest Masonic Lodges in the state.

quicksilver was hauled 68 miles from the mine to San Juan by freight teams, six to twelve horses or mules to a team, with bells ringing and the driver sitting on a wheel base for guiding the team by means of a jerk line that was fastened to the bit of one of the lead horses.

ⱬ The Zanettas

Angelo Zanetta had two sons, Ferdinand and Ernest, who was always called CC, and two daughters, Vicky, who was organist at the mission, and Mary or Mariquita. Mariquita married William Breen who was the youngest son of Patrick and Margaret Breen. He was stricken with a fever and lived only a few months after they were married.

Mariquita later married P. E. G. (Lupe) Anzar, son of Don Juan Anzar and Maria Antonia Castro Anzar, who previously owned the building where the Plaza Hotel is now located. Lupe was born in what was to become the barroom after Zanetta restored the building.

In an interview in the *Los Angeles Times* in 1936, telling about life at the Plaza Hotel, Mariquita said:

It speedily became the best liked stopping place between Los Angeles and San Francisco. San Juan was some place in those days.

We were virtually slaves to the horn. At any hour of the day or night a toot-a-toot-toot reverberating across the San Benito Valley apprised us that a stage was plunging toward us on El Camino Real. The old Bixby coaches were drawn by six horses. Then what a hustle and bustle there would be!

First I would dash into the bar and beg the *caballeros* to please take out their horses to make room for arriving guests. Horses in the bar? To be sure! The young bloods used to ride right in and sip their drinks from the saddle. They used to play billiards on horseback too. We had two tables and they were seldom idle. The senoritas could ride as well as the men. After the evening meal we used to move the furniture out of the dining room and dance. Later, beds covered the floor.

During a conversation with Clara Abbe Zanetta in the spring of 1975, just two months before her death at the age of 96, this remarkable little woman talked about her husband Ernest, or CC, and life in San Juan. She said that he served as constable for 56 years until his death in 1945 and that he never lost an election.

"My husband never carried a gun," said Clara Zanetta. "He knew everybody in town and had his own way of handling things. If a Mexican got sick he'd call him. CC would go over to see if he was sick enough to go to the hospital.

"One night some neighbors called about a lot of singing and noise in the Casa Rosa (an old adobe, now a restaurant). It wasn't midnight yet, but he went over and joined them in singing for awhile. Then he said, 'Okay, boys, it's time to go home,' and they all left."

CC never drove a car, always a buggy. In his later years his niece, Grace Matthews of Santa Cruz, said if he was called to break up a fight she would drive him over with two of her children in the back seat. She said she often drove him over to Hollister with prisoners. The quaint little jail used by Zanetta stands across the street from the Breen Adobe on the plaza. Lawbreakers liked to be put in this jail, she said, because the food was good.

Reminiscing about life in San Juan in the early days, Mrs. Zanetta told about a time when Miller and Lux were running cattle through town. "One of

Antoine (Tony) Taix, owner of many commercial buildings in San Juan.

the steers got into the barroom at the Plaza Hotel," she said, "and they had quite a time getting him out."

She talked about contests of the San Juan Eagle Hook and Ladder Company of which her husband was a member, along with such familiar names as Thomas Flint, W. S. Prescott, George Beuttler, and Tom Nyland. There were eight buckets on each side. 15 men pulled or pushed; the fastest pulled. There would be a 300 foot dash down a crowded street—the ladder was pulled from the truck and raised, and one man climbed to the top. The time was tallied from the start of the run to the top of the ladder. Recalling one of these contests in Gilroy at which San Juan won, she said, "Of course that was very exciting when we won."

When they were first married she said they lived in the Zanetta House. Then Vicky Zanetta, her husband's sister, fixed up the little white cottage next door, directly across from the mission, for them. It looks down on the rodeo grounds and the valley. Their next move was to the house at the corner of Franklyn and First behind the stables, where they spent the rest of their lives, CC preceding his wife in death by 30 years.

Her husband, she said, "was always called 'CC' — never anything else. I was told that the nurse who took care of him when he was a baby called

The San Juan Eagle Hook and Ladder Company was organized after the fire of 1867 by George Beuttler, who is holding the banner. Timed races with neighboring communities created great excitement. Thomas Flint, Jr., lower left front row, was trainer in the 1880s.

Judge Edward F. Pearce and family in front of his house in San Juan Canyon. His son, Edward A. Pearce, and grandson, E. F. Pearce, were born in this house, which is still standing.

A group of the "boys" in the bar of the Plaza Hotel. Left to right: Louis Raggio, Art Baker, F. French, Jack Welch, Ben Ahern (behind bar), Federal Judge Edward Murphy, who fell in love with San Juan Bautista when he was a student at Santa Clara and came to take part in the pageant, and CC Zanetta.

15

Prominent citizens of San Juan, all natives of the town: W. S. Prescott, Supervisor; Edward A. Pearce, Justice of the Peace; Lupe Anzar, pioneer rancher; CC (Ernest) Zanetta, Constable; and George Abbe, Mayor and co-owner of Abbe Co. General Merchandise Store.

Ernest "CC" Zanetta and his wife, Clara Abbe Zanetta. CC was born in the old Plaza Hotel, which was operated by his father, Angelo Zanetta.

him 'Cissy' because he had curly hair and from that came 'CC'. He knew everybody in town and when he walked along the street everybody said 'hello'." Zanetta ran the livery stables on the plaza until the state took over the plaza as a national monument in 1934.

Clara Zanetta's face lighted up as she told of the social life in San Juan in earlier days. She obviously loved to dance, but was quick to add, "Of course, I never did any of the kind of dances they do today—we liked to waltz and foxtrot. We always had a New Year's Ball and a big celebration for St. John's Day on June 24." They started St. John's Day with mass at the mission. "If it came on Saturday or Sunday they would have it on Friday," she explained, "because if they had it on Saturday they could only dance until midnight." She said they would dance until almost dawn. Her first ball at the Plaza Hall was the Centennial in 1897. Senator and Mrs. Thomas Flint, Jr. from the San Justo Ranch led the Grand March. After the regular Saturday night dances they would go across the plaza to the mission for supper.

Clara Zanetta was born at the north end of town on First Street (the house is still standing), but didn't meet her husband until after she was grown because, she explained, he lived at the other end of town. After her father, Andrew Abbe, had to leave the San Justo property, where he had a farm, in the mid 1850s, he purchased 20 acres of land and set out one of the first orchards on the far north side of town, planting apples and then apricots. He was also superintendent of roads and in those days in

San Juan with a "low" budget and no paving, it must have been a thankless job. In 1883 they issued a decree for one month to permit cattle to graze in the streets because there was so much grass.

Andrew Abbe, his daughter said, was born in Marion, Iowa, in 1848, and as a boy came to California with his father, William Abbe, from New York on a sailing vessel around the Cape. They were shipwrecked and lost everything they had. After going to the gold fields like everybody else, they returned home, later coming back to California by covered wagon. Her brothers, Frank, George, and Fred, operated the Abbe Mercantile business in San Juan; their brick building is still standing.

The Pearces

One of the Abbe daughters, Nellie, married Edward A. Pearce of San Juan Canyon, who served as Justice of the Peace for the San Juan Township for 32 years, retiring in 1947. His father, Edward Frank Pearce, who also served as judge in San Juan in the 1800s, came to California on a sailing ship around Cape Horn in 1849. As he crossed over the San Juan Pass, he looked out on San Juan Canyon and decided then that he wanted to return there some day to live.

Before this was to come about, however, as a teenager he teamed up with a Portuguese by the name of Silveira and hunted game in the area of Niles Canyon. They killed deer, antelope, geese, and ducks, which they shipped by boat from Alvarado Landing to San Francisco for the hotel

Zanetta House. Plaza Hall is upstairs. Using the adobe bricks from the old nunnery, Angelo Zanetta built the home for his family and the hall for public use.

Above, Clara Abbe Zanetta on her 96th birthday in 1975. Her father, Andrew Abbe, set out orchards in San Juan on First Street in the early 1850s. Her husband, CC Zanetta, served as constable for 56 years and never carried a gun.

Plaza Stables, built in 1870 by Angelo Zanetta and his partner John Comfort to accommodate horses for stage lines and for livery stables.

market. They would return with their larder stocked with flour, bacon and beans, shot powder and shells, along with a supply of rattlesnake medicine. After five years he returned to Gloucester, Massachusetts, where his family had been among the original settlers. He married Sarah Eaton of Halifax and returned to California to homestead 53 acres of land in San Juan Canyon. A number of Mormon families settled there, among them Jasper Twitchell, whose large home the Pearces later bought. It was a beautiful place with an almond orchard, grapes and elderberries. The large barn is still standing.

A third Edward Pearce, son and grandson of the two judges, was born in San Juan Canyon shortly after the turn of the century. His brother, Donald Abbe Pearce, lives in Piedmont. They share many memories of their childhood in San Juan and of the canyon where Ed and a brother and sister were born. This house, where their father was also born, is still standing. They talked about the creek where Ed would catch his limit of trout (at that time 50) before school, of shooting enough quail and rabbit for the family's dinner table, of the Ferry Morse seed property—that at certain times practically the whole valley was planted in sweet peas and of what a grand sight that was to look down upon. They said 150 Chinese were employed by the seed company.

There used to be mountain lions in the Canyon. Once a lion came up to the door of the porch where the Pearces were sleeping. It was frightened away but took a pig as its loot.

Donald Pearce said he was born in the second house from the corner of Main Street (Third Street) and Muckelemi. The streets in those days were referred to as Mission Street (Second), site of the mission; School Street (First); and Back Street (Fourth), on which is located the Native Daughters' Adobe. This building, built in 1840, was the

17

The dressmaker's cottage, on the edge of the plaza facing the mission church. Vicky Zanetta, daughter of Angelo, lived here. She was organist for the mission church.

The Plaza Hotel. Reconstructed by Angelo Zanetta in 1858 from the adobe garrisons that had housed soldiers to protect the mission. During the 1860s and '70s stagecoaches arrived at all hours. Businessmen who came to buy grain and cattle made the hotel their headquarters.

residence of Don Jose Maria Espinosa. "We boys were forbidden to ever go on that street for there were many places of ill repute in that area."

He also recalled there were 17 saloons and four newspapers in town at one time and that the famous desperados, such as Tiburcio Vasquez and Cleodovio Chavez, were in and out of town. Vasquez's mother had a tamale parlor on Third Street.

After Vasquez's hanging in San Jose in 1875, Chavez set out to avenge this deed. A price was put on his head, and Louis Raggio, it is said, brought it back to San Juan in a gunnysack to collect his bounty. It was put on display—an ironic ending for this bandit.

The Pearces used to have Mariano Castro's old adobe on their property on Third Street south of town, and the boys would walk along the top of the thick adobe walls. Judge Pearce found a gold wedding ring with the initials "M.C." They believed this identified it as Maria Castro's (cousin of General Castro) so gave it to a relative of the Castro family.

Still more memories were of parades in Taix's

grove on the Alameda, horse cart competition, picnics on the sand beach at the confluence of the Pajaro and San Benito Rivers, chautauquas at Hollister, Ringling Brothers and Barnum & Bailey circuses in Salinas, and Buffalo Bill Cody—of going to see the great white fleet of Admiral Dewey sailing into Monterey Bay, and of the time their uncle drove an early model automobile into town on his way from San Francisco to Monterey and they tied sacks over the horses' eyes to avoid runaways.

Kemp House

Many a visitor to San Juan stops to admire the Kemp House at the corner of Third and Muckelemi Streets, with its white picket fences and old fashioned flower garden. It has been preserved with great care by Carroll and Martha Hayes who, when they purchased it in the 1960s from the Kemp heirs, acquired all the furnishings. The Hayeses are well attuned to early California and appreciate the treasure they have in this house. They have also owned the old Lazard Lion Ranch in San Martin for 50 years.

In front of the Hayes (Kemp) house are old water troughs hand carved out of sandstone that used to be in front of Kemp's Bola de Oro Saloon, caldrons for boiling tallow or skinning pigs, an old water pump, and at the front door a light fixture that came from one of the early California Governor's carriages.

Frederick William Kemp bought the house in 1864 from a man named Hollenbeck who had built it in 1860. Kemp had left his home in Philadelphia to come to California during the Gold Rush in 1849. He became associated with cattleman Tom Hildreth in the San Joaquin Valley, the same Hildreth who sold cattleman Henry Miller his first ranch in the valley. It was through Hildreth that Kemp met his French wife, Mary Louise Deslandes, in San Francisco.

Originally the house had only four rooms, two upstairs and two down. As can still be seen, some of the beams were hand hewn. As their family grew, so did the house. A lean-to that served as a kitchen was converted into a dining room and living area, and a new kitchen, pantry, bathroom and laundry added. By 1890 the girls were growing up, and Kemp added a "courting room" on the front of the house where the girls entertained their beaux. Several family weddings and funerals were held in this room. Pictures of Fred and Mary Louise Kemp still hang on the wall.

Outside Mr. Kemp built a stone fireplace, a unique arrangement into which an iron cauldron was filled for heating water which was funneled by a pipe through the wall. The same procedure was used to the laundry. Another unique feature is the tin chimney. Apparently with San Juan's location on the San Andreas Fault, they got tired of bricks falling as a result of earthquakes and built this chimney of tin. Still in the house is a three-foot square box lined with tin, a forerunner of the icebox, a big iron woodburning stove, a pine table with flour bin, and a handsome oak table. Among the conversation pieces are the long-handled bed warmers in which were inserted hot coals, and a lightweight rawhide vest with pockets on the inside that served as a money belt for men coming from the New Idria Mines.

San Juan Bautista Jail.

Across the back of the property in a line were a carriage house, a wood shed, a water pump and a windmill. Still standing is the little house that Kemp built in 1900 for his mother-in-law, Mme. Gingras. Usually called the "Granny House," it is also referred to as the "Mother-in-law House." Mme. Gingras was said to have come from a well-to-do family with a house in Paris and a place in the country. The unadorned simplicity of life in San Juan Bautista must have been an adjustment for the Frenchwoman. The last addition to the house was the sewing room for Mary Louise Kemp, completed in 1905, just after the death of her husband. It was said that until her death in 1936 at the age of 92, this was her favorite room. She liked to sit there and look up at Fremont Peak.

Fred Kemp owned the whole block between Second and Third and Muckelemi and San Jose

Left: Frederick William Kemp, who came to San Juan in 1864. Originally from Philadelphia, he owned the block between Second and Third Streets and Muckelemi and San Jose Streets. Right: Mary Louise Deslandes Kemp. She met her husband, Fred, in San Francisco through a friend of the family, Tom Hildreth, a San Joaquin Valley cattleman.

The Twitchell Ranch, later bought by the Pearce family. The large barn is still standing. The Twitchells were part of a Mormon colony which settled in the Canyon.

Judge E. F. Pearce, Judge E. A. Pearce, and E. F. Pearce II, taken in 1910. The senior E. F. Pearce came to California by sailing ship in 1849.

A mountain lion killed in San Juan Canyon about 1905. Holding the animal are the village blacksmith and Judge Ed Pearce. Leaning against the pole is Donald Pearce.

Streets. On one corner he had the Bola de Oro Saloon. Although it was said to be a respectable place, according to a report in the *Monterey Journal* of 1864, Kemp's saloon was the scene of a shooting—a man was killed by sixteen balls of buckshot.

During the Civil War when the National Hotel was taken over by the government for barracks and called Camp Low, for Governor Frederick Low, both the officers and soldiers used to come to Kemp's bar and, as the story goes, learned a few lessons in playing poker from San Juan residents. The bar must have been a popular place because when the signs were posted by Frederick Mac-Dougall in "three prominent places" to announce the auction of Estolano and Patrocinio Larios' share of the Rancho Santa Ana, Kemp's saloon was one of the places chosen. The election for the incorporation of San Juan in 1869 was also held at Kemp's saloon.

Included with the house when the Hayeses pur-

chased it, along with the furniture, was a scrapbook going back about 90 years that had been kept by a member or members of the Kemp family. They were assiduous clippers, but for some reason did not think it important to include the date. Nevertheless, much of the life and times in San Juan is revealed in the book. There are wedding stories which, according to the prevailing custom, listed the wedding gifts received by the bride and the name of the giver.

The Kemp marriages formed links with old and well known families of San Juan. Willis Kemp, whose father, Fred Kemp, Jr. died early, and who was raised by his grandparents, married Antoinette Anzar, daughter of the P. E. G. Anzars (Mariquita Zanetta), and granddaughter of Juan Miguel Anzar and Maria Antonia Castro.

Another prominent wedding reported is that of Marie (Mary Louise) Kemp to William Reid Flint, son of Benjamin Flint of the prestigious Flint-Bixby Company and owner of the San Justo Rancho. Flint

20

Fred Kemp behind the bar of his saloon, the Bola de Oro, a popular meeting place. The election for the incorporation of San Juan in 1869 was held here.

Kemp house, built in 1860 and bought by Frederick Kemp in 1864. Originally there were only four rooms, but Kemp added rooms as the family increased. In back can be seen the "the mother-in-law house," which was occupied by Mme. Gingras, mother of Mary Louise Kemp.

was in the Assembly and State Senate. They lived for many years in the house they built on the family ranch, San Joaquin o Rosa Morada, which is now owned by the Paul Hudner estate. Another daughter married Frank Breen, son of John Breen.

In 1885 Fred Kemp's niece, Elizabeth (Lizzie) Prather, of Tennessee was married in this house to William Sims Prescott before 80 guests. According to their daughter, Viola Archibald, who resides in San Juan, they received many beautiful gifts of silver and crystal and, on the practical side, chickens, and from the San Juan Eagle Hook and Ladder Company, of which her father was a member, five gallons of coal oil.

The Crane House

The Crane House at the corner of Second and Polk Streets in San Juan Bautista has been in the family of Nita Harrell, who lives there with her husband Milton, for over a hundred years. Although the quaint little white frame house with its high pitched roof, well tended garden, and white picket fence all around, has a Cape Cod look, it was shown in an 1853 drawing by artist Henry Miller of the village of San Juan Bautista. According to Milton Harrell, it was built by early American settlers traveling through for a trading post before being converted into a residence.

It was to this house that Maria Encarnacion Ortega came in the early 1870s to spend the last years of her life. A great-granddaughter of Jose Francisco Ortega, who brought the first settlers to California in 1774, she was born at Rancho San Ysidro which her grandfather, Ygnacio Ortega, had settled sometime around 1796. This area is now known as Old Gilroy. Her uncle was John Gilroy, for whom

the town was named. Upon the death of her first husband, Don Jose Maria Sanchez, in 1852, she became the wealthiest woman in California. Unfortunately, she and her six minor children were to be cheated out of this fortune. What is more, she had five husbands, all of whom died tragically.

She lived with her husbands in the Sanchez adobe. When she moved into town she chose this house because it was across the street from the convent school, and, a typical Spanish mother, she could watch her two youngest daughters, Virginia and Lydia, walk across the street to school. It was also convenient to the mission where she could walk to mass. In this house Nita Harrell has family mementoes including a framed piece of her grandmother's embroidered Spanish shawl and a teak desk of Jose Maria Sanchez in oriental design which he no doubt acquired from one of the sailing ships from the Orient that put into port at Monterey. There are also old family tintypes, including a portrait of George Crane with Encarnacion and their two little daughters. Lydia, the younger, was the mother of Nita Harrell.

George Crane was an attorney who came to California to join Fremont's regiment as an intelligence agent under the guise of supply officer. He was attorney for Dona Encarnacion and her third husband, Dr. Henry Sanford. After Sanford's death in a barroom duel in the Washington Hotel in Monterey, Crane married the beautiful widow.

In a series of stories in the *Salinas Daily Post* on the story of Encarnacion de Ortega y Sanchez, Crane was described as a young man who liked to drink and gamble—that because he was Dona Encarnacion's fourth husband he was known as

The Crane family, from an old tintype. George Crane, his wife, Encarnacion Ortega, and their daughters, Virginia and Lydia.

The Crane House, so named because the widow of George Crane spent the last years of her life here.

"George the Fourth." The story also said that the widow deeded her land to Crane and that he spent most of what was left of the Sanchez fortune with his gambling, lavish entertaining and running for the state senate.

On the other side of the coin, it was said that he served well in the Assembly, received special recognition from the Texas Masonic Lodge in San Juan (this document is framed and hangs in the Crane House), and that his death in 1868 from smallpox was due to his efforts to try to help victims of the dreadful disease which killed many of San Juan's citizens that year. Shortly after his death, title to the Sanchez ranchos passed to Henry Miller.

Encarnacion's last husband was Anastacio Alviso whom Nita Harrell said she only learned about in recent years. He met his death in a hunting accident the year following their marriage.

Nita Harrell's mother, Lydia Crane, married Spyro Raicevitch, a San Francisco restaurateur, in the early 1880s. Raised in San Francisco, Nita went on the stage in 1906. Her first job was with Kolb and Dill. In 1908 she played at Gold Field, Nevada, where the miners threw money up on the stage. She was in "Prince of Pilsen" with Wallace Beery before he became a famous movie star, and performed with, among others, Walter Catlett. Her husband said that she can out-dance anyone on the dance floor now, at the age of 86.

San Juan's Jehu: Mark Regan

A legend in anybody's time was Mark Regan, San Juan's stagecoach driver for 50 years. Old-timers recall with a smile the tales he used to tell as they rode in his Concord coach from San Juan Bautista to Gilroy, and back, that is if they were fortunate enough to have the seat in front next to him. Although Mark was only 25 years of age when he came to San Juan, he had already had enough adventures to fill an anthology. It was from these that he drew the material for his stories.

He was born in 1847 in Cape Girardeau, Missouri, between St. Louis and Cairo on the Missouri side of the Mississippi. Unlike that of other boys his age, who dreamed of becoming river boat pilots, Mark's first love was horses and his ambition was to become a Wells Fargo stagecoach driver. His equine interests were undoubtedly inherited from his father, James Regan, who died by drowning in the Mississippi when Mark was three years old. Born in Ireland, the senior Regan was an importer of thoroughbred horses. Mark later lived in St. Louis with an uncle and aunt, was a telegraph messenger, and knew General Grant well.

The Civil War was sweeping toward Missouri, a border state, and young Mark, at 14, was eager to get into the action. Caught up in the momentum of an unorganized rabble of men called out by General Price to resist "the Yank and the Hessian" (General Siegel and the Union Army), he figuratively jumped over the seminary wall. Actually he was attending a private school from which his Irish Catholic family hoped he would matriculate to the seminary. He headed for the Confederate camp and enlisted in the Third Missouri Ambulance Corps, the only branch of the service that would take a boy his age. This was his "bag of oats." He was working with horses and they were getting ready to move into Northwestern Arkansas for the spring campaign of 1862. However, a few weeks later he was captured by the

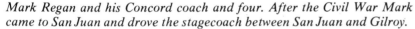
Mark Regan and his Concord coach and four. After the Civil War Mark came to San Juan and drove the stagecoach between San Juan and Gilroy.

Mark Regan

Union troops in the battle of Pear Ridge and was a prisoner until the end of the war. He became acquainted with many prison camps in the west, such as Forts Upton, Laramie and Leavenworth, where he recalled how he would lie on the banks of the Mississippi at night, listening for skiffs under instructions to catch and arrest men fleeing from the draft.

During his three years of frontier life (young prisoners were kept as far away as possible from combat), he developed his expertise with horses, hunted buffalo, and acquired an understanding of Indian sign language and Indian fighting. While driving an ambulance for the militia under Colonel Clavington on an expedition from Denver he was shot in the leg by an Indian arrow at the battle of Sand Point. He was at Fort Laramie during a Sioux and Cheyenne conference and said that Father Deserett, who spoke several Indian languages and had the rank of captain, was there and that he knew him well.

It was because of these experiences, he would tell his stagecoach passengers, that at the end of the war he was asked to drive for General Sherman in his buckboard on a tour of inspection of western forts. His opinion was that Sherman wanted to get away from the politicians.

Leaving the military he realized his dream of becoming a stage driver for the Overland Stage on the route from Cheyenne to Salt Lake City. One of his favorite stories was of the time he drove Susan B. Anthony, the early day pioneer for women's rights. They stopped at a little station called Bitter Creek for lunch. On the menu was "white fish," which she ordered and liked so much she reordered it. It was not until they got to the next stop that she learned from a waitress, annoyed at her raving

about it so much, that what she had eaten wasn't fish at all, but rattlesnake meat.

Years later Regan received a letter from Miss Anthony in which she recalled the incident, saying, "It is now a quaint memory, but at the time it impressed me as the most repugnant and horrible incident of my life."

Another incident that stood out in Regan's memory was driving Charles Crocker from Sage Brush Plain to the Promontory in May of 1869, for the ceremony of the driving of the golden spike that marked the completion of the transcontinental railroad. He realized that this event was the signal that his days with the Overland stage were over. He came west with his Concord coach, planning to drive for the Coast Line out of San Luis Obispo, but he got as far as San Juan Bautista and fell in love with this little village set on a plateau looking out on the green valley and the hills towards Gilroy. He went no further.

With his Concord coach and four he established his line between San Juan and Gilroy. Another famous lady was a passenger from Gilroy to San Juan—Helen Hunt Jackson, author of *Ramona*. Mark always maintained that if it hadn't been for the animosity of a certain Mrs. O'Flynn, who was running the Castro-Breen adobe, Miss Jackson might have stayed on to make San Juan the locale for her novel. During her stay in San Juan she was entertained by the children in the orphanage who showed her samples of their handiwork. Their sweet singing made an impression on her and near the end of her book, the young lady is advised to go to San Juan, where at the hospitable convent, "she might find knowing grief at the loss of her lover." When the orphans were transferred out of San Juan after one of the earthquakes, Mark, as did most of the citizens, took great offense at the bishop who issued the order. They missed hearing the happy voices of the children and seeing them walk in file down the street to the mission for mass.

Two years after he came to San Juan, Regan met a serious looking young man at the station in Gilroy. Mark suggested that he ride up in front with him, that a lot of Mexicans smoking cigarettes were getting in and that the air would be better up there. As they drove up the hills the traveler asked about the town and its people. He said that he was a priest sent from Los Angeles by his bishop to look over the parish, that his health was delicate, and that he might become the mission's pastor.

Mark, of course, was a total convert to San Juan and waxed eloquently on its climate and scenic beauty. The priest, Father Valentine Closa, then wanted to know about the parish. Mark told him that there had been six protestant churches in town, but that now there was only one, and that the pastor of it was a gentleman. He said, "You will have no trouble if you are tolerant and strive for harmony and good will and are not too ambitious." A long time later, speaking from the pulpit, Father Closa told the people that the stagecoach driver had given him some good advice and that he had never forgotten it.

Father Closa was a native of Barcelona, well educated, a handsome, austere aristocrat, but loved by his people. He stayed in San Juan for 45 years, and although Mark had long ago given up the faith of his family, the two men became close friends and grew old together in San Juan.

One of the more colorful stories told about Mark Regan was about a drive from Gilroy to San Juan on a stormy night in 1888. The favored passenger in the seat beside Mark noted through the dim yellow rays of the coach lanterns that the San Benito River was up. Mark agreed, but he said, "Watch my beauties take to the water." He reined in his mustangs before descending the steep decline. The animals swam across while the women passengers stifled their screams. In a moment he was lifting his mustangs up on the opposite bank and back onto the pike. The favored passenger agreed, probably with a sigh of relief, that Mark had his horses well broken.

One of Mark's favorite topics was the by-passing of San Juan by the railroads in favor of Hollister because the town fathers voted not to give land for the railroad. When he came to San Juan, it was a thriving trading center in grain, cattle and sheep. It could have been one of the most important points south of San Francisco, Mark believed, but the merchants who had made their fortunes were indifferent to the future. San Juan's fate was sealed, and she lapsed into a deep sleep.

The paradox of progress is that if the railroad had come to San Juan, it would have lost its identity and would no longer have been the same little Spanish town that Mark Regan and everybody loved. Fate has saved it for history and the several hundred thousand tourists who come every year to enjoy its unique charms.

With the arrival of the age of mechanization, Regan finally faced the fact that he would have to give up his coach and four. And so it was that after 40 years he bought a fine 12 passenger automobile. Two years later he sold his old Concord to a moving picture company.

"The automobile is an abomination," Mark told people. "The horse was man's best friend. What has the automobile done? It has increased crime and ruined manners. It has changed human nature and made the world a less pleasant place. But it is here to stay."

John Marentis

Probably no other person in San Juan Bautista is identified as closely with the past and present of the town as John Marentis. His parents, Pedro Marentis and Claudia Estrada, were married in the mission church in 1857. The youngest of 14 children, John was born in 1888. He still lives in the two-story Victorian house on Monterey Street near the cemetery, built by his father in 1873. "My father paid $10.00 for that lot," he said. When John was a child the population of San Juan was around 600 and about half were Spanish and half Americans, he said, adding that he didn't learn to speak English until he started school.

The house, like so many of the Californian's homes, had a large *sala* downstairs for fiestas, and the family had many of them there. John said he played the violin (he still has his instrument and is very proud of it), and one of his brothers would play the guitar. His mother made enchiladas. They were the best. In fact, old-timers still talk about Mrs. Marentis' enchiladas. She also used to make them for the Plaza Hotel.

For 51 years Marentis served as town treasurer. He retired in April of 1976, saying, "I want to have more time for hunting and fishing. Besides, there's too much red tape these days." He said he owns

Marentis house on Monterey Street in San Juan where John Marentis was born in 1888. His father, Pedro Marentis, bought the lot for $10 and built the house in 1873.

John Marentis, who retired as treasurer of San Juan Bautista in April 1976, after serving for 51 years. He is holding his first gun, a Winchester rifle, and some of his hunting trophies can be seen behind him.

four hundred acres in the Gabilan hills which he keeps for hunting.

Speaking of his parents, he said that his father, Pedro Marentis, left Guadalajara, Mexico, at the age of 18 during a revolution. He went to the gold fields near Sonora with Refugio Echeverria and Liberado Corona. "My mother, Claudia Estrada, was born in Baja California in 1841. Her family had a lot of land in Monterey County." On the mantel in his living room is a picture of his mother and his grandfather, Jose Antonio Estrada, a distinguished looking Spanish gentleman.

Marentis said his father was manager of the Aromitas ranch, that Tiburcio Vasquez sometimes stopped over to change horses, that he was always nice. Continuing, he said that the bandit's mother lived in San Juan at one time, on the Alameda, and that she was friends with his parents and with other Spanish families such as the Rozas.

On the subject of the Aromitas ranch, Marentis was of the opinion that his father had owned the ranch at one time and was cheated. The deed that he had, however, named Frederick MacDougall as buying from Pedro Marentis a share in three ranches for the sum of $18,803 in gold dust. MacDougall paid Marentis $4,847. Still due was $14,000 in gold, but the deed indicated that it was to be paid to A. Lewis. John Marentis didn't know who Lewis was. In fact, the whole transaction was not clear, but John said that losing the ranch was the downfall of his father. He was in an accident and unable to work the rest of his life.

"I went to work when I was 13 years old for Arthur J. Trafton at the McAbee Ranch," John said. "At first I milked cows, but I didn't like that and then I convinced him I could drive a team." He also worked driving cattle for Henry Miller from Bloomfield, haying in Watsonville, and for Ferry Morse Seed. But he decided that he wanted to become a butcher. He learned the trade from Tony Taix, working for him for 12 years, and then had his own butcher shop on Main Street for 26 years.

In talking about life in San Juan, he told about Jim Jack, the mustard king, who had a process for making mustard from the wild seed, and that with the money he made from selling the mustard he would buy candy to give to the children. Jim Jack (pronounced as one word) was one of the loved characters in town. Another Chinese man that Marentis remembered was Tom Get, who would come down to San Juan to hide out. He ran a gambling place. "I lost money there," he said, and added "but he was nice." Get was killed by one of the tongs. When asked if it was true that there were once 17 bars in San Juan, Marentis replied, "Yes, and I drank in every one of them. Frank Anzar and I used to drink a pint of whiskey before breakfast. My dad used to give it to me when I was a child, but I don't drink any more—don't like it." And to the question about there being four newspapers, he said, "Sure, there was a lot to write about in those days."

Always active in the life of San Juan Bautista, Marentis said he was a volunteer police officer for Constable C. C. Zanetta for 15 years. He said Zanetta knew how to handle people, that he helped him put many a man in that little jail at the corner of the plaza across from the livery stables. Until his 85th year Marentis rode horseback up to Fremont Peak for the annual flag raising ceremony with a group of townspeople such as the Flints, Abbes, and Anzars. George H. Moore always gave the address. John took part in the rodeos and said he has led the parade for the fiesta since 1961. "I was a flagbearer and last year was grand marshall."

Viola Prescott Archibald

A contemporary of John Marentis, Viola Prescott Archibald was born in San Juan in the farmhouse off First Street built in 1850 by her grandfather, William Sims Prescott, a native of England, who was said to have planted the first orchards in San Juan. He also hauled lumber from Santa Cruz Mountains to New Idria Mines and built the first San Juan school on Rocks Road.

Viola's father, who was also named William Sims Prescott, was a long time supervisor of San Benito County and active in town affairs. He was born in this house in 1860, and Viola in 1889. She and Mamie Lavagnino Avilla attended the old grammar school, built in 1869 on First Street, with John Marentis, 80 years ago. In 1907 the school was moved to the corner of Third and Polk Streets and is now owned by the Odd Fellows.

In memory of Hazel Prescott Beck, Viola's sister, her husband, Kenneth Beck, presented a 24-bell carillon to the Glad Tidings Church. The bell rings out at noon and at six in the evenings. Now non-denominational, this church at the corner of Third and Muckelemi Streets has been called "the little church that would not die." Built by the Baptists in 1863 in the Protestant section of the cemetery (the

Americans were predominantly from the south at that time), in a few years it was purchased by the Congregational group who moved it to its present site.

Tuccoletta Hall

One of San Juan's oldest adobes still in use is the Tuccoletta Hall (Indian for owl) at the corner of Third and Washington Streets. Built in the early 1800s, it was once a tavern, then a bakery operated by Adolph Vache and, after Lorenzo Lavagnino acquired it around 1850, it became a grocery and general merchandise store. Today it is known as the Plaza Market.

Lorenzo's son, Stephen, who came down from Angel's Camp near Sonora where many of the Lavagninos had gone during the gold rush, took over the running of the store. He and his family lived upstairs in what had been the hall, sometimes the scene of wild parties. On the more sober side, Judge Pearce held court there for awhile. Ernest Lavagnino said that after the earthquake of 1906 his mother refused ever to go up there again. He was a boy of seven at the time and he remembers his mother carrying him downstairs. To appease his frightened wife Steve Lavagnino built a Queen Anne style house for her, which was later moved to the corner of the Alameda.

Ernie Lavagnino, who was postmaster of San Juan for 25 years, said his father started the first bank in San Juan. In his scrapbook he has a picture of A. P. Giannini, who was a friend of his father, on a visit to San Juan. Ernie remembered that there was a bar in his father's grocery store, and that they had big 50 gallon kegs of whiskey. The cheapest cost $1.50 a gallon. They called it the "Chinee" whiskey because the Chinese drank a lot of it. The medium grade was $2.50, and $3.50 was the tops. "They used to sell a shot glass of whiskey," he said, "for ten cents." Mixed drinks weren't popular then, but beer was five cents and wine 25 cents a gallon.

Lumber being hauled from the Santa Cruz Mountains by oxen. William Sims Prescott hauled lumber to New Idria Mines.

Group assembled in front of the mission, circa 1912, before riding up to Fremont Peak for the annual flag-raising ceremony.

Glad Tidings Church. "The little church that would not die" was built by Baptists in 1863, later owned by Congregationalists, and is now non-denominational.

"My father made his own wine and would sell it in those old rattan jugs, mostly to the Japanese for $1.25 for five gallons, and I would deliver it in the horse and wagon."

Ernie Lavagnino and his wife live on the Alameda across from Taix Grove where Tony Taix had his home and where many picnics were held. "Blanche Taix," he said, "willed the property to the Maryknoll sisters to use as a home." When the highway was put through to Hollister, it cut the property in half.

"Blanche was the good samaritan for the town," he said. "She fed many people during the Depression." He added that in the early days the creek ran past the Taix property, across where the highway is now, through the John Breen place, around the mission to below the Anderson-Pearce place, and emptied into the Pajaro River.

Also living on the Alameda is Ernie's sister, Mamie Lavagnino Avilla, who was born in 1888. Her memories of the old days include those of the Indians who used to live on Fourth Street near the Native Daughters' adobe. She remembers them as fine people. One in particular, named Hovita, worked for her mother doing laundry and housework. She said there were also many Indians at Indian Corners where the San Juan Grade and the Mission Vineyards Road form a "Y" and that she owns several little houses there which she rents, mostly to descendants of the Indians, including Hovita's daughter, Margie Hall.

Mamie Avilla is the last surviving charter member of the Native Daughters of the Golden West, San Juan Parlor.

Theophile Vache Adobe

On the other corner from Adolph Vache's adobe

on Third Street, his brother Theophile had a one-story adobe. Theophile, who came from France by way of New Orleans, had learned the art of making table wines and of growing grapes in France. He planted 320 acres in grapes in the Cienega Valley and built an adobe winery building which was standing until a few years ago. In 1883 he sold the winery to William Palmtag, a Hollister banker. In recent years it was taken over by the Almaden Winery.

In Isaac Mylar's book, he told about Filoucheau, a saloon keeper in San Juan who acted as Vache's agent. Vache used to send two or three barrels of his wine in a carreta for Filoucheau to dispose of. The driver would return to the vineyard late at night through the dark canyon, over what was the mere semblance of a road, arriving without mishap.

Camp Low

"The stars and stripes shall not fly over San Juan" was the cry of a large segment of the San Juan population during the Civil War. They were southerners who had come to San Juan, tried to convert it into a rebel town, and had in mind taking California out of the Union and into the Confederacy. They did not make good their boast, however. Federal troops were sent into the town to establish Camp Low, named for Governor Frederick Low, and the Union flag was raised in the plaza. The army officers and their wives were housed at the Plaza Hotel and the enlisted men were quartered at the National Hotel and in tents pitched north of the mission buildings.

The plaza square served as a parade ground for the infantry and the cavalry did their maneuvers on the flat to the north of the mission orchard. On Sundays, hundreds of the townspeople, who had always had an inclination for horses anyway, would line the hillside and watch the cavalry perform.

Left, General Jose Castro, one-time Governor of California. He was the leader of the California forces in the war with the United States, with his headquarters in San Juan Bautista.

Right, Juan B. Castro, founder of Castroville, son of Simeon Castro, brother of Manuel Castro, and first cousin of General Jose Castro.

CHAPTER III

The Castros

The story of California is more than generously sprinkled with Castros. There were 70 Castro ranchos, both Spanish and Mexican grants, and a conservative estimate was that members of the Castro families controlled more than ten percent of land held privately in California before it was taken over by the United States.

After secularization of the missions by Mexico, the Castros played leading roles at Mission San Juan. Jose Tiburcio Castro became Civil Administrator of the mission, and for a short time the town became known as San Juan de Castro. He was the son of Macario Castro who came to California in 1784 from Sinaloa, Mexico, as a sergeant in the Spanish Army. In accordance with his authority, Tiburcio Castro divided up the mission lands and, as a result, many of his relatives and friends received grants. His brother, Mariano Trinidad Castro, was given the Rancho El Solis which he had occupied for many years and also received three lots near the mission; the Lomerias Muertos went to his brother, Jose Antonio Castro; another brother, Angel Castro, who was mayordomo of San Juan in 1835, received Cienega de los Paicines, three lots near the mission; the San Justo originally held by Rafael Gonzales went to General Jose Castro, Tiburcio's son.

As Prefect of the Northern District with his headquarters in San Juan, General Castro led two revolts against governors. He is probably best remembered for the incident when John C. Fremont made his famous stand on Gabilan Peak above San Juan. Femont was forced by Castro to retreat after three days, with his band of 62 men, including the colorful Kit Carson. They headed for Sutter's Fort at Sacramento.

Another Castro active in the defense of Mexico against the United States was General Manuel de Jesus Castro, who, when he received word that horses were being delivered to Fremont, attempted to cut them off at the pass. He led the Battle of Natividad, also, which was fought near the Joaquin Gomez Adobe and was the only battle of the Mexican War fought in Northern California.

Rear view of the Castro adobe. This adobe was built in 1840 and was the scene of the planning for the overthrow of two governors, as well as strategy for the Mexican War.

29

John Fremont leading his men to Monterey. In his memoirs he commented that he had tipped his hat as he passed Gabilan Peak,, from which he and his men had been forced to retreat earlier.

Maria-Mercedes Castro

Although Maria Mercedes Castro was never included in the history books, her story, as told to a reporter for the *San Jose Mercury* in 1917, was an excellent first-hand account of the life of the Indians in the years following the secularization of the missions. Mercedes and her twin brother, Rafael, were baptized at the San Juan Bautista Mission in 1836. Her baptismal record was signed by Padre Anza. (The spelling without the "r" would bear out the opinion of the Anzar descendants that Anza was changed to Anzar because of the anti-Spanish feeling in California at this time). Their parents were Jose Antonio Castro and Maria del Merced Ortega de Castro. Their mother had also been baptized at San Juan Bautista Mission, in 1799, and was the daughter of Don Ygnacio Ortega, who received the Spanish Grant San Ysidro. When Mercedes was a little girl her sister, Modesta, married Jose Castro, who was to become the noted general.

They all lived at San Juan Bautista Mission. Maria became greatly interested in the mission Indians who lived in their rancherias beyond the pear orchard. She liked the Indians, and they taught her their songs and dances. Mercedes never forgot these songs and dances and during her later life would sing for fiestas at San Carlos church at Monterey. One of the priests at Monterey transcribed one song and wrote the music for it. She also taught the Indian dances to the young people.

According to the newspaper story, despite her rheumatism and blindness Mercedes demonstrated for the writer the hopping Indian movement, the body moving a very little to either side, always proceeding in a horizontal line from right to left, and the sudden shooting out of the arms to the right, accompanied by expressive Indian grunts.

In describing the San Juan Indians, Miss Castro said that they varied in height and their complexions were a brownish-yellow not unlike a toyon

berry after it had been put in the oven. The women wore their hair over their shoulders "banged" in front as was the American fashion years ago. Sometimes a band of beads or red berries kept their hair out of their eyes. Their dresses were loose little chemises coming halfway to the knees.

Almost every Saturday night the Indians gave a fiesta in an arena-like place near the rancheria. For this they would put on skirts trimmed with bird feathers and tails of squirrels and rabbits. With these they wore bracelets and necklaces of beads.

The feet of the Indian women impressed Mercedes because, she said, they had "never been marred by boots." The men wore only a diaper and did not tattoo themselves, but for the Saturday night fiestas wore red and green plumes.

Another phase of the Indians' lives that fascinated Miss Castro was their treatment of death. With them it was an art. When there was a death in the family the women cut their hair and burned it, painted their faces black, and wore black beads and earrings. She imitated for the writer their weeping and the rhythm of their moans, adding that professional weepers were employed for the occasion. Not everyone, however, had a talent for weeping, she said—it was a special talent.

The Indians' treatment of mothers of newborn babies, as described by Mercedes, is not something a modern mother would be likely to take to. After the birth the other Indians would dig a hole in the ground the size of a woman, which they filled with estafiate, an herb good for poison oak. The mother would have to lie in this hole while the others pressed upon her stomach with their feet, the purpose being to press the poison out of her and make her well. The Indian mothers carried their papooses on their backs in baskets woven of tules, which Mercedes said gave the babies no room to move.

The oldest and most interesting Indian Miss Castro ever knew was Lupisina at Carmel. She said Lupisina had a crooked back and was wrinkled like a monkey, that she lived so crudely that at night she slept on warm ashes from her fireplace. Little Mercedes Castro of San Juan Bautista, who had moved to Monterey, had the greatest reverence for Lupisina, because she had been baptized by Father Junipero Serra. With Father Serra and others she had carried the timbers from the mountains to build the Carmel Mission. This had helped bend her back, and for this Mercedes also had reverence. Once Mercedes gave a bright red shawl to old Lupisina. The most treasured compliment ever received by Mercedes was the Indian's grunt, "Pretty little girl."

Shortly before the American occupation, the Castro twins were taken to Monterey to live in General Castro's house. She said that when the troops marched into town in 1846, the doors were closed on Alvarado Street, not so much in anger as in fear and grief. The Spanish Californian boys, curious to see their future rulers, gathered in the street. She described how the women wept when the Mexican flag fell and the stars and stripes were raised, and remembered how her mother prayed and how she, at the age of ten, got down on her knees and pleaded, "Oh, God, don't let the American men kill us."

As she grew to womanhood and looked back on that day, she smiled. The American men did not kill the Spanish and Mexican women; they wooed them. In fact, one American named Benjamin Upton wooed Mercedes but didn't win her. "In those days," she said, "young ladies were most correct. They did not thrust out their feet nor cross their knees as they do so shockingly today, but they did play with fire, 'un poquito' (a little)."

She said she pretended not to understand young Upton when he told her he wanted to marry her, nor did she respond when he wrote poetry for her. Finally she fled to her grandfather's rancho San Ysidro near Gilroy, and Upton fled from Monterey, swearing never to return.

Mercedes Castro never married. At 81 she was poor and blind. The reporter asked her, "Where is Upton now?"

"Quien sabe," she answered with a deep sigh. This sigh was not for the blindness of age, but for the blindness of youth.

Old drawing of Rancho Aromitas y Agua Caliente.

Mariquita and Lupe Anzar with their family beside the lake in front of their home.

Ramon Anzar and his daughter, Laurita. He was the brother of Padre Anzar and Don Juan Anzar.

Left, Lupe Anzar and Sheriff Jerry Croxon leading the fiesta parade from the Camino Real to the Plaza.

CHAPTER IV

Rancho Las Aromitas y Agua Caliente

The name Anzar in San Juan Bautista dates back to 1833 when Padre Antonio Anzar, the last of the Franciscan friars to serve at the Mission, and his brother, Juan Miguel Anzar, arrived from Colima, Mexico. Both were considered men of wealth at the time. Juan Miguel Anzar served as Juez de Paz (justice of the peace), occasionally acted as prefect at San Juan Bautista, and was Suplente de la Junta at Monterey.

During this time he was also acquiring vast land grants: the Santa Ana y Quien Sabe, 48,822 acres, which he received with Don Manuel Larios in 1839 and divided in 1848, Don Juan Miguel taking the Quien Sabe portion; the large Rancho Real de Aguilas of 31,052 acres; the Vega del Rio del Pajaro of 4,310 acres; and Los Carneros of 1,628 acres. His brother, Ramon Anzar, lived on Los Carneros and is said to have buried $14,000 in gold there. He would never tell anyone where it was, saying they would only quarrel over it; then suffered a stroke and was unable to talk.

It was the Rancho Las Aromitas y Agua Caliente (Little Odors and Warm Water) of 8,700 acres, however, where Don Juan Miguel chose to live with his wife, Maria Antonia Castro. Located four miles west of San Juan, it is also the ranch where his youngest son, P. E. G. (Polocronio Escolastico Guadalupe), always called Lupe, and his wife, Mary (Mariquita) Zanetta Anzar, lived with their family of 12 children. The ranch, which has the distinction of being located in three counties—San Benito, Santa Clara, and Monterey, has long been divided into small parcels.

Of their large family who were such a vital part of life in San Juan, only Reginald V. Anzar and his daughter, Mary Dolores, are still in the area. They live in a house on what was part of the Aromitas ranch. The house in which Reg was born on the rancho is still standing in the Anzar Hills above Highway 101, but the house he remembers best was on Anzar Road overlooking Anzar Lake, where he lived as a boy growing up. Only one other of the children of Lupe and Mary Anzar, Antoinette Anzar Kemp of Sacramento, survives. A daughter

Right, the Guadalupe Anzar family at their Las Aromitas y Agua Caliente ranch. Seated on the steps in front of his father is Reginald Anzar, the only member of the family still living in San Juan Bautista. Others are, left to right, Mrs. Anzar (Mariquita), Aurelia, Gertrude, the cook (standing in background), Lupe, and Lizzie (standing).

33

CC Zanetta and a friend named Bassett who used to come down from San Francisco to shoot birds on the Aromitas ranch. CC's sister, Mariquita, lived on the ranch with her husband, Lupe Anzar, and their family.

Johnny Anzar, son of Lupe, carried the flag in the Fiesta parade for many years and was a popular man in San Juan.

of Frank Anzar, Lolita Lizotte, lives in Palo Alto; a son, Eugene Anzar, lives in Twaine Harte, and another son, Guadalupe, in San Bernardino.

Looking back on his boyhood, Reg recalled boating on the lake, the dances and good times in this house, Henry Miller in his horse and buggy visiting his parents (and eventually owning a good part of the ranch as did another land baron, Jesse D. Carr). Always the Anzars identified with San Juan and took part in all its events—the dances at Zanetta Hall, the rodeos, the Fiesta parade, Lupe leading it, in costume. Later his son, John Anzar, who was an outstanding horseman, led the parade.

Lupe's mother was Maria Antonia Castro, daughter of a first cousin of General Jose Castro, Mariano Castro, who had the Spanish grant Rancho El Solis at the base of Mt. Madonna. He also owned a long spacious adobe on the Alameda where a big fiesta was held after Maria Antonia's marriage in the Mission to Don Juan Miguel. Seven years later Angelo Zanetta, father of Mariquita, who had owned the Sebastopol Hotel, bought the adobe and the one next door belonging to Don Jose Maria Sanchez, and built the Plaza Hotel.

Anzar also owned the adobe building directly across the plaza from the mission known as the

Dr. Frederick MacDougall, a native of Scotland who came to San Juan in the early 1850s. He married Maria Antonia de Castro y Anzar, widow of Juan Anzar. She lived only a year after their marriage and Dr. MacDougall became the guardian of her three sons.

Haying on the Aromitas.

Iron caldron brought from Mexico by the Anzars. It was used for dipping pigs, making tallow, etc.

monjerio, which was used during the Mexican War by General Castro as headquarters for the cavalrymen. Later it was the home of Juan Anzar's sister, Chona, and her husband, Julian Ursua. Still later Angelo Zanetta bought the building and used the adobe bricks in constructing the Zanetta House where Mariquita was raised.

Juan Anzar died in 1853 when Lupe was two and one-half years old. His mother, who was also ill, married her physician, Dr. Frederick MacDougall. They moved into the house of her mother, Dona Rufina Castro, on the Alameda, but Dona Maria Antonia was to live only a year longer.

Two of her three sons, Juan and Anatolio, died young. The family said that Dr. MacDougall educated his three charges and that when Lupe went to Santa Clara College he sent 50 head of cattle to pay his tuition. Lupe was a handsome, dashing and colorful personality. He loved race horses, had a livery stable in Los Angeles at one time, and a gold mine in Mexico.

Although the comparison has been denied by her family, Maria Antonia Castro y Anzar will forever be associated as the Rose of the Rancho in Richard Walton Tully's play of that name. Lupe said she received the appellation because of her generous, kind qualities. She was buried in Mission San Juan Bautista. One story was that Maggie Salas, housekeeper at the mission for Father Closa, was showing visitors through the mission and, pointing to the grave of Dona Maria Antonia, said it was the grave of the Rose of the Rancho. She didn't intend it seriously, but the story went over so well she continued to tell it. Later she was sorry for ever having said it.

In the mission files were found a sheaf of notes concerning San Juan and reminiscences of early residents, including those of Soledad Rodriguez. Much was said about the charitable and thoughtful

Reginald V. Anzar and his daughter in front of the Plaza Hotel which his father-in-law owned and where his father, Lupe Anzar, was born.

nature of Dona Maria Antonia—that she was always inviting children into her parlor and giving them shoes and dresses. Soledad, Anzar's god-daughter who lived with them, told about a time when some Indians were passing the ranch with an Indian boy tied to the saddle, so sick that his head hung over the horn. Mrs. Anzar was very moved and asked a man how much they wanted for the boy. He said a hundred dollars. Mrs. Anzar said promptly, "I will give you two hundred dollars." The Anzar family raised the boy. He had a peculiar gait and was known to everybody as El Troton (the trotter). Another time a cub was captured at the ranch and was going to be killed, but Mrs. Anzar would not allow it. The cub grew up to be a big bear.

Another story told by Soledad happened when she was a little girl. She used to help dust in the mission church. Her father made her a ladder so she could climb up to reach the statues. One time she was cleaning the statue of San Ysidro about half way down the side of the church. Her ladder began to give way and when she got down she found that one of the tiles in the floor was loose. Under it she found two sacks of gold coins. She had always been taught "see, but do not talk." When she got home she told her mother. Years later her mother told her she had told Dona Maria Antonia and learned that it was Padre Anzar's money that he had buried under the tile.

In describing Juan Miguel Anzar, Soledad said that he was prepossessing in appearance and a man of wealth. She believed that pressure was brought upon Maria Antonia by her parents to marry him. When he was dying in San Jose he sent for Soledad.

Mariquita Zanetta Anzar grew up during one of San Juan's most exciting periods and at the place where the action took place, the Plaza Hotel. With the stagecoaches coming and going, there was never a dull moment. In an interview in the *Los Angeles Times* in 1936 she said that on festival days her father used to stage bull fights in the plaza, which in those days was a smooth, barren rectangle. People came from miles around to see the fights and afterwards there was a big dinner and dance. The dance was five dollars a couple and they had to turn people away.

One of Mariquita Anzar's most vivid recollections was of the great flood of 1862. It must have been a big one, for San Juan was marooned for a week and for once the stagecoach horns were silent. All San Juan Valley was under water, but presently the ground was dry again and the nine-year-old Mariquita climbed into the carreta with her parents to see the damage as a pair of oxen whirled them along at a breathtaking three miles an hour.

Another recollection concerns a man who got out of the stage from Visalia with one side of his face covered with whiskers and the other smooth shaven. He was Casper Behrendt of Los Angeles, enroute to San Francisco to help establish the Masonic Lodge in that city. He was only half finished with his shave when the stage was ready to leave Visalia and finished it at the Plaza in San Juan.

A controversial subject in the same interview, open to question and unanswered, is the subject of the disposition of the Anzar ranchos, the Quien Sabe, Real de Aguilas, Vega del Rio del Pajaro, and the Aromitas. Mrs. Anzar said that after the death of Maria Antonia, Dr. MacDougall lost little time in disposing of all but the Aromitas, which Lupe received. What arrangements MacDougall had made with Lupe are not known. The records in Hollister show that the two largest ranches, Real de Aguilas and Quien Sabe, were sold in the 1870s by MacDougall, his wife, Francesca, and others, to Jose De Laveaga. Lupe's name was not listed. Dr. MacDougall at this time had moved south. He was mayor of Los Angeles from 1872–74.

Around 1909 or 1910 Lupe and Mariquita moved with their family into the house in town that had been Judge James Breen's and then Edward Breen's, where Cademartori's Restaurant is. They later moved to a house on Monterey Street near First Street. It is now the home of Mrs. Charles Vacarezza. With them they brought the huge iron kettle that had been brought up from Mexico by Juan Miguel Anzar and used for cooking a whole hog and to make tallow for candles. Also prized possessions were the rosas de Castillas which had been brought from Spain by the mission padres in the 1790s and from which Mariquita took cuttings.

Just before Lupe's death in 1932, the couple celebrated their 55th wedding anniversary. There were so many people there that their son Reg said that in order to get out of the house he climbed through a bathroom window.

The vast ranchos of Lupe Anzar's father had long since passed into other hands, but Lupe and Mariquita could look back, he was quoted as saying in an interview, "on the fiestas of earlier days—the bull and bear fights—the cock fights in the stockade in the enclosed arena of the present plaza; of days of feasting, the nights of dancing, the vivid life and romance of the old, old days."

CHAPTER V

B The Castro-Breen Adobe

Six generations of the Patrick Breen family have lived in San Juan Bautista. When Patrick and Margaret Breen arrived in February of 1848 with their six children (a seventh was born in San Juan), they became the first American family to settle in the mission community. It was shortly after the signing of the treaty ending the war between Mexico and the United States. In 1846 the war had started and one of the motivating factors in Patrick's decision to leave Iowa and bring his family to California was the anticipation that California would be joining the Union.

The Breens had survived the harrowing crossing of the Sierras with the Donner party and that unforgettable winter of cold and starvation at Donner Lake. The snows came early to the Sierras that year, in October, and it wasn't until March that they got out. Of the original members of the party, 39 died of starvation or exposure. The Breens made their way to Sutter's Fort, camped at the Robert Livermore Ranch, and were taken in by the Franciscan padres at Mission San Jose. At each stop they were given household goods, beef, and information. When they arrived at San Juan Bautista and looked out over that valley, Patrick Breen knew they had reached their promised land.

Padre Antonio Anzar took them in at the mission first. Then General Jose Castro let them live in his adobe house across the plaza. Shortly after their arrival, two prospectors came through town, and the Breens' eldest son, John, went off to the gold fields with them. He dug at Mormons' Bar and Placerville, returning home with $12,000 in gold dust. With this he bought the adobe for his parents and some of the mission lands Castro had acquired at the time of the secularization of the missions. For a time the Breens ran an inn. It was always busy—there were so many travelers passing through San Juan, going to the mines, and there was no other place for them to stay.

In his book, *Crusoe's Island*, J. Ross Browne described a trip by muleback in 1849 from San Francisco to San Luis Obispo, and spending the night at the United States Tavern. Connected with the revenue service, Browne was on his way to San Luis Obispo to see a wrecked boat full of riches. He described the inn as an adobe house, part of the mission establishment, and the only tavern in town. He said it was run by Americans, survivors of a party who were snowbound crossing the Sierras. This description leaves little doubt as to where he was. Bayard Taylor, in his book, *Eldorado,* also told of staying at an inn run by Americans when he passed through on foot on his way to Monterey to attend the convention.

On a visit to the Castro-Breen adobe, James Breen, great-grandson of Patrick and Margaret Breen, talked about the family. He said that generations of Breens have known this house, that it stayed in the family until it was taken over by the State of California for an historical landmark park in 1933. It was built in 1840–41 by Jose Tiburcio Castro, prefect of San Juan Bautista after the secularization of the missions, with Indian labor, for his son, General Jose Castro. The handsome Monterey colonial house has a classic style of architecture featuring balconies and porches front and back, and beautiful old trees. It was intended to serve as headquarters of the northern prefecture, but Don Jose was so busy as commanding officer of the Mexican forces that he spent little time there. He did use it as his headquarters during his campaign against Fremont and on two occasions when he served as interim governor of the state for Mexico. It was here, too, that together with Juan Bautista Alvarado, he organized a revolt against Governor Micheltorena which resulted in his being recalled to Mexico. Earlier in 1836 Castro had led a revolt against Governor Gutierrez which resulted in Alvarado's being made governor.

Castro-Breen adobe, one of the finest examples of Monterey architecture in the state. General Castro gave the Breens permission to live in the house when they first arrived in San Juan. They had crossed the Sierras with the Donner Party and were the first American family in town.

In speaking of the Breens' life in San Juan, as told to him by his father, William James Breen, and his grandfather, Patrick Breen, Jr., Jim Breen said that they worshipped at the old mission church cater-corner across the plaza from the family adobe, where Breens have traditionally been baptized and married, that after mass on Sundays they would walk over to the adobe for family gatherings.

"His great-grandmother, Margaret Breen," he said, "was noted for her hospitality and entertained prominent personages at the adobe." Her warm personality was described by Patty Reed in her book about the Donner-Reed party. When her father, James Frazier Reed, went ahead to San Jose for help, Margaret Breen befriended her.

Margaret was considered by many to be as capable as her husband, or more so. When Patrick was sick, according to George R. Stewart in *Ordeal by Hunger,* she oversaw the slaughtering of the cattle. She probably could have headed the family.

Patrick Breen was the only member of the Donner party who kept a diary—the original is in the Bancroft Library in Berkeley. He recorded the weather, measured the snow, and told of trying to proceed but of having to return to the shanty on Donner Lake time and again.

The children and grandchildren of Patrick and Margaret Breen grew up in an atmosphere that was Spanish and French (many French families moved into the village in the '50s), and they soon learned to speak Spanish and some French. All attended school in San Juan. James went to Santa Clara College (now University). He was one of its first graduates, studied law, was superior court judge of Monterey County, served in the 22nd Assembly, and was superior judge of young San Benito County

from 1880 to 1897. He married Catherine McMahon, daughter of a San Juan merchant who moved to Hollister and had extensive holdings in San Benito County, including Hotel Hollister, formerly the McMahon House. The present site in Hollister of the Sacred Heart Church and school was donated by McMahon. Jack Breen is the only descendant living on McMahon property. He farms on Union Road outside of Hollister.

Judge Breen's sister, Isabel, known as Bella, the only daughter of Patrick and Margaret, who was a baby during the Sierra crossing, married Thomas McMahon, the brother of Catherine. Bella was educated by the Dominican sisters. In a newspaper interview late in life she said she wished she had paid more attention to the stories told by her parents and brothers about the crossing, because she, of course, had no recollections of the experience.

Well preserved and restored is the old adobe with its four-inch thick walls. The bedrooms upstairs face on the balcony. To the sides of the main entrance hall are the living room and the large dining room, furnished in the period of the 1870s, mostly gifts, Jim Breen said, from the family. In the office is the Wells Fargo desk and gold scales of Judge Breen. The piano was donated by Joe Cullumber, great-grandson of Simon Breen (son of Patrick and Margaret). Simon had it shipped around the Horn as a present for his daughter, Mary Catherine Breen, who learned to play at the convent. In an upstairs closet is hanging the wedding gown of Bella. On display are Breen branding irons, lariats, and braided rawhide *riatas.*

A curious feature of the house are the low doors, which Jim Breen said he heard were measured to a

The Breen family. Clockwise from bottom: Patrick, Edward, Simon, William, Peter, James, Patrick, Jr., John, Margaret (lower center), and Isabella.

James Breen, grandson of Patrick Breen, Jr., with his sons Paul and Patrick and his granddaughter, Leslie Breen.

short Indian, as Castro himself was a tall man. In the back of the house are beautiful old pepper trees, one with a trunk approximately eight feet in diameter, believed to be the oldest in California. The pepper trees were brought to California originally by the mission padres, who planted them along El Camino Real. Nearby are huge iron caldrons, holdovers from the Mexican days. They were used for rendering fats and tallow. The *peleadors* (hide strippers) stripped the hides from the cattle quickly and the fats were cut up and dumped into these great kettles. After being rendered, the fat was poured into *bolas* and loaded into carretas, to be pulled by oxen to Monterey. Here they would be traded to Yankee or English clipper ships for merchandise.

After our visit to the Castro-Breen adobe with Jim and Betty Breen, the next stop was the Breen Ranch. As the Breen boys married, most became ranchers and branched out into the valley. In fact, at one time they owned most of San Juan Valley. The land acquired by Jim's grandfather, Patrick Breen, Jr., was along the San Benito River. He married Amelia Anderson who came to San Francisco on a sailing vessel from Australia. They built a house to which he kept adding rooms, and

he also continued to add land to his holdings, including part of the Lomerias Muertas rancho which was originally granted to Jose Antonio Castro, a piece of the San Justo from the Flint family (this too was a Castro grant which had been sold to Don Francisco Pacheco), and a section of the Rancho San Antonio from the Don Manuel Larios family.

Five generations of Breens have lived or worked on the ranch, including Jim's sons, Paul and Patrick. The ranch covers more than 15,000 acres, and there has always been a Breen to manage it. It is now owned by 15 descendants of Patrick Breen Jr. The original brand was a capital "B." When Patrick, Jr. started out for himself, he turned his father's brand around, making a B backwards. About 1930 it was altered again to "B." There had been confusion because the vaqueros would forget to put it on backwards.

Simon Breen, who was seven years old when the family came to California, married Marie Constance Pidancet, a native of France. They lived in San Juan Bautista at Third and San Jose Streets, and owned several blocks in town. Their daughter, Geneva, married Albert Beuttler, the brewer who was so noted for his fine product that it was shipped over the Pacheco Pass to the San Joaquin Valley. The Beuttler place, built in 1870, is still standing on the Alameda.

Two talents for which Simon is especially remembered were his horsemanship and his violin playing. His favorite trick was riding a bucking horse in the plaza. He would bet some unsuspecting person that he could put a gold piece on the stirrup under his boot and could buck the horse all over the plaza square without its falling. He always won and everyone would repair to the Plaza bar for a drink, including the horses—horses in the Plaza bar in those days were common.

Patrick, Sr. raised mostly sheep. He apparently leased out land and was also quite a good businessman, to judge from one of his account books found in the old mission among Harry Breen's books and papers. The U.S. Patent to Castro's mission lands signed by President Grant was also found among those papers.

In the account book which starts August 1, 1857, appear names that tell the story of San Juan in those days—Twitchell, who headed the Mormon colony that came to San Juan Canyon, is listed for one white mare at pasture for $2 per month on 7-22-58; Refugio Echeverria, 30 head of sheep; Antonio Castro, $87; October 4, 1859, sold to Miller & Lux 47 head of cattle at $27 per head; more large cattle purchases by Miller and Lux; Manuel Larios, the beloved owner of Rancho San Antonio, which he called "El Ranchito," and Rancho Santa Ana, borrowed $22 at 3% interest per month on April 8, 1862; on June 1 that same year Butterfield with teamster put head of oxen at 10 cents per day in pasture; October 30, Negro Bill—wood for John, seven cords; October 13, 1862, Gregorio Sanchez, horse in pasture $2. (He was the son of Jose Maria Sanchez, the vast land owner, and Maria Encarnacion Ortega of the famous Sanchez treasure story.) Other names appearing include W. W. Hollister for whom the town of Hollister was named; Miguel Castro, who put his mules and one mare for pasture; Angelo Zanetta; Andrew Abbe, whose daughter, Clara, married Zanetta's son, "CC"; and Miguel Gilroy, son of John Gilroy of San Ysidro ranch, for whom the town was named.

CHAPTER VI

The John Breen Adobe

After staking his parents to the Castro adobe, in 1852 John Breen decided to have an adobe of his own for his bride, the former Leah Smith, daughter of San Juan Bautista's first postmaster. He chose his site well. The house sits on the bluff with the fertile valley land below at the end of Nyland Lane off the Alameda.

On a visit to the adobe his three granddaughters, Adele McConnell of Hollister, Agnes King of San Francisco, and Leah Rosborough of Menlo Park, talked about John Breen and the house. They said that he first built a kitchen and dining room. He then hauled an old adobe building from the Castro property, in back of his parents' house, bringing it on logs by oxen, to add on to the house. Apparently he added on to it several times, they said, because their mother always talked about the new part and the old part. A substantial structure, the house has large buttresses of adobe bricks and three-foot thick walls.

The three sisters were the daughters of Thomas Nyland and Catherine (Kate) Breen, daughter of John Breen. Nyland was an orphan boy from San Rafael who was befriended by Patrick Breen, Jr. Their brother, the late Arthur Nyland, was the father of Dorothy (Mrs. Frank) Avilla, who now owns the adobe and 38 acres. She lived there for a time with her husband, son Robert and daughter Cathleen, who are sixth-generation Breens.

The Nyland family lived on the old San Juan Road across from the McKee family. Arthur Nyland eventually bought this property where Dorothy Avilla and family now live.

Arthur Nyland became a rancher of prominence, raised thoroughbred horses and rode at the head of the Fiesta parade for many years. His ranch, which includes part of the San Antonio grant, is at the foot of the Gabilans. It is now owned jointly by his son, Harvey Nyland, and Dorothy Avilla, who raise Herefords.

As we looked over the house with its typical deep overhang, Agnes said there had been a porch on three sides with all the doors opening onto it (the front has been enclosed with glass). "We used to run around it, unless Grandfather was asleep at his favorite place by the window in the kitchen. In that case we would have to wait until he woke up. We always used to ask Grandma why all the doors opened outside."

Adding to the charm of the place, there is a grove of trees in the fenced-in portion in back of the house with water troughs serving as planters. The sisters remember that often when they came, their grandmother would be working in the garden. She didn't like housework, but then she had the girls to do that.

Looking over the fence to the valley floor, Dorothy Avilla said that the Breens owned practically all the land over to the Flint Hills and that the Patrick Breen, Jr.'s ranch is at the base of those hills. To the left just below are potato fields, which

John Breen adobe, on bluff overlooking the San Juan Valley. It was built by John, the eldest son of Patrick and Margaret Breen, after he had come home from the gold fields with $12,000 in gold. He also gave money to his parents to purchase the Castro adobe.

Dorothy said had been Tony Taix's property. He was an early San Juan settler and had a butcher shop. His house was where the new school is now, just off the Alameda. "His property adjoined my grandfather's; the highway to Hollister cut through both pieces," she added.

One of the fondest memories the sisters seemed to have of the adobe was of the springs below the house. They said that on Sundays the family would go to mass at the mission in the carriage. "Later in the day," said Leah, "we would come to the adobe to visit our grandparents. The first thing we would do when we got here was to run down to the springs for a drink. There was something about that water that tasted so good." She pointed to a place where some willow trees were growing. "Mama told us that the Indian girls used to come here to get water and would carry it in brown jars."

Above left, the present owner of the John Breen adobe, Dorothy Avilla, and her aunt, Leah Rosborough, grand-daughter of John Breen. Note buttresses adding strength to the already three-foot-thick walls.

Above, a view of the porch which at one time ran all the way around the house.

In the notes found in the mission, Tony Taix wrote about the spring where the Indian girls got the water for the rancheria. He said it was too steep for the ox carts, and that one of the old Indians used to have a colored picture showing a string of the Indian girls carrying water in clay jars up the hill. There were two springs below the Breen adobe. The other one was where the Indian women used to bring clothes in big bundles on their heads to wash.

Taix also told of a stream that came down from the San Juan Canyon and flowed along the hills across the Alameda on down to the mission orchard. The Indians told him that the Alameda was planted with willow trees in 1800, that it was originally an eighth of a mile long, and that there was an "L" that ran from the Alameda to the Breen Spring. The four willow trees near the John Breen spring are all that are left. Taix said he chopped down those on the Alameda.

From the front of the house, the Breen and Taix property can be seen. Adele McConnell reminded her sisters of how they used to cut across Taix's property. Both had groves where picnics were held. The centennial celebration was held there as well as Fourth of July picnics.

Reminiscing about their childhood days at the farm on San Juan Road, the sisters said that they weren't allowed to go into town. "San Juan was pretty wild in those days," said Agnes. "There were saloons all over." They remembered that if they

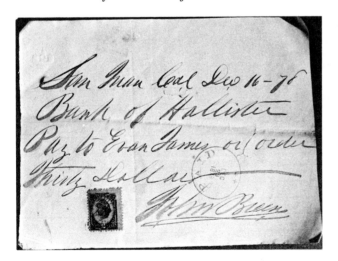

John Breen wrote this check on a piece of foolscap paper. It was drawn on the Bank of Hollister and is dated December 16, 1878.

42

were walking down the road and Mark Regan came along in his stagecoach, he would stop and give them a ride.

After Margaret Breen's death in 1874, the Breen family no longer occupied the Castro-Breen adobe. A Mrs. O'Flynn took care of the house. Adele, who is the oldest, said she remembered going with her mother to visit Mrs. O'Flynn.

Back to John Breen—apparently that winter at Donner Lake made its imprint on his life in many ways. Beside the front of his house is an enormous pine which he planted when he built the adobe. It has a special significance. During that winter at Donner Lake, it was his job to climb up a certain large pine tree to see if he could spot help coming. It was his mother, Margaret, however, who took turns with him in climbing the tree, who spotted rescuers coming.

Another reflection of the Sierra experience was John Breen's love for dogs. At a certain point that winter, the family's dog, Towser, had to be killed. John never forgot that. "Grandpa always had dogs," said Leah. "He took them everywhere. Grandma didn't especially like having them in the kitchen, but wherever he was his dogs were with him. He even took them to the school board meetings and when he was on the board of supervisors of Monterey County and later of San Benito, he took his dogs to those meetings. I guess they were a little surprised at first."

After experiencing want and near starvation, none of the Breens ever wasted anything. Nevertheless, John Breen was regarded as a generous man—he gave away land or anything, said his granddaughters.

In his book, *Early Days at the Mission San Juan Bautista,* Isaac Mylar tells of John Breen's incorruptibility and generosity. When a road was to be built between his father's and his own property, Breen insisted upon giving the land.

Another carry-over from his Donner Summit days was an aversion for snow. Kate Breen Nyland told her daughters that when there was snow on the Gabilans, she and his other children would beg him to take them up, but he would turn his head away and his eyes would fill with tears.

She also told them a story about their grandmother. During that terrible winter Margaret carried her baby, Isabel, close to her. In her blouse she kept a little sack of sugar. From time to time she would put her finger to her lips, touch the sugar and give it to little Bella.

Patrick Sr. died in 1868 during the smallpox epidemic that hit San Juan. That same year Margaret's son, Peter, who was soon to be married, was on an errand for the sisters at the convent. Crossing the Pajaro, he fell from his horse. The animal apparently kicked him, and he drowned. His funeral at the mission was one of the biggest San Juan Bautista had ever seen.

In 1874 tragedy again struck the Breens. William, the youngest, who was a hotel man, died of a fever, a few months after his marriage to Mary Zanetta. This was the last straw for Margaret Breen. She said the winter at Donner Summit was easier than having to give up her sons.

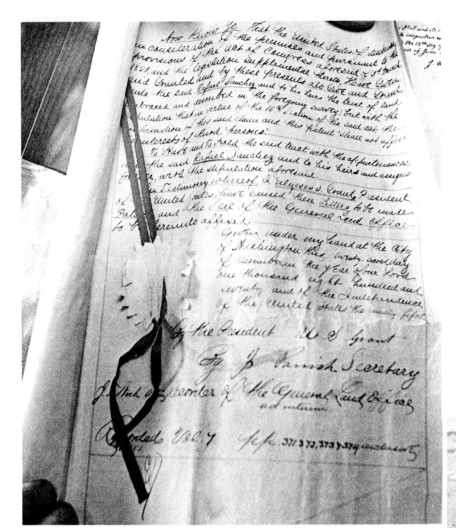

Left, U.S. patent for Topo ranch (San Lorenzo) to Rafael Sanchez, signed by President U. S. Grant.

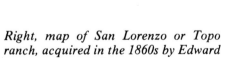

Right, map of San Lorenzo or Topo ranch, acquired in the 1860s by Edward Breen and James Dunne.

CHAPTER VII
Rancho San Lorenzo
(The Topo Ranch)

As it was for most of the Breens, ranching was a way of life for Edward Breen, second son of the Patrick Breens, and said to have been Margaret's favorite. He had 400 acres of farming land in the San Juan Valley, but he chose the Rancho San Lorenzo, better known as the Topo, for his home base. Together with James Dunne, in the 1860s, he had bought the 48,000 acre grant to Rafael Sanchez, which spread over San Benito and Monterey Counties.

His first wife, an Irish girl, died at 28 years of age leaving him with three sons who passed away in their twenties and early thirties. In 1880 he married Mary Burns of San Francisco, 30 years his junior, only to make her a widow ten years later, leaving her with three sons and 20,000 acres of the Topo ranch. Very much a San Franciscan and described by some of her family as "lace curtain Irish," Mary Burns Breen raised her sons, Edwin, Harry, and William in San Francisco.

In my visit with Barbara Breen Rolita and Edwina Breen Kump (Mrs. Peter) of San Francisco, granddaughters of Edward Breen and daughters of Edwin, they said that Mary Breen and the boys used to stop over at the Castro-Breen adobe on the plaza in San Juan on their way to and from the ranch. Barbara added that Henry Miller was an old friend of her grandmother and used to visit her when she was at the adobe while his driver took his carriage around and around the plaza. Barbara now lives in the house Edwin and Harry built for their mother in 1929. It is located on Franklyn Street backing up to the old Zanetta property on the plaza and looks out on the San Juan Valley.

Barbara has kept her father's den intact. In fact, it looks like a mini-museum with the walls lined with old photographs, mostly of the original house built in the 1860s when her grandfather acquired the Topo, and the house her father built in 1915,

where she and Edwina were born. There are also scenes of cattle roundups, some with Edwin working with just a rope around his horse's neck to show the skill of the horse, a picture of Edwin with Gary Cooper when Cooper made his first western on the ranch, pictures of Julius Trescony, an old friend of the family and well known cattleman, panoramic photographs of the Salinas Rodeo, and pictures of Edwin with cavalry horses he bought for the army during World War I. In the corner is a hatrack with a marvelous assortment of hats, and Edwin's branding iron with the big "E."

Edwin Breen as photographed by Ed Borein, noted western painter, when he was working on Topo ranch.

Dominating one wall is a handsome photograph of her father taken by the famous western artist, Ed Borein, who worked on the Topo. There is a handwritten bill of sale, made out during the overland crossing of the Donner Party, to Edward Breen in St. John, Missouri for one roan horse. Over the signature, Joseph Davis, is an "X." A sad message is contained in a telegram addressed to Edward at the Topo from his brother John Breen: "William died last night." In another vein is a sign warning poachers—"Wanted - $1,000 Reward." It bears the names and brands of Edwin Breen, James Dunne and others, including Matt Williams, O. H. Willoughby, and Martin Griffin Co.

Speaking of the Topo, Barbara said it was considered to be a fine cattle ranch because it had water. "Frank Grimes, who was foreman, told me of the time he saw 1,000 head of cattle watering out of one spring," she said, adding that during the Depression the Bank of America repossessed the ranch and 400 acres of farming land in the San Juan Valley. Edwin stayed on to run the ranch until 1950 when it was sold and he retired. A man named Tannehill from New Mexico bought the Dunne portion, and the Topo is now known as the Albert Hanson Ranch. Hanson formerly rented the Sam Mathews Ranch.

"Grandmother held a tight rein in raising the boys," said Barbara. "One time they rode their horses to San Francisco, and then to Yosemite, visiting friends along the way. When they arrived at Yosemite, who do you suppose was waiting for them on the porch at the Curry Hotel but Grandma!

"Then there was the time on the ranch when Grandma heard a Mexican whooping and hollering

Edwin Breen with Gary Cooper and cowboys during filming of one of Cooper's first westerns made on the ranch.

and went outside to see her young Harry going through a row of gum trees on a bucking bronco. She threw the big white apron she always wore over her face and cried, 'Oh, my baby!' and passed out, while the Chinese cook went for the Florida water (alcohol).

"Another time Grandma was going through San Juan on her way to Gilroy and discovered her sons

Barbara Breen Rolita and Edwina Breen Kump sitting in old family surrey in front of Plaza Stables, where it is presently housed. They are great-granddaughters of Patrick and Margaret Breen.

46

Left: Edward Breen, who crossed the Sierras with his parents, Patrick and Margaret Breen, in the Donner Party. Right: Mary Burns Breen, wife of Edward, was widowed ten years after their marriage and raised their three sons, Harry, Edwin, and William in San Francisco.

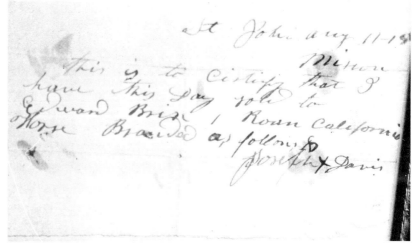

Bill of sale written in St. John, Missouri, for one roan California horse, with brand listed. Note "X" over name Joseph Davis.

in a time race in which they had to stop the horse and jump off. It was very dangerous—a test of horse and rider with a stop watch. Grandma arrived just in time to see one of her sons, Edwin, jump off. She shook her umbrella at him, crying, 'I didn't raise my children to be wild Indians.' ''

Still another story about Mrs. Edward Breen concerned a time she went into court over some debts owed to her husband. She always wore her widow's weeds—a big black hat with a black or purple veil. She wasn't in the courtroom long before she left in a huff, saying, "This court is packed from the bench on down." The judge, of course, was Superior Court Judge James Breen.

There are stories, too, of Fat Ed, who was also called the Topo Pigeon. His name was E. P. Breen, but nobody seemed to know where he fitted into the family. "He was smuggled out of San Juan," said Edwina, "during a smallpox epidemic, in a wagon that was going to the Topo. While the boys were growing up he ran the Topo. When he would go out

to ride the range, he would attach to the back of his saddle a container of cream, and when he came back it would have turned to butter.

"Fat Ed had a cabin on the ranch and when my dad would leave he would take him 12 mince pies and 12 cans of tomato sauce. That was his favorite food."

Edwin died quietly in 1960 at the age of 76. It was a more peaceful death in a way than that of his father, who like all of his generation of the Breens was never able to forget completely the ordeal at Donner's Lake.

According to Barbara, her grandfather, Edward, died in the house on First Street which he had bought from his brother, James, the Superior Court Judge. "My Aunt Annie told us that Grandma wanted him to take some jello. All his life he couldn't stand the looks of anything that resembled gelatine because he still remembered his mother boiling the hides at Donner Lake for food. Finally Aunt Annie said, 'Let the man die in peace.' ''

47

The San Justo ranch. The large house, built in 1863, is now the St. Francis Retreat Center. The small house was originally Hollister's. Horses were kept in the large barn, and the smaller one was used for sheep. During the Civil War, although most of the townspeople were pro-Confederate, the Union flag was flown from the flagpole.

Map of San Justo land grant, purchased from Francisco Pacheco in 1855. The Flints and Bixby paid $25,000 for 34,615 acres. By pre-arrangement they sold half to Colonel Hollister who in turn sold his portion to the San Justo Homestead Association for the town of Hollister, for $375,000.

The Flint-Bixby house. Three families lived in this house together, in apparent harmony.

CHAPTER VIII

Rancho San Justo

The saga of Dr. Thomas Flint, his brother, Benjamin, and their cousin, Llewelyn Bixby, who bought Rancho San Justo in 1855, is truly an American success story. From a trip to the gold fields of California between 1849 and 1851 by these three young men from New England, one with only five dollars in his pocket, evolved the Flint-Bixby and Company empire in California, which included vast ranches from Central to Southern California and the San Joaquin Valley, ownership of the Coast Line Stage Company, and other ventures. The headquarters for their widespread enterprises was always San Juan Bautista and the San Justo Ranch. Still standing, proud and strong, is the staunch New England home they built against the foothills of the Gabilan Mountains. It is now the St. Francis Retreat Center.

Ben Flint had heard tales of the great wealth being found in the mines of California. After completing his education at the Academy of Yarmouth in civil engineering, he became fired with the desire to go to California to find his fortune. On the boat trip by way of the Isthmus he was to make the acquaintance of a James Irvine, an event which was later to be important. When his brother, Dr. Thomas Flint, and his cousin, Llewelyn Bixby, received glowing letters about the placer mining, they decided to join him. They also traveled by ship, and on their arrival in San Francisco headed immediately to Volcano in Amador County to join Ben. With their Yankee instinct for business, the three young men soon decided to abandon mining and take on business enterprises such as the meat business, fattening cattle for market. They also built the National Hotel at Volcano and weighed gold for the miners.

After a year and a half at Volcano, they had accumulated a considerable sum. They agreed they would take their fortune back to Maine and return

overland with sheep and cattle. The problem, though, was how to get the gold dust safely back to the mint in Philadelphia. They had special buckskin jackets made with compartments in the lining, but they proved to be too heavy. The boat going back was not as full as the one on which they had come to California (everybody was coming but nobody was leaving), so they decided to take an extra cabin. They put their gold between the mattresses and at least one of the three stayed in the cabin at all times.

Their next concern was how to take the gold across the Isthmus of Panama without being robbed. They packed a chest with blankets and clothes so as not to arouse curiosity, put it on the back of a mule, and practically ran across. At Aspinwall they booked passage on another sailing ship for New York and arrived home in Maine in 1853.

After several months' stay in Somerset County, visiting family, they were ready to begin their return trip to California. Dr. Flint kept a detailed diary starting with their train trip from Boston to its western terminus in Terre Haute, Indiana. Along the way they visited relatives who had moved west from Maine. At Terre Haute, before starting for Quincy, they organized the firm of Flint, Bixby and Company. Because Benjamin had come to California two years earlier, he held four-tenths, with Thomas and Llewelyn each holding three-tenths. With careful buying they accumulated 1,034 head of sheep and six yoke of oxen.

By the time they reached Warsaw, Illinois, it was time for shearing, and they reaped an early return on their investment with the wool bringing in $1,570.45. Now with 1,880 Spanish Merino sheep (increased to 2,400 by the time they reached California), eleven yoke of oxen, two cows, four horses, two wagons and complete camping outfit, and

Mr. and Mrs. Thomas Flint with their daughters, Marjorie and Dorothy, and Dr. and Mrs. Thomas Flint on upper steps.

three dogs and four men besides the Flints and Bixby, they began their overland journey. At Keokuk, Iowa, they had the animals ferried across the Mississippi at a cost of $62. Keokuk, by the way, was the home of the Patrick Breen family, the first American residents of San Juan Bautista, before they made their trip to California with the Donner Party. Later, Benjamin Flint's son, who was named for him, was to marry Mary Catherine Breen, daughter of Simon Breen.

Dr. Flint stayed on at Keokuk to receive payment for the wool sold in Warsaw, and then took the river boat to join the party near Council Bluffs.

With the exception of a few encounters with Indians, their trip across the plains was quiet. In their first meeting, an Indian tried unsuccessfully to run off with some horses. Four nights later one of the camp guards was killed when he saw an Indian trying to steal Dr. Flint's horse.

Dr. Flint wrote in his diary about another experience:

Soon after halting, half a dozen Indians bounded out of the bush and commenced to pillage the wagons. The teamsters, Johnson, Palmer, and Jennings were scared out of their wits and offered no resistance, but Mrs. Johnson went after their hands with a hatchet when they went to help themselves to things in her wagon. I found it necessary for me to put on airs, so went to the wagons...ordering the Indians to put everything back they had taken from the wagons. They were sulky and one of them taking an ox bow by the ends made a motion to strike me with it whereupon I brought my pistol to bear upon him with the intention of shooting when he dropped the bow...Then I knew I was master of the situation...

Two more Indians joined those already present—one

of them with a certificate that they were good Indians. It was written in faultless penmanship, expressing the hope that we would treat them well, so we gave them a sheep that was lame...We found they were a hunting and marauding party of Arapahoes from Texas.

A short time later Flint and Bixby overtook an emigrant train of Mormons from England who had been robbed of all their provisions by these "good Indians" and shared their supplies with them. Had it not been for the Flint-Bixby train, they might not have survived.

This incident was to serve them well when they reached the valley of the Great Salt Lake. Two men approached them and asked if they were "saints or sinners," in other words were they Mormons or not. When the men learned, however, that this was the party that had aided the Mormons who had been stranded, they were treated very well. Their flocks were permitted to graze in church pastures, and they were given vegetables from the Mormons' gardens and repaid for supplies.

In the diary Dr. Flint also tells of meeting other parties driving sheep, one a Colonel William Welles Hollister who had a herd of 4,000 with his sister, Lucy Brown. They sometimes joined forces against the Indians who were trying to run off with some of the stock. The hardest part of the trip was crossing the Mojave Desert, a hundred mile stretch with only one water hole. On the eleventh day they reached the Mojave River. From here the going was easier. They crossed through the Cajon Pass in Southern California to San Bernardino and then to the Mission San Gabriel. That winter the flock grazed at Rancho San Pasqual where the city of Pasadena is now located.

Hollister and Lucy Brown did not tarry but continued north by way of Ventura, Santa Barbara, San Luis Obispo and Paso Robles. Along the way they passed the Tecolotito Canyon and the Dos Pueblos Ranch. Hollister was so impressed that he became obsessed with the desire to own the beautiful property.

In the spring Flint and Bixby drove their sheep to San Jose where they rented grazing land on the Santa Teresa Rancho for 14 months. By then the sheep had more than doubled in number. Although the Spanish had brought sheep to the mission ranches, the first American sheep in California marked the beginning of the wool industry. The Flints and Bixby lived south of San Jose on Rancho Santa Teresa for a time. In his diary Thomas Flint told of selling their "clips" to Messrs. Moore and Folger.

In 1855 they decided to buy the Rancho San

Justo where Colonel Hollister and Lucy Brown had been staying, having reached an agreement with Hollister that he would become a partner. They purchased the property from Francisco Perez Pacheco for the sum of $25,000. Pacheco had acquired the rancho from General Jose Castro for $1,400. It was previously granted to Rafael Gonzales in 1836 who abandoned it, giving up his claim to the land. According to the agreement beforehand, Hollister purchased half the grant for $12,500. In 1868 he sold his portion to the San Justo Homestead Association for $375,000. They named the new community Hollister because some of the members were tired of "all those Spanish names."

Rancho San Justo, which covered 34,615 acres, extended from the crest of the Gabilan Mountains to the present town of Hollister. It ran the width of the valley, bordered by the Cienega del Gabilan Ranch on the south, the Lomerias Muertas and San Juan on the west, and the Bolsa de San Felipe ranchos to the north.

Hollister lost no time in heading down to Santa Barbara. He was now in a position to purchase the Tecolotito ranch which he had dreamed of owning.

The House at San Justo

The handsome Flint-Bixby house, set in the San Juan Hills of the Gabilan range, with a natural lake in front and 73 surrounding acres, has been owned since the early 1940s by the Franciscan Order of Friars Minor who operate a retreat house. In the ecumenical spirit of the day other denominations also come to hold their retreats there. At the invitation of Rev. Gilbert M. Zlatar, O.F.M., and Rev. Gratian Goebel, Marjorie Flint and her sister, the late Dorothy Flint, granddaughters of Dr. Thomas Flint; Eva Galli, daughter of Ben Flint, Jr.; and Mrs. William Bradford Flint, whose late husband was a son of Benjamin Flint, Jr., visited the old family home. It was a return to the scene of their childhood for Marjorie and Dorothy. Although they were born in San Francisco where their father, Thomas Flint, Jr., always kept rooms at the Palace Hotel, they grew up in this 113-year-old house which seems as durable as its New England heritage, and yet is only two miles from the mission town of San Juan Bautista.

Marjorie and Dorothy Flint told the story of their grandfather, Dr. Thomas Flint, and his brother, Benjamin—that after the success of their sheep venture and the purchase of this fine property, they

Benjamin Flint, left, and his brother, Dr. Thomas Flint. Benjamin came to the gold fields in 1849 and wrote such glowing letters home that he was soon joined by his brother and a cousin, Llewelyn Bixby. This was the beginning of a great American success story.

decided it was time to find wives. Where else were they to look but in their native New England. Llewelyn Bixby stayed in California to look after business. Ben Flint was married to Caroline Lavina Getchell, descendant of Governor William Bradford, and Thomas married Mary Ann Mitchell, daughter of Joshua Mitchell. Bixby followed their example two years later and married Sarah Hathaway in Maine.

The two young married couples, joined by Ann Flint and Nancy Dinsmore Bixby, who later married William Lovett, sailed from New York. The brides recorded the story of their trip in letters to their parents. When they landed at Chagres, the railroad was not yet completed so they started up the river on a small stern wheeler, tying up at the bank at night—a trip that took two days and two nights. At Gorgona they transferred to a smaller boat propelled by six natives with long poles. Three or four days were spent in leisurely tramping over the mountain trail leading to the western port. At Panama City they boarded the *SS Northerner* for San Francisco. What an adventure it must have been for these sheltered New England girls. They wrote home of their experiences, telling of the crowded conditions on the boat and of stopping at Acapulco where the Spanish galleons used to call on their way from Manila and the Orient before 1600 A.D.

On reaching their destination at Alviso, they took a stage to San Jose where they stayed, visiting friends and family, while they purchased fur-

Tom Landrum and his wife lived in this house. Landrum, with Lester Morse and Albert Hart, selected the San Justo land for the seed farm.

nishings for their house. In their letters home they described this new country—mustard ten feet tall, fields of golden grain ripened, the live-oaks dripping with moss and mistletoe.

At Rancho San Justo the couples first lived in a house on the San Benito River. Dorothy Flint recalled that when they used to drive to Hollister in the carriage their father would point out a spot on the San Benito River and say, "Look over there and you can see where I was born." It was just about at the division line of the Flint-Bixby and Hollister portions of the San Justo.

After the settlement of the division of the property as pre-arranged with Colonel Hollister, the Flints and Bixbys moved to the house where Hollister and Auntie Brown had lived until their big house was built.

What a stir this two story white New England house with its green shutters, high pitched roof and gables with icicle trim, and the white picket fence around the front garden, must have made with the townspeople of San Juan Bautista.

Although many Americans had come into San Juan after the American takeover and built rather simple frame houses, the town was still half composed of adobe buildings, and Spanish was still the predominant language. Signs were posted in Spanish and English. Many of the Spanish dons were still around. Don Manuel Larios was on the Rancho San Antonio or "Ranchito," as he called his ranch near town, staging bullfights and fiestas, and only a short distance away was the El Camino Real, a path made by the Indians and Spanish explorers. Bayard Taylor, the author of *Eldorado*, described the path in 1849: "...[it] started up a canada to cross the mountains to the plain of the

Aerial view of Ferry-Morse Seed Company plantings, which since 1910 have provided the valley with a riot of color. 910 acres of the San Justo ranch were purchased for a headquarters, and 383 acres of the Flint Hills were purchased for winter pasture for the company's 150 horses. The growing operation has expanded to 1800 acres.

Salinas River. It was a mule path, impractical for wagons, and leading directly up the face of the dividing ridge."

He described the madrone filling the ravines, purple branches and trunk and glossy leaves, and thickets of a shrub with snow-white berries. "From the summit there was a fine mountain view, sloping off either hand into the plains of San Juan and Salinas."

As the Flint descendants looked about the house with Father Gilbert, they told about the three families who lived in the house in apparent harmony. Each had its own sitting room and bedroom, and shared a common parlor which was a good-sized room. The wives took turns running the main household, including the kitchen, for a month at a time.

They were reminded of the way the house had looked in their day, noting that after Madame Butler Hedges bought it in 1922 she made many changes. (The title "madame" was used at her request.) The original kitchen and pantry were incorporated into the dining room, and a new kitchen was added on. There were five fireplaces downstairs, all marble except for the one in the dining room.

Much of the lumber in the house came from Maine, and the moldings around the doors were made at a mill in Santa Clara. Their furniture came mostly from New England. Marjorie has some of it in her home in Hollister—the square Steinway piano which came around the Horn, the spinning wheel, desk, grandfather clock, and a painting of a pastoral scene in Maine.

In the back of the house were the old stone retaining wall which the sisters remembered well, and the old oak tree with its graceful spreading branches. Dorothy said there used to be a porch where guests arriving by carriage could alight. With three families living in the house and the family business being conducted there, there were many comings and goings. Before this porch was incorporated into the house by Madame Hedges, there was room for a carriage to turn around in back. Behind the kitchen were the auxiliary buildings, one for laundry, another for wood, a milk house, a meat house, and a dining room for the men. The house towards the lake where Colonel Hollister had lived housed the vaqueros. Nearby was the barn with long rows of stalls for the horses on one side and on the other the carts, buggies and hay mow. There was also a cow barn where the cows were milked; the Spanish Merino sheep were kept in a

barn up the hill. In a picture taken in 1865 of the lake, house and buildings, a weathervane in the shape of a sheep can be seen on top of this barn.

Dorothy and Marjorie had many memories of life on the ranch. A big thrill for Marjorie was to ride from the gate with Refugio Echeverria, the head vaquero, on his white horse, Old Sam. Dr. Flint wouldn't let his daughters ride on the ranch because of the squirrel holes. They talked of the boat they had on the lake, of having school on the ranch in the Hollister house, of walks through the orchards on the other side of the lake to the orchardist's cottage. The family orchard, Marjorie said, was closer to the house. It had started first with vegetables, then fruit trees, a vineyard, an almond orchard, and olive trees. It was probably some of the olive trees from this orchard which were moved down to the village and planted along the Alameda leading into town. A path led into the center of the orchard where the family burial ground was surrounded by a white picket fence.

Marking off the picturesque lake area are mossy weathered fences, low stone walls, pepper trees and bay and oak. From here the group looked down on the flatland which at one time was a solid mass of sweet peas planted by Ferry-Morse Seed Company, and before that was planted by Flint-Bixby in grain. Marjorie said the hills that we saw were called the Flint Hills and that the ranch originally extended across from San Juan Canyon to beyond Hollister.

Eventually Llewelyn Bixby and his family moved to Southern California to look after interests there. His daughter, Sarah Bixby Smith, was to carry childhood memories of the ranch with her. In her book, *Adobe Days,* she wrote, "...it was among rolling hills whose velvety slopes bounded my world. Over all was the wide blue sky, a bit of it having fallen into a nearby hollow. This was a fascinating pond, for water ran uphill beside the road to get into it. There were many fish, none of which ever would get caught on my bent pin hook. It was into this water that I once saw some little ducks jump."

Around this time, in 1871, there was a description of the Flint-Bixby holdings in the *Monterey Republican:*

Flint, Bixby and Company of San Juan own about 200,000 acres of land, 19,000 in the immediate vicinity of San Juan, 140,000 in Los Angeles, 53,000 in San Luis Obispo and over 18,000 in San Joaquin and Washington Territory on which graze 75,000 sheep and thousands of cattle. Their wool clip this spring will realize them about $95,000—over 300,000 pounds have been sheared...

The Benjamin Flints moved to Oakland, considered at that time a fashionable place to live. Eva Flint Galli said her grandfather, unlike his elder brother, did not take part in fraternal or civic activities, but had a reputation for being a sharp businessman. In 1860 he was elected first president of the Southern Pacific Railroad Company, but did not accept. Instead he became vice-president. He and his partners had actively assisted in securing the franchises and grants of land so necessary for the railroad.

Although Dr. Flint never practiced medicine unless needed for an emergency, at one time he did serve as the chairman of the County Medical Board. As a member of the Monterey Board of Supervisors one of his accomplishments was to lay out the Old Stage Road. The Camino Real was too steep for a coach. He went out on horseback up San Juan Canyon, a man following him with a horse and plough, and they planned the route. This stage road is still passable except during the winter months. He was elected state senator from Monterey and San Benito Counties, and in 1884 was a delegate to the Republican National Convention.

Active in Masonry, he was grand master of the Lodge for nine terms, the beginning of the "Reign of the Flints." He was followed by Thomas Jr., who served a number of terms as did his cousin, William Reed Flint. This is interesting inasmuch as Dr. Flint did not join the Texas Lodge, Free and Accepted Masons in San Juan Bautista (one of the first founded in California) for 16 years after he came to the town. The reason was probably that it was dominated by Southerners. Their feeling about Yankees was particularly strong during the Civil War.

The Flints' sympathies must have been equally strong for the Union, for they decided to raise the American flag on their ranch still under construction in 1863. The women made a tremendous 18-foot-long flag by hand. The men went over to the Santa Cruz Mountains and got a flag pole and brought it through San Juan at night because they didn't dare risk trouble in San Juan. The huge flag flew over the Hollister house for some time. Marjorie still has it.

In addition to his San Justo home, Dr. Flint kept a suite of rooms at the Palace Hotel in San Francisco and also made frequent trips back to Maine. As a matter of fact, most of the Flints and Bixbys were what might have been regarded as cross-country commuters for their day. Mrs. Jotham Bixby was a passenger on the Pacific Railroad on its return trip east after the initial run, to visit her family. She had come around the Horn to marry Jotham in 1862.

Dr. Flint took over the running of the ranch at the death of Ben Flint in 1881. When Bixby died in 1896, the property was divided, with the Bixbys taking the Southern California property. In dividing the San Juan-Hollister property, Ben Flint's heirs received the San Joaquin o Rosa Morada ranch and Dr. Thomas Flint the San Justo.

Thomas Flint, Jr. meanwhile had gone east to school, graduated from Dartmouth College, and married Ada Mary Fisk. Upon the death of his father in 1904, he took over the management of the ranch. Like his father, he was interested in civic affairs. A member of the State Senate from 1889 to 1904, he was prominently mentioned as candidate for the Republican nomination for governor in 1898, but withdrew on the eve of the convention.

With five children he had found it feasible to have a school on the property, but when Marjorie and Dorothy were ready to enter high school, the family decided to move to Hollister. Only one of the three sons is still living, Dr. Thomas Flint of Vallejo. He is tenth in line to carry the name of Thomas. The first Thomas Flint came to Salem Village from Wales and died in 1663.

Flint-Bixby had done well with their cattle and sheep, especially during the Civil War, risking the blockade to ship wool to the east coast. They were in a position to buy land and in 1866 acquired the Los Cerritos Ranch from Don Juan Temple for $20,000. In other words, they purchased what turned out to be the town of Long Beach for 72 cents an acre. The sale was facilitated by the fact that Temple wanted to go to Paris.

Jotham Bixby was made manager and permitted to buy half interest in the sheep ranch. He and his family occupied the old adobe that is now the La Casa de Rancho Los Cerritos Museum. About this same time Don Juan Sepulveda, who was deeply in debt, was forced to sell his 50,000-acre San Joaquin Ranch for $18,000. This was to become Orange County. The purchasers were James Irvine and Flint-Bixby. Irvine and Ben Flint had first met on that long 103-day voyage to San Francisco in 1848.

In 1883, Flint, Bixby and Company purchased the Rancho Los Alamitos in conjunction with I. W. Hellman, Jotham Bixby and John W. Bixby. It was operated by John W. Bixby and his son, F. H. Bixby, as a stock ranch.

About this same time, William Wolfskill's

interest in the Rancho Santiago de Santa Ana became available, and the Irvine-Flint-Bixby firm became owners of Rancho Lomas de Santiago of eleven square leagues, 47,226.61 acres. The Irvine, Flint and Company ranch was now 110,000 acres. Eventually James Irvine bought out the partners for $150,000 and it became known as the now famous Irvine Ranch. By a coincidence Dorothy Flint, granddaughter of Dr. Thomas Flint, was later to have Joan Irvine, granddaughter of the partner who played a prominent part later in the Irvine Ranch lawsuits, as a student in one of her classes in school in Pasadena.

Goats

Their operation with cattle and sheep successful, Flint and Bixby decided to try raising goats, thinking their pelts might have commercial value.

Captain James Cook was said to have left some goats on Guadalupe Island off the coast of Lower California on one of his voyages. By the 1860s there were 30,000 wild goats on the island. Flint and Bixby imported Angora goats to the island to improve the quality of the pelts. Although several shipments of the goats were made, the project was eventually abandoned, but to this day, black and white goats populate Guadalupe Island.

Although Flint, Bixby and Company branched out into other enterprises, they were most noted for their high-grade, full-blooded sheep which were shipped to Panama, the Sandwich Islands, and Nevada. They were the first to import Merino sheep to California and the first to pay $1,000 for a Merino ram—a price which to most seemed

ridiculously high but was justified by the quality of their sheep. With the 2,000 head of Merinos they brought to California, they built up a fortune and empire in the sheep and wool industry.

Stagecoaching

Highly successful was the Coast Line Stage Company which ran coaches from San Jose to Los Angeles and which Flint and Bixby had acquired from William E. Lovett in 1869. One reason for the success of the stage line was the inadequate steamer transportation between San Francisco and Los Angeles. It wasn't until 1901 that there was through railway passenger service between the two cities. The coaches carried mail, passengers, and Wells Fargo Express.

There seems to have been a bit of political maneuvering in Lovett's securing the mail contract. He had campaigned all over the state for Abraham Lincoln and was a good friend of the Commissioner of Indian Affairs, who had an "in" with the government. Lovett got a job as a special agent to investigate any and all matters between the Indians and the whites in the southern counties, so that he was on the inside when the Post Office Department asked for bids for the mail route. He underbid Charles McLaughlin, builder of the railroad from San Francisco to Gilroy in 1869. The thrice-weekly service began July 10, 1866 with San Juan an important stop and headquarters for the company. The transfer to Flint-Bixby was involved with Lovett's indebtedness to them. In charge of the stagecoaches for Flint, Bixby and Company was William Buckley.

Furnishings for the house, including this Steinway piano, were shipped around the Horn.

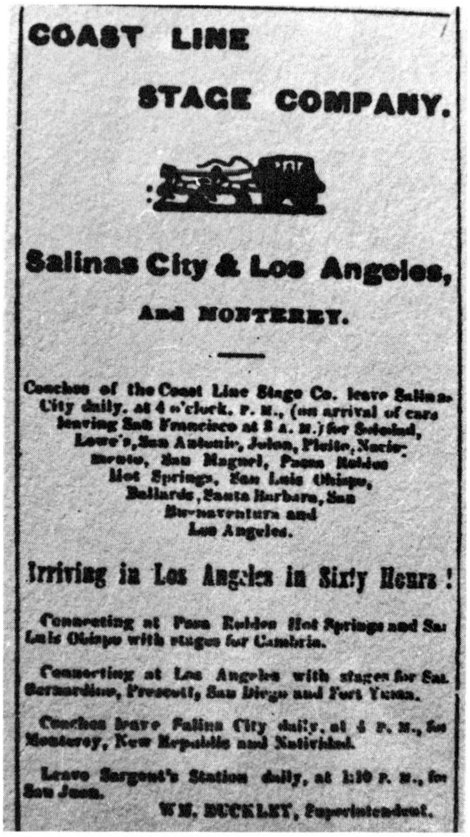

COAST LINE

STAGE COMPANY.

Salinas City & Los Angeles,

And MONTEREY.

Coaches of the Coast Line Stage Co. leave Salinas City daily, at 4 o'clock, P. M., (on arrival of cars leaving San Francisco at 8 A. M.) for Soledad, Lowe's, San Antonio, Jolon, Pleito, Nacimiento, San Miguel, Paso Robles Hot Springs, San Luis Obispo, Ballards, Santa Barbara, San Buenaventura and Los Angeles.

Arriving in Los Angeles in Sixty Hours!

Connecting at Paso Robles Hot Springs and San Luis Obispo with stages for Cambria.

Connecting at Los Angeles with stages for San Bernardino, Prescott, San Diego and Fort Yuma.

Coaches leave Salinas City daily, at 4 P. M., for Monterey, New Republic and Natividad.

Leave Sargent's Station daily, at 1:10 P. M., for San Juan.

WM. BUCKLEY, Superintendent.

Schedule of Coast Line Stage Company owned by Flint-Bixby. Headquarters were always in San Juan Bautista.

The inventory on the bill of sale listed the Coast Line, San Juan, and Los Angeles Stage Company as owning 270 head of horses, 22 stations with buildings, hay and grain necessary to care for stock, 23 stages (four of which were mud wagons), one freight wagon, 49 sets of four harness horses, and six sets of six-horse harnesses.

From San Juan the coaches passed over the Gabilans on the road Dr. Flint laid out, to Natividad, Soledad, San Luis Obispo and Santa Barbara, and other stops.

Madame Leila Butler Hedges

In 1923, after the Flint family had been in the San Justo home for 60 years, the main house, including the lake and 2,400 acres, was sold to Madame Leila Butler Hedges for $150,000. The new owner, who requested that she be addressed as "Madame," had first been married to L. Hedges, and divorced him to marry a man named Stoddard, whose name she eventually dropped. The daughter of Gates Butler, who made his money in railroading, Madame Hedges lived in a style to which San Juan Bautista was unaccustomed. After purchasing the Flint property, the first thing she did was to hire the firm of McLaren and McElroy, who had planned Golden Gate Park and Villa Montalvo, to redesign the landscaping.

At the far end of the lake she built a house for her son, Walton Hedges and his wife Betty, which she called "La Casita," meaning little house, (a relative term in comparison to the size of her house). She started almost immediately adding on to the main house—glass in the veranda across the front, a wing

Coast Line stagecoach crossing the Gabilans. Flint-Bixby bought the line from William Lovett in 1869. Where the grades were steep the gentlemen would have to get out and walk.

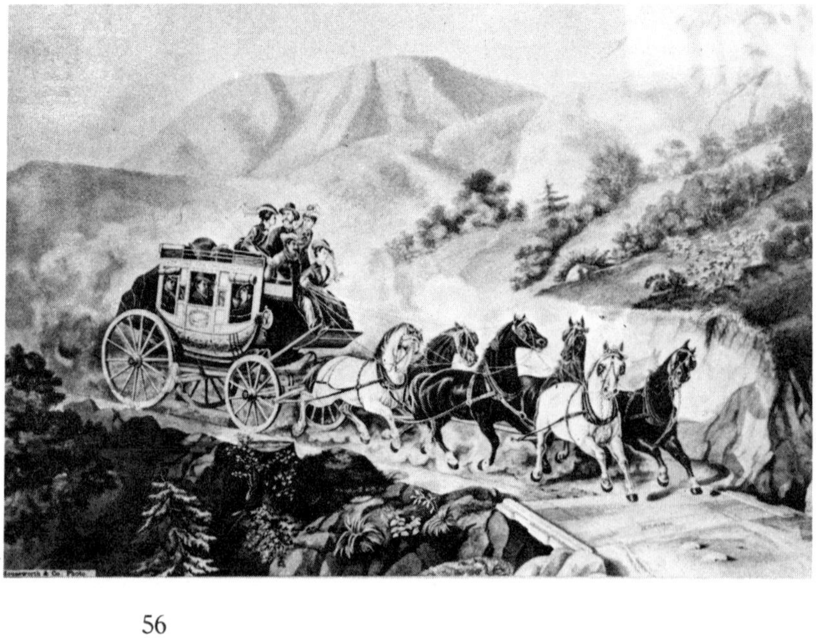

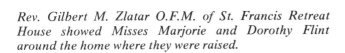
Rev. Gilbert M. Zlatar O.F.M. of St. Francis Retreat House showed Misses Marjorie and Dorothy Flint around the home where they were raised.

at each end, and a gazebo. In fact, she was referred to as a latter-day Sarah Winchester. Palm trees were planted along the drive and patios added and she gave her place a new name, "Hacienda Del Justo." There were nine steady gardeners and 15 day laborers who worked in the yard. In the house she had a butler, a butler's helper, a maid, a social secretary, and a chauffeur who took care of her four automobiles including two Cadillacs. According to members of the family, her daughter-in-law always had to do all the planning of the menus and over-seeing of the running of the house. Sometimes Madame Hedges would decide to change houses, and she would move into the Casita. In addition to her home at the ranch, she always kept an apart-ment at the Mark Hopkins and another place at Pebble Beach.

According to the Edward McNears of Palo Alto (his stepmother, Mrs. Fred McNear, was Madame Hedges' sister), she would have houseparties for as many as 15 guests. Dorothy McNear said that in redecorating, Madame Hedges had kept the New England feeling, even having wallpaper removed from old houses in New England and rehung on the bedroom walls upstairs. The bedrooms had canopied beds and were done in great taste. Mrs. McNear also said that Madame Hedges furnished the house with beautiful antiques, but that a somewhat discordant note was the painting of her pet Pekingese dog which hung over the marble fireplace in the living room. The McNears remem-bered taking a boat trip to the Islands in 1930. His aunt happened to be on board with her son and daughter-in-law. Madame Hedges told them she

had engaged two trained nurses to look after the dog at home. The last time they saw her was in Santa Barbara where she moved as her health failed (she weighed 250 pounds). She spent her last years at El Mirasol Hotel, passing away in 1953.

San Justo has had its third set of owners for almost 30 years and is enjoying yet another way of life. The Franciscan order, which has the main house, lake, and 73 acres, added a chapel, rooms for overnight guests, and a conference room where they conduct their retreats.

In October of 1947 the Armand Holthouses pur-chased 2,300 acres of the San Justo, which they operate as a cattle ranch. Bud Holthouse's family formerly owned land in Mountain View which they sold to the Navy for Moffett Field.

Living not far from the Holthouses on the San Justo are the John Baumgartners. John, who first came to San Juan Bautista in 1928 and lived at the Plaza Hotel, learned about cattle on his family's 45,000-acre Santa Margarita Ranch in Southern California. His maternal grandfather, Richard O'Neill, in partnership with James Flood, pur-chased the ranch in 1882 and held the property until it was sold in 1941 to the Navy for Camp Pendleton.

After he married his wife, Eleanor, in 1932, he moved into the house Edwin and Harry Breen had built for their mother, Mrs. Edward Breen, on Franklyn Street, now the home of Barbara Breen Rolita. The Baumgartners' present home is on a knoll surrounded by 300 acres, and they enjoy a superb view of the Gabilans on one side and the vast sweep of San Juan Valley below.

View of the Cienega del Gabilan ranch house high in the Gabilans near Fremont Peak. The late Dr. Rollin Reeves gave part of the ranch to the State of California for Fremont Park. The ranch is now owned by Reeves' widow, his son, Dr. William Reeves, and his daughter, Marilyn Baldocchi. It was formerly the property of John and Jessie Carr Bryan (granddaughter of Jesse D. Carr, who received the patent in 1867.)

The Reeves ranch house on the upper reaches of Cienega del Gabilan ranch, built over 100 years ago.

Thomas Oliver Larkin, first and only U.S. Consul to Monterey, purchased the 48,000-acre Cienega del Gabilan ranch from Jose Y. Limantour. His heirs sold the ranch to Jesse D. Carr, who made many trips to Washington over a period of years before he finally secured clear title.

Dr. William Reeves and Donald Baldocchi on Carr Ridge. From here Pacheco Peak can be seen in the distance. Nearby three fences come together at right angles, marking the division of this ranch, Jim Bardin's, and Ky Scillacci's. Elevation is 3,169 feet.

CHAPTER IX

Rancho Cienega del Gabilan

Scenically beautiful and historically colorful is Rancho Cienega del Gabilan. The original grant of eleven square leagues (48,780 acres) to Antonio Chavez by Governor Micheltorena in 1843 straddled San Benito and Monterey Counties. On the San Benito side it bordered Rancho San Justo, Rancho La Cienega del Paicines (along the San Benito River), and Rancho Los Vergeles, which extended down the west side of the Gabilans.

Chavez, the original grantee, was a tax collector brought from Mexico by Governor Figueroa. He served as a lieutenant to General Castro, was wounded in the Battle of Natividad, and escaped capture with protection by Californians. It was he, incidentally, who had kidnapped Thomas Oliver Larkin from the Gomez's adobe during this same battle and took him to the Californian's camp. Chavez eventually went to Baja California with Castro, but before he left he gave a deed to the Gabilan rancho to one Jose Y. Limantour. This transaction is regarded by historians as somewhat cloudy. At any rate, Limantour gave a quit claim deed to Larkin, who died just before the patent was signed in 1858.

Jesse D. Carr bought the ranch from the Larkin heirs and from then on, for Carr, it became a *cause celebre*. Carr hired Washington attorneys, including Attorney General Blair of Lincoln's administration, to represent him. It took him ten years and many trips to Washington before the U.S. patent was finally signed by President Andrew Johnson. There was some question as to whether Chavez ever had a legitimate grant. Carr also had a multitude of problems with squatters, including Jasper Twitchell of the Mormon colony, with whom he made some sort of deal. James Bardin, with his brother, Henry, acquired 17,000 acres of the ranch from Carr. He used to say that every time there was a new president Carr would get out his stovepipe hat and head for Washington.

Carr, who came to California in 1849, was obviously a man on the move. He acquired five ranches, ranking with Henry Miller and David Jacks as the top landowners of Monterey County. He was a banker and a politician, his interests extending to several states. He was also a stock breeder, importing in the early 1870s Durham cattle, a prize bull named "Old Sam," Spanish Merino sheep, and Kentucky racing stallions. A contingent of Japanese came to see Carr's shorthorn cattle in 1877 and purchased several head for shipment to Japan. In 1880 the Japanese government ordered 100 Spanish Merino ewes to improve their breeds.

7 *The Reeves Ranch*

Mrs. Rollin Reeves, her son, Dr. William Reeves of Los Altos, and her daughter, Marilyn Baldocchi (Mrs. Donald) of San Francisco, share ownership in a 10,000-acre parcel of the Gabilan grant. It is just below Fremont Peak at an elevation of 2,700 feet, at the place where, during the Mexican War, John C. Fremont and his band of 62 frontiersmen in their buckskins raised the American flag on March 6, 1846, only to make an ignominious retreat three days later when out-bluffed by General Jose Castro.

The late Dr. Rollin Reeves of Salinas acquired this property from John Bryan and his wife, Jessie, granddaughter of Jesse D. Carr, in the financially disastrous year of 1929, but, according to his son, Dr. William Reeves, he managed to hold on to it. Dr. Rollin Reeves donated a part of the ranch for Fremont Peak State Park.

The setting for the 100-year-old house is so picturesque that it is almost as though someone had found a painting of how a western ranch should look and brought it to life. There is a large oak tree in front of the two-story house, set in a hollow beside a lake which reflects the trees and red ranch buildings. This entire area is marked off by stone walls and mossy picket fences.

In back of the house is Mare Pasture, a name given to it by John Bryan. In front of the house is parked an old wagon piled high with hay, and under the oak tree are mortars and pestles found near the house, formerly the property of the now extinct Castanoan Indians.

Quite a different story is attached to the solid copper water storage tank with a weathervane on top. It is an old still which Dr. Reeves spotted and managed to buy in Monterey during prohibition, just as it was about to be destroyed. The iron pot below it to catch water came off a whaling vessel from the Lahaina coast of Maui. It was used originally for boiling whale blubber.

In remodeling this charming old place that was built with square nails, the Reeves have kept the simplicity and old California ranch feeling of Jessie and Johnny Bryan's home. There is a large iron pot-belly stove in the kitchen and a big stone fireplace in the living room, but everyone gathers around the long hunting table in the kitchen, which, although refinished, retains its scars.

On the walls are prints of paintings by the famous western artist, Charles Russell, and Ed Borein. It is a coincidence that John Bryan was a cousin of Russell and also of Charles Howard (Seabiscuit). Johnny is remembered not only as a colorful character who wore a big diamond ring, but as a superb horseman. He rode in the San Juan Bautista Mission fiestas and received special mention from the judges for his riding in the fiesta of 1908 which was held to raise funds for restoring the mission after the earthquake of 1906.

Although it is hidden away in the Gabilan Mountains, the ranch was spotted from the air by the Marlboro cigarette people who sought out the owner and asked if they might photograph their commercials there. The company gave Bill Reeves copies of the photographs, which now hang in the front hall. Bill noted that it is easy to spot that they are commercial pictures, because the cowboys are wearing white hats and no real cowboy ever wears a white hat.

The plant life on the Gabilan is indeed varied. A dirt road leads up to Pine Ridge where Coulter pines covered with large pine cones with sharp spines can be found. On the way, past a forest of mossy oak trees, is an area called Bear Tree, where one sees an old oak tree that has fallen. Carved on its bark is, "Bear killed here, 1900." Silhouetted against the sky, as we crossed a nearby hill in the late afternoon, were a family of deer, and an uncharacteristic touch—here and there could be seen old iron bathtubs. They came from the San Francisco fire of 1906, Don Baldocchi said, and are used for salt for the cattle.

A great place to take in the view is Carr Ridge. In the distance can be seen Pacheco Peak—closer by a knob of a hill is called Dowdy Hill, named for an old San Juan family. Nearby three fences come together at right angles—this is the meeting place for three ranches, Reeves', Jim Bardin's, and to the left Ky Scilacci's. Directly in front is Fremont Peak at 3,169 feet. It is from this point that the Marlboro people photographed the riders on horseback going down that hill with the sun setting behind them, Dr. Reeves said.

Most impressive of all, however, is the view of the Salinas Valley with its color patchwork quilt of agricultural lands, and on the other side the Santa Lucia Mountains.

This valley was described by two early-day travelers in 1849. J. Ross Browne, in *Crusoe's Island,* described what he saw as he crossed over the El Camino Real from San Juan:

The view from the summit was magnificent. Beyond a range of sand hills toward the right stretched the Pacific. Ridges of mountains singularly varied in the outline swept down in front to the broad valley of Salinas. The pine forests of Monterey and Santa Cruz were perceptible at the distance; and to the left was wilderness of rugged cliffs as far as the eye could reach—weird and desolate as Cape Horn suddenly petrified in the midst of a storm.

Descending through a series of beautiful little vallies, clothed in golden drapery of wild oats and charmingly diversified with groves of oak and sycamore and rich shrubbery of ceonosa, hazel and wild grape, I at length entered the great valley of the Salinas, nine miles from the Mission of San Juan. At that time innumerable herds of cattle covered the rich pastures of this magnificent valley.

He noted, incidentally, that a couple of years later there were not so many cattle.

Another traveler and a writer of that same period, traveling by foot from San Francisco to Monterey to attend and cover a constitutional convention in 1849, Bayard Taylor writes in *Eldorado* (published in 1861) of crossing the Gabilans:

Descending a long canada in the mountains, I came out at the Great Salinas Plain. At an Indian ranch on the last slope several cart-loads of melons were heaped beside the door, and I ate two or three in company with a traveler who rode up, and who proved to be a spy em-

Jesse D. Carr, large landholder, politician, breeder of racing and trotting stock, and owner of Rancho Cienega del Gabilan.

ployed by General Scott in the Mexican campaign. He was a small man with a peculiar, keen gray eye, and a physiognomy thoroughly adapted for concealing all.

Some 60 years later Katharine Bixby Hotchkis, granddaughter of Jotham Bixby of the Bixbys of Flint & Bixby, who had the adjoining San Justo Ranch, described a 500-mile ride on horseback in 1916 in her little book *Story of a Trip from Piedmont to Los Angeles.* She made the trip with her father, Fred Bixby, and two sisters. As they crossed the Gabilans they passed the family's San Justo Ranch. Their father pointed out Fremont Peak saying that was where he thought the house was. She describes it:

The narrow wagon road that twisted up through a canyon full of elderberries and poison oak turned into a trail and came out on a ridge. What a view! We were looking out over the Salinas Valley—a wide expanse of flat country smoothed out between two mountain ranges.

We were on one range and behind the opposite one a round orange-y sun was just about to disappear. The different shaped sections of farming land, dark and light green, brown or yellow, all spread out there, looked like pieces of a giant's jigsaw puzzle. Some tiny puffs of smoke and dust spiraled up from a few little far-apart towns, attached to one another by a long continuous thread of road. Right below us (San Juan Valley) were dabs of bright color which were the fields of sweet peas we had ridden by [Ferry Morse] earlier in the day.

As they followed one trail that split off to another she said her father managed to stay on the ridges and that before long they were among pine trees and ferns. They finally found themselves blocked by a barbed wire fence. It was dark and Fred Bixby, according to his daughter, finally admitted he was lost. "I must have zigged when I should have zagged," he explained.

Before long they saw the light of a bonfire and a big black saddle horse beside a man who looked enormous in his orange-colored hairy chaps, red jacket and flaring black Stetson. It was Johnny Bryan who had come out to look for them. Bryan led them to the house where his wife, Jessie, took the chilled girls in to give them an alcohol rub. They then warmed themselves in front of a fire on a thick polar bearskin rug. Before retiring they all gathered around the piano and sang old songs.

The next morning they continued their journey. The Bryans rode with them a few miles to be sure they got started down the right trail. As they looked down into the miles of valley they saw the town of Chualar, "a clutch of tiny houses with four crossing streets like a minute tit-tat-toe pattern." Their father said that was where they were going to have lunch.

Before the Fremont Peak Road to the park was put in, the access to the Gabilan ranch was by way of Bird Creek Canyon. It was in this area, Don Baldocchi said, that during prohibition bootleggers held forth under the guise of woodcutters. They would put their liquor on trucks and cover it with chopped oak firewood to take it to San Juan. The boards from the woodchopper's cabin were used by the Reeves to panel a family room added on to the house. On one of the boards is burned the name "A. Garibiotti - Value $20."

Bill and Marilyn's mother's father, Harvey Abbott, remembered coming to the ranch to see Carr. Abbott told his son-in-law, Dr. Reeves, when he was considering buying the ranch, "If you buy that ranch, you will have a principality." Harvey Abbott managed the Topo Ranch for Sam Mathews. His father, Carlisle Abbott, who crossed the plains in 1850, was a prominent dairyman who came to the Salinas Valley in 1856, driving 500 head of dairy cattle from Marin County. He leased 9,000 acres of Rancho Llano de Buena Vista from David Spence, later exercising his option to buy half the land at $3.40 per acre. According to his book, *Recollections of a California Pioneer,* he increased his herd to 15,000 and produced 200,000 pounds of butter. He told of hauling lumber from Watsonville and

James Bardin, whose family started buying part of the Gabilan ranch from Jesse D. Carr in 1883 and eventually owned 17,000 acres. In 1906 he established the James Bardin Hospital in Salinas.

building his home and out-buildings on the site of what was to become Spreckels Sugar Company's big factory. "In those years," he wrote, "there were only two other buildings between my residence and the Oak Grove House below Soledad—one of which was at the Deep Well stage station, and the other a cabin occupied by David Spence on the river road."

In 1874 the California dairy industry gained international recognition when Carlyle Abbott sent 25 head of dairy heifer to Yokohama. These were busy years for him—he built the Abbott House which he described as a "popular hostelry," an impressive building and popular hotel, in 1874; was a delegate to the National Republican Convention in 1872, when Grant was nominated; was elected to the California State legislature in 1875 and 1877; and also purchased 12,000 acres of San Lorenzo ranch, in partnership with R. M. Shackleford. Jesse Carr invested $15,000 for purchase of stock.

Another of Abbott's ventures was the Monterey and Salinas Valley Railroad Company of which he was president. It was narrow gauge, 20 miles long, and enabled farmers to ship grain to the tide waters at a great savings in freight. His competitor made a large reduction in freight charges, and the farmers gave their business back to the Southern Pacific.

Along with his railroad problems, Abbott lost 6,000 acres of wheat in a single day, due to unseasonable June rain followed by sunshine, causing rust. Also a shipping company in San Francisco appropriated $45,000 of his money. He left the Salinas Valley to go to Arizona to recoup his losses.

Ⓑ *Jim Bardin Ranch*

Rancho Cienega del Gabilan is one of the few Mexican land grants that is still devoted entirely to ranching. What is more, its major owners are descendants of early California pioneers. Jim Bardin, who has 7,000 acres on the eastern slopes of the Gabilans, is the grandson of James Bardin who came to California in 1855. D. A. Eyre, who has several thousand acres on the Tres Pinos side, is a descendant of Faxon Dean Atherton, who arrived as early as 1836, and Mrs. Rollin Reeves' family is descended from Carlisle Abbott, who came in 1850.

Although his gates are on the Old Stage Road, Jim Bardin's ranch actually starts where his house is built at an elevation of 350 feet and extends up to Fremont Peak at an elevation of 3,000 feet. His uncle, Henry Bardin, was one of the first to acquire a piece of the ranch from Jesse D. Carr, something over 6,000 acres, in 1883. His father bought an additional 10,000 acres from Carr just a few months before he died in 1903, so that together they had

Jim Bardin and his stepdaughter, Margaretta Swanson. Bardin's father, James Bardin, was known as the "Potato King."

Aerial view of Jim Bardin's Gabilan ranch. To the right is the home Bardin built on the site of the old Jesse D. Carr house. The old Carr barn is on the left.

The Bardin ranch rises from an elevation of 350 feet to 3,000 feet, with Gabilan Canyon running through the middle. Oak and sycamore trees predominate, but at higher elevations are madrone and tan bark oak trees.

A close-up of the Jesse D. Carr barn on Bardin's Gabilan ranch. Carr kept his thoroughbred trotting horses in this barn. Note the picket fence corral, one of the few to be seen today.

17,000 acres. Henry's daughter, Mrs. Grover Tholke, sold 6,000 acres to Ky Scilacci in 1923.

Jesse D. Carr's beautiful old barn where he kept his trotting horses (the most famous was known as Carr's Mambrino, which he purchased in Kentucky), is still in good condition, having received good care and reinforcing from Bardin. Between the barn and Jesse D. Carr's house was a practice track. Jim Bardin took down the old house a few years ago and built a California ranch house, incorporating the oak trees into his patio and taking advantage of the view of the Salinas Valley from his living room.

The Gabilan Creek, along which grow alder and maple trees, flows down the Gabilan Canyon through the middle of the ranch. Mud Creek, which also goes through the Church (Vergeles) Ranch and joins Gabilan Creek, is on the north edge, and on the west the Bardin joins the Natividad rancho. The most predominant trees are the oak and sycamore, but at the higher elevations are madrones and tan bark oak trees. There are deer and quail and some coyotes, skunks, fox, bobcats and badgers. Although Jim Bardin's parents were living in town (Salinas) at the time he was born, he was raised on the ranch and has hunted all of his life.

His son, Bob Bardin, who lives across the creek from Jim's house, is following the family ranching tradition. He leases the Molera Ranch at Big Sur, where he runs cattle. Jim's wife, Dorothy, also has a

Vineyards of Theophile Vache planted on the Gabilan ranch in 1850. Vache later received the patent for the land. It is now the Almaden La Cienega vineyards.

son named Bob Swanson, who farms in Hollister, and two daughters: Lillian, who teaches, and Margaretta Swanson, who attends Cal Poly and rides in the shows.

When Coleman Younger, a leading cattleman of his time from San Jose, visited the ranch in 1875, he was impressed with its beauty and described it as:

...a little vale running up into the mountains...waving grain fields, the countless herds of sheep, the distant Monterey Mountains...This immense domain is fenced with substantial fence...cross fences running in every direction...stocked with blooded horses, runners and trotters, sheep and Angora goats and above all the Shorthorn.

Younger said that he remembered coming to the valley when it was full of wild Mexican cattle.

Jim Bardin's grandfather, James Bardin, came overland to California in 1855 from New Albany, Tippah County, Mississippi. Aware of the slave question brewing, he decided westward was the way to go. According to the diary he kept, he and four companions went to Independence, Missouri, the starting point for most wagon trains. Their terminating point after 103 days was Yreka. Inasmuch as Bardin had been a farmer in Mississippi, he didn't like the looks of the farming land in Yreka so he moved south to Monterey County. Here he began with 1,000 acres of land near Blanco.

The following year Bardin returned to New Albany, Mississippi by way of the Isthmus, picked up his wife and six children, and returned to the Salinas Valley. He also brought one slave whom he set free after they arrived in California. The black man used his gift of freedom to advantage by conducting a blacksmith shop on the Blanco-Salinas Road for several years. Jim Bardin's father was born on the ranch near Blanco and also named James. Grandfather Bardin later purchased 6,000 acres of Rancho Nacional where he lived until his death in 1888. For a man who came to California with nine yoke of oxen and a horse, he did pretty well. His son used to quote his father's saying about how cheaply he could live:

No coffee, tea, sugar, whiskey nor tobaccer
No vest, socks, undershirt, nor drawers,
No high-heeled boots, gold-headed canes or jingling watch chains.

Although it's certain his son James didn't follow that advice, he did manage to do very well for himself. He started by farming at Blanco and was the first to grow sugar beets of more than an acre or two for Claus Spreckels. By getting an advance from Spreckels on the crop to be planted, said his son, Jim, he "was able to buy the 'home place' at Blanco from his brothers and sisters." He rotated his crops of barley with potatoes and was called tne "Potato King" of the world. He built the James Bardin Hospital in Salinas in 1906.

HK *Dean Atherton Eyre*

The family of Dean Atherton (Appy) Eyre, who owns 3,500 acres on the Tres Pinos side of the Cienega del Gabilan ranch, goes back considerably further than that of the Reeves (Carlyle Abbott) or of Jim Bardin. Eyre's grandfather, Faxon Dean

Lilla Bell, daughter of Lilla Renshaw Hunter, with sons John and Dean on Cienega del Gabilan ranch.

Atherton, a native of Massachusetts, came up the coast on a sailing ship from Chile and engaged in the hide and tallow trade. He wrote about his travels in *California Diary of Faxon Dean Atherton 1836–39.*

In 1860 Atherton purchased 400 acres at Fair Oaks on the San Francisco peninsula (later changed to Atherton in his name). Here he built his magnificent estate, Valparaiso, named for the birthplace of his wife in Chile, a city where he had spent a number of years. That same year he acquired the Rancho Milpitas in the San Antonio Valley from Ygnacio Pastor, the original grantee.

Finding squatters to be problems, he sent his son George with his family down to manage the Rancho Milpitas near Jolon along the San Antonio River. It was about this ranch that George's wife, Gertrude Atherton, wrote in *Adventures of a Novelist.* Their accommodations were primitive, and there were other problems, and Gertrude made it plain that this wasn't her cup of tea. But it was there that Appy Eyre had many happy times.

He used to spend summers there as a boy. He said in 1900 the ranch became part of the Milpitas Land Co., organized by James Brown and the Atherton heirs, and sold in 1924 to William Randolph Hearst. It is now the Hunter-Liggett Military Reservation, and the mansion Hearst built overlooking the San Antonio Mission is now the officers' club.

Jesse D. Carr dairy barn on Cienega del Gabilan ranch. It was put together with square nails.

Cienega del Gabilan ranch of Lilla Renshaw Hunter on the Tres Pinos side of the original grant. At the far left is the wagon shed, next the big dairy barn, the foreman's house, and the milk barn. The L-shaped house with chimney is the old Jesse D. Carr house.

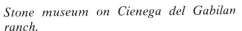

Stone museum on Cienega del Gabilan ranch.

Still wanting to have a ranch, but on a smaller scale, Eyre and his late wife, Katherine Wigmore Eyre, a well-known writer, bought 3,500 acres of the Gabilan from Paul and Bill brown.

Lilla Renshaw Hunter, whose parents, the Howard Renshaws, owned the adjoining ranch, remembers the excitement in the little town of Tres Pinos when 350 head of cattle arrived by freight train for Eyre. She was a child at the time.

Lilla Renshaw Hunter

From Long Island, New York, the Howard Renshaws first came to Tres Pinos to be houseguests of old friends, the Kingsley Macombers, at their Cienega de los Paicines ranch. It was a custom of the Macombers in those days to invite friends for a six-week visit. The two men,

Renshaw and Macomber, were fond of race horses and used to go to the races together at Saratoga, New York.

Lilla said her father was attracted to the western country around Tres Pinos. One day he casually remarked to Macomber, "If I had a thousand acres around here I'd move out from New York."

Macomber said, "Great, you've got them." A Captain Sudden sold Renshaw part of Gabilan ranch, and he moved his wife and their small children to California in 1917. They built their attractive country house on a knoll, and Lilla, together with her brothers, John, who now lives in Hillsborough, and Howard, who lives on a ranch across the river, grew up there.

On the flat below is a big white house and the old Jesse D. Carr house. Jessie Carr Bryan, who lived on the Reeves portion of the ranch with her husband, told Lilla Hunter one day when she was visiting them that she was born in that house. One time when the Renshaws were having some work done they uncovered newspapers in the walls dated during the gold rush days. Both Jessie and Johnny Bryan loved children, and they in turn held a fascination for the young people. Jessie raised Arabian horses and Johnny was regarded as a superb horseman. One time Jessie made a trip to Arabia where she raced across the desert with the Arabian chieftains on their steeds, an experience that almost proved to be her undoing.

Johnny Bryan was a great story teller and the Renshaw children used to love to hear him tell about his Miller-Lux days—of the bandit, Vasquez, and the shootout at Snyder's store—in fact, he gave Vasquez's gun to John Renshaw.

To appreciate the beauty of this ranch one should go in the spring and drive over it by jeep, first to "Big Hill," a circuitous route up and down back hills which are covered with yellow daisies, here and there Queen Ann's lace, bright red Indian paint brush, California poppies, and perky fiestas in yellow and white, all set off by the gnarled old oak trees draped dramatically with Spanish moss. Along the way you will shoo cattle off the narrow road or send a covey of quail scurrying as you pass such places as "Rattlesnake Springs" and an abandoned old mine in the bottom of the canyon. On the far hill can be seen rows of grapevines which Lilla says originally belonged to Mission San Juan Bautista and where there used to be an old adobe winery building.

There is not as much wild animal life around their ranch any more, but Lilla recalled one time her mother was taking them to Johnny and Jessie Bryan's for a picnic and suddenly from nowhere a mountain lion jumped across the hood of their car.

The wild beauty of Lilla Hunter's countryside is still untouched and there for her numerous grandchildren to enjoy.

Jesse Whitton, surveyor and mapmaker for John C. Fremont. He first saw the land when he camped overnight beside Bird Creek with Fremont and his men during their retreat from Gabilan Peak.

Seven of the nine daughters of Jesse and Missouri Swope Whitton. Back row, Angie Crow, Emma Crow, Ella, and Betty. Front row, Nancy Ware, Sara Robinson Miller, and Mary May. Picture taken in 1888 or 1889.

Marion Crow married the youngest of Jesse Whitton's daughters, Emma, and lived on the ranch. He drove in the pickets for the fence which forms the dividing line for the ranch. They are still standing.

CHAPTER X

Howard Harris Ranch

When John C. Fremont and his men made their famous retreat from Gabilan Creek they camped for the night beside Soto Creek. A large oak tree marks the site. Nearby is the house which Howard Harris, great-grandson of Jesse Whitton, who was a surveyor and mapmaker for Fremont, built for himself and his family.

Fremont's retreat was one of several low points in his career. He had gone to Monterey alone to ask permission to spend the winter in California before proceeding to Oregon. Neither General Castro nor Governor Pio Pico objected. A short time later, however, when Castro learned that Fremont and his men were camped along the Salinas River, he sent a dispatch to Fremont requesting their departure from the territory.

Instead, however, the willful Fremont moved his camp to Gabilan Peak, the summit of the Gabilan Mountains above the little village of San Juan Bautista, on March 6, 1846. The first thing Fremont ordered his 62 men to do was to build a log fort and raise the flag of the United States. The 62 included five Delaware Indians; the rest were mostly frontiersmen.

In the meantime Castro's diplomatic efforts to make Fremont retreat failed. Consequently he assembled an army of 300 to 400 men at San Juan Bautista. Bancroft says that Castro sent a message with John Gilroy, who found Fremont's camp deserted. After three days, Fremont, realizing he could not defend from there, had started down the mountain, heading for Sutter's Fort.

According to Howard Harris, who recently moved to Hollister, the stories Whitton told the family about Fremont were not too flattering. He said that Fremont was out to make a reputation for himself and that the Fremont Peak affair was against the orders of his superiors. Whitton said that Fremont was cruel to his men, that even when they were physically depleted he would insist upon pushing on.

The streams were flowing, the hills were velvet green, the wild azaleas were in bloom and the birds were singing, and surveyor Whitton was enchanted. As mapmaker he renamed the stream "Bird Creek" and vowed he would return some day and own it when the area was developed. He kept that promise to himself, returning with his wife, Missouri Swope, in the latter part of the sixties, after the San Justo Homestead Association had purchased Colonel Hollister's share of the Rancho San Justo. To his dismay a man named Ike Lewis had already purchased the site he had set his heart on. It took him several years to finally purchase the 600 acres. Instead of the $15 an acre Lewis had paid, it cost him $50 per acre. Whitton wanted the land badly enough that he sold his mines in Arizona and holdings in Virginia to pay the asking price.

Whitton was soon to become active in the forming of San Benito County. According to his great-grandson, he was one of five commissioners appointed by Governor Booth. It was decided to take the Gabilan mountains as the boundary; from the watershed everything that flowed into the Salinas was Monterey County, and where it flowed into the San Benito River it was San Benito County. Whitton was in Arizona on mining business when the election was finally called. Receiving word, he rode horseback to Hollister, arriving just in time to cast his ballot, only to learn that he was disqualified because he had not been in the precinct the required length of time. He died of a heart attack that same day.

For many years the ranch was known as the Crow Ranch. The youngest of Whitton's nine daughters married Marion Crow. They lived in the little house started by Ike Lewis and added on to it. The pickets for the fence that forms the dividing line for the ranch, driven in by Marion Crow, are still standing. One of their daughters, Ella, married John Jacob Harris of Oakland. Harris's son, Howard, when he was nine years old, moved down to the ranch to live with his Aunt Casse and went to the little Vineyard school. In time, after his graduation from the University of California at Berkeley as a geologist, he and his Aunt Casse started adding parcels of the Cienega del Gabilan Ranch and of the Cienega de los Paicines until they held 3,200 acres. The Harris's four grandchildren were the sixth generation of Whittons to live on the ranch.

The scenic beauty of the ranch today is everything Whitton remembered it to be on his first visit. There is Azalea Canyon with woodwardia fern buckeye trees blooming beside the road, azaleas, of course, and at the top a waterfall where tiger lilies grow six feet tall, but are a delicacy to the deer so they don't last long.

In another direction Mountain Canyon goes up to the border of the Reeves' Ranch. At this point there are a series of pools formed of solid rock graduating down the canyon; there are wild fern, flowers, and 27 varieties of oak trees. Occasionally a gabilan, the hawk with a red tail for which the mountains were named, flies overhead.

Seen on a distant hillside are olive trees planted by an English sea captain named Pierce and his partner, William Robson, almost a hundred years ago. The captain had seen the success of olive trees in Italy, Spain and Portugal, grown at an elevation of 2,000 feet on granite soil 15 to 20 miles from the sea. On this road between the grass and the timberline, all but hidden by shrubs and trees, is a recording station for the ominous San Andreas Fault.

Another completely modern aspect to the ranch, beyond the wildest dreams of Whitton, and to the dismay of neighbors, are the motorcycles. Harris said he was the first rancher to go into recreation. He has laid out motorcycle trails so that cyclists take the lower roads going up and the upper roads coming back as a safety factor. There are ten lakes and camping grounds on the ranch, so families can spend the weekend.

The Harris ranch also has its mysteries. One is about a hidden treasure. Some visitors who came in 1924 told Harris they were heirs to a treasure of gold that was buried on the ranch. The gold had been stolen from General Francisco Pacheco at his large home on the Ausaymas rancho on the Pacheco Pass. Harris said he agreed to their proposition that they would give half of what they found if he would permit them to dig. According to the map and instructions they would first find a horseshoe at a certain place. They did find the horseshoe, but that is all they found. The gold seekers have never returned, but Harris said he thinks maybe some day he will look for it again. He thought about using his bulldozer, but was afraid the leather pouch supposedly containing the gold coin might be destroyed or covered over.

Another intriguing story concerns silver mines located on the ranch. There are deep shafts and tunnels visible, and the remains of ancient smelters, but Harris chooses not to reveal their location because he said it would create a furor. There was always mining in the Gabilans years ago, he said. A reporter came to him one time and expressed interest in finding a lost silver mine. Harris swore him to secrecy and took him to it. The writer was so jubilant that he forgot his promise, and his story was sent out over Associated Press, published in *Life* magazine, and broadcast over radio and television. Harris had a hard time denying the claims and there was general confusion. People even tried to stake out silver claims in the area.

Nevertheless, Harris claims the mines are real, and that if you walk to the summit of a nearby hill as the sun goes down, in the horizon to the west you can see the Soledad Mission—this is just a part of the clue.

Since this story was written Harris has sold his ranch to the State Department of Parks and Recreation, and there are no longer any members of the Harris family or descendants of Jesse Whitton living on the property.

Elena Sayers

Elena Sayers, a full-blooded Mutsun Indian who lived most of her life in the Indian lands of the Cienega district in the hills above the Almaden Vineyards until 1973, corroborated Howard Harris's story about the silver mines. Her grandfather, Sebastian Garcia, she said, worked in the silver mines. Years later men would come to try to find out where it was. "My grandfather just stood there and wouldn't say anything. If he didn't want to talk nobody could make him. He was like a wooden cigar store Indian. So the men went away." She said there was always a mystery about the mine. Men would ply her grandfather with liquor, she said, but he would never take them up the canyon. Referring to rains, the growth of shrubs and soil movement, in her poetic fashion she said, "Mother Nature with her tears covered it [the mine] up pretty good."

Another story she told about her grandfather Sebastian was of his uncanny sense of being able to tell whether there was going to be a freeze. A rancher would say, "Well, Garcia, what do you think? Is it going to freeze tonight?" If Sebastian liked the man, he would turn the faucet, feel the water, and tell him. But if he didn't like him he would just stand there. A lady in Gilroy told Elena that her grandfather used to make clothes out of deerskin. He also made ropes out of horsehair, and hobbles for the horses.

Elena Sayers' father, Romola Sanchez, was a full-blooded Mutsun Indian of one of the Castanoan tribes. He was also a good vaquero who worked the ranches around Chualar and Gonzales as well as roping in the rodeos at Soledad. Elena said that the fact that he was an Indian and a cowboy used to puzzle the children—in their minds he was both a "good guy" and a "bad guy." They would say, "How come you're an Indian and a cowboy too?"

Elena explained that the reason for the family's Spanish names was that the mission padres couldn't pronounce the Indian names, so they changed them to Spanish when the Indians were baptized. Elena was fourth generation San Juan Bautista Mission Indian, she said, and one of the last two full-blooded Mission Indian descendants left. The other, an uncle, Fagundo Batron, who lives near Watsonville, came up the canyon to see her the previous year at three o'clock in the morning, with friends who were helping him celebrate his 78th birthday.

Elena's great-grandmother, Maria Garcia, was born at the mission. "She was short, but she was boss," Elena said. She had 12 children, but only two grew up to be married. Elena's mother, Evangelista Garcia Sanchez, like her brothers and sister, succumbed to galloping consumption when Elena was a small child.

She had a snapshot of her great-grandmother with Indian Joe Wellina. It was taken by Casse Crow in 1906 with her box camera. Joe Wellina died in 1910 at the age of 110. Elena said the records at the mission prove this. Wellina lived at Indian Canyon, and Elena's grandparents, Sebastian and Maria Garcia, looked after him. He was just three years old when the padres started building Mission San Juan Bautista. Before the mission was completed in 1812, like Elena's great-grand-

Elena Sayers was one of two remaining full-blooded Mission Indians still living in 1973. She died in that year.

parents, he probably helped make the adobe bricks. He lived under the flags of Spain, Mexico, and the United States.

"They had four or five tepees at the head of the canyon," Elena said. "One day they had a fire. All the neighbors down below brought them food and clothes. My grandmother said they never had it so good. After that they built a little wooden building."

Elena Sayers and her son, Chris, had moved into town the week before this interview because of her ill health, but a visit to her house at the Indian lands off Cienega Road was rewarding. To reach Indian Canyon one turns in at the Almaden wincry off Cienega Road and drives up a steep narrow dirt road past orchards to a clearing among oak trees. Her small frame house was built along the edge of a ravine with oak and sycamore around it, and a thicket of blackberries. In the deep canyon are madrone, willow, chaparral and manzanita. In the higher elevations of the Gabilan mountains rising up around it are bull pines. As for the wildlife, Elena said there were fox, mountain lions, bobcats, and wild pigs. The total scene was one of wild, natural beauty.

Elena told a curious story about how this has always been Indian Canyon, that as one family would leave, without any communication whatsoever another Indian family would appear the next day and move in. For food there was plenty of venison. Rattlesnakes were used for stew and to make medicine. She demonstrated how, taking only the center part, they would chip off a man's hand-

Elena Sayers and her son, Christian, in the Indian Lands of the Cienega district of San Benito County. Her grandfather, Sebastian Garcia, received title to the land from President Taft in 1911.

length from each end. Every child had his own *metate.* The acorns which were found in abundance were peeled, roasted until soft, and mashed for use in various dishes. The herbs had many uses, she told us. The wild martynia was used for infection; stickmonkey, a yellow blossom, for upset stomach; and yerba buena for tea. There was always plenty of water at Indian Canyon. Elena said Hollister used to get its water from there. "William Palmtag would come up in his horse and buggy to see if anything was obstructing the flow of water. If it was, he would clean it. At the same time he used to visit my grandparents." The Palmtag winery, which was just below, was started in 1854 by Theofile Vache, a Frenchman from San Juan Bautista. He set out several hundred acres in grapes and built an adobe building that was standing until a few years ago. The vineyards are now owned by Almaden.

When Maria Garcia, Elena's grandmother, went into town she would stop at the winery and have lunch with Mrs. Palmtag. When she worked for families down below they would pay her with potatoes, a pig, or some other kind of food. Later, Elena said, she would trade a load of wood for a sheep or some such thing.

In 1894 Sebastian Garcia applied for homestead rights, with assistance from Casse Crow, who was always a friend of the Indians, and received title in 1911 from President Taft. Elena, who inherited the land, received her title in 1945 from President Truman. Her husband, Elliott Sayers, was the first white man to live in Indian Canyon.

Elena remembers many of the stories her grandmother Garcia told her, such as how her mother (Elena's great-grandmother) had helped make the adobe bricks for the mission San Juan Bautista where Elena's grandmother was born. A more romantic tale, however, is how Sebastian took a wife. Maria was working at the time on a ranch at Arroyo Seco. "Along came my grandfather on horseback, swooped her up on his horse and took her away. They were married in the little Catholic church in Tres Pinos. This was how they worked it in those days," she said, adding, "sometimes they would have another Indian do it for them."

Apparently Maria had to keep close tabs on her husband. "When my grandfather worked, Grandmother told his bosses they had to give her the check. Otherwise, you know what my grandfather would do," and with a knowing look she pantomimed lifting a glass to her mouth. "My grandfather would drink up all the money if he had a chance."

She said her grandfather used to cut the wood and take it into town with the horse and wagon to sell. "In 1910 after the wood had all been cut, they left the Indian lands. In 1936 I brought my grandmother back. She looked around and said, 'This isn't the place.' I told her, 'Yes, it is. It's all grown back.' "

A group of Mutsun Indians standing beside the building which was constructed after their tepees burned. Left to right, an unidentified man, Sebastian Garcia, Indian Joe Wellina at the age of 106, Maria Garcia, a San Juan Bautista Mission Indian and four of her 12 children.

"You know," Elena said somberly, "we had good planters. The blue jays. They scattered the seeds all over."

Although Elena at times showed a wry sense of humor, she never laughed nor was there a flicker of a smile in her serious brown eyes. In talking about herself she said that because of her diabetes her eyes were failing and she could no longer make the hairpin lace shawls and ponchos to sell. "I'm 63 years old—over the hill and in the valley." These proved to be prophetic words, for within two months she was gone.

Joe Wellina and Maria Garcia. Wellina was a Mutsun Indian who lived to the age of 110. This photo was taken in 1906 by Casse Crow.

Paddock built during the long ownership of the ranch by George Uhl of the wallpapaer family of Los Angeles. Patricia Uhl, who had been an actress in movies before she lost her hearing, raised and showed thoroughbred horses. Beyond this paddock is a canyon which is used by Church heirs for growing lettuce seed. Church was one of the Big Four of the lettuce industry.

Old barn, probably built during the era of Miles Hills, is on the del Gabilan ranch of the Bruce Church heirs.

Corral on the Church ranch.

74

CHAPTER XI

Rancho los Vergeles

Beautifully situated on the eastern slopes of the Gabilan Mountains was the two-story adobe of Don Joaquin Gomez. Because of its strategic location at the entrance to the pass, it was to have its place in the history of California. The adobe sat on a hill above what is now called the Old Stage Road (at one time called Gomez's Pass) near the junction of Mud Creek and Gabilan Creek. Many a well known traveler in the 1830s and '40s stopped to accept Don Joaquin's hospitality before starting across the mountains to San Juan.

Earlier Spanish explorers and padres had taken this path, the El Camino Real, that had been made by the Indians on their excursions inland. Juan de Anza and his party camped at the base of Sugar Loaf Mountain on the border between Los Vergeles and Rancho La Natividad. It was here that the Battle of Natividad was fought during the war with Mexico, the Americans making their headquarters at the adobe. In the 1850s and '60s enormous cattle drives passed by, headed for the gold fields, and it became the route for stagecoaches heading north or south.

Don Joaquin Gomez was a prominent trader from Guadalajara who came to California on the sailing ship *Leonor.* He was customs officer at Monterey where all ships planning to make calls at California ports first had to stop and pay a duty. Shortly after his arrival he was also put in charge of the secularization of Mission San Carlos. For the performance of this work he received from Mexico, in 1834 and in 1835, two land grants of one league each, Canada en Medio and Canada de Ceboda, which made up his rancho. He named it Los Vergeles or "Ranch of the Flower Gardens." All that is left of the original buildings are the stone foundations of the house and adjacent corrals. They are at the far end of the Agostini Ranch, and can be reached by jeep.

William Agostini was born 74 years ago on the Vergeles Ranch. His father, Attilio Agostini, had come from Switzerland in 1886 and worked for Miles Hills of San Jose, who had come to California shortly after the Civil War. When Hills died, according to Agostini, he left 5,000 acres (part of which is now owned by the Bruce Church heirs) to his son, Ed, and 3,000 acres to his daughter, Mrs. J. Hills Wythe. The latter part was purchased by Attilio Agostini in 1913. It has remained in the Agostini family, who run cattle on it.

As one enters the complex of ranch buildings from the San Juan Grade, the old cheese house is to the right. Attilio was a dairyman. The old bunkhouse, which William and his daughter Jean use for a ranch office, was there when he was born, he said, and he doesn't know how long before that. He said that the Agostinis are joined on one side by the Church Ranch (the Old Stage Road is the dividing line) and on the other side are Walter and Gus Settrini. The Settrinis have the portion of the Vergeles bought by James Hebbron in 1866. Hebbron leased additional lands and stocked purebred cattle and horses. He was at one time president of the American Livestock Association.

The terrain of the El Gabilan ranch of the Bruce Church family has changed little since the days of Joaquin Gomez, except for weathered old barns and fences here and there, and trees not indigenous to the area, including clusters of eucalyptus and olive trees which must have been planted after the American occupation by squatters. But the iron entrance gates and the clean white board fences at the headquarters are more contemporary. According to Irene Church, after the main ranch house burned they enlarged the guest house of the former owners, the George Uhls of the wallpaper company.

She said her late husband had leased the ranch from the Uhls for a number of years before buying it 25 years ago. It is now owned by her three daughters, Marion McNamara (Mrs. Tom), Joanne

William Tecumseh Sherman, one of the many famous people of the era preceding U.S. occupation of California. Sherman accepted the hospitality of Don Joaquin Gomez before going over the Gabilans to San Juan.

Taylor (Mrs. Ted), and Sally Church. They have moved practically all of their cattle to their big ranch at Yuma, Arizona, where they have a large feed operation.

On one of the hilltops under a grove of oak trees is a barbecue area where a giant barbecue attended by 1,000 men is given every summer in memory of Joe Gheen, to benefit cancer research and the Multiple Sclerosis program at UCLA.

There are two large canyons on the ranch, one used for cattle (now leased) and the other for growing lettuce seed. Bruce Church was a part of a fabulous success story in the Salinas Valley—Nutting, Merrill, Harden and Church, who pioneered in combining lettuce growing with related products, such as ice and cartons; their operation included everything from planting to shipping.

According to Irene Church, the handsome red paddock with cupola on top and the corrals were built by Patricia Uhl, who raised and showed thoroughbred horses, especially five-gaited horses. Another person who remembers Patricia Uhl is Eileen Rose of Hollister, who used to ride on the ranch. She said that Patricia Uhl had been an actress in films, but after losing her hearing had to give up her career. Her friends from Hollywood, however, often came up to the ranch and stayed for a couple of weeks to ride and relax.

Willis Towne, who bought from the Hills family, was the owner of this ranch before the Uhls. He was a butcher from Santa Cruz.

The adobe of Don Joaquin Gomez, just across the road and creek from the Church Ranch, was described by early-day travelers. In his *California Diary 1836-39,* Faxon Dean Atherton wrote that he spent a night at the adobe in 1837 and again in 1838, that after arriving in the afternoon he had time to look around and that he was "very much pleased with the appearance of the land and the building." Here he could get food and lodging which was more than he could say for his overnight stop the previous year at Natividad, where Isaac Graham, the wild and unruly Kentucky rifleman, had recently leased land and started a distillery for making *aguardiente* (an alcoholic beverage). There Atherton had slept on a soft side of a hide and had nothing to eat.

Another visitor at the Gomez adobe was Bayard Taylor, author of *Eldorado,* who also stopped at Blanco's place close to the river in the El Tucho area (later known as the Bardin Ranch). The artist, Henry Miller, who did a drawing of Mission San Juan Bautista in 1853, was one of those stopping by, as were Sir James Douglas and William Tecumseh Sherman. Sherman arrived in 1847 with another officer from Monterey. He described their visit:

...In the morning we crossed the Salinas Plain, about 15 miles of level ground, taking a shot occasionally at wild geese which abounded there, and entering the well wooded valley that comes out from the floor of the Gavillano.

He went on to say that it was almost dark when they reached the house of Senor Gomez, whose son, Vincente, had entertained them rather well the night before in Monterey. In describing the meal, he said:

I was helped to a dish of rabbit with what I thought to be an abundant sauce of tomato. Taking a good mouthful, I felt as though I had taken liquid fire; the tomato was chili colorado, or red repper, of the purest kind. It nearly killed me, and I saw Gomez's eyes twinkle for he saw that his share of supper was increased. I contented myself with bits of meat and an abundant supply of tortillas. Ord was better case-hardened and stood it better....the next morning we crossed the hill by the bridle path to the old Mission of San Juan Bautista.

The most descriptive account of Don Joaquin and his rancho was given by Dr. William Maxwell Wood in 1944 in his *Wandering Sketches of People and Things* which included his travels in South America, Polynesia, California, and other places visited during a cruise on the U.S. ships *Levant, Portsmouth* and *Savannah.* The account includes the following:

...It was a barn of a looking place, two stories high, with balconies in front, above and below; not a tree, scrub, or flower to relieve the barren waste about the building.

La Lagunita Rancho of James Hebbron, who purchased part of Rancho Los Vergeles, originally granted to Joaquin Gomez in 1835. The Battle of Natividad was fought near here.

The gardens must have been gone by that time. He described debris around the house:

The noise of our arrival brought out old Don Joaquin Gomez and his housekeeper. By the glare of the light in his hand, we saw several quarters of beef suspended in the upper porch, and our appetites had some interest in the discovery....Although he had not expected us until the following day, Don Joaquin gave us a hearty reception. [He was] about sixty years of age, with a short, squat figure....His head was round with short curly gray hair, and was supported upon a short neck, and surmounted by a large, old greasy gig-topped cap, hanging over the back of his head, while the visor projected from the top of his forehead. His clothes were old and soiled but there was in his whole appearance a 'devil-may-care' good humored air.

Wood judged that the large fortune which Gomez had inherited had been freely spent in having fun and at the disposition of all his friends.

He was now reduced to a remnant of worldly goods, but still his hospitality knew no check, and he was laughing his way into the grave as merrily as he had laughed along the journey of life.

In telling about the house he said the furniture was worn and the dishes mismatched and cracked. The sala, as in all the adobes, covered much of the lower floor. Wood's party was given a porch room with three beds of unpainted wood, calico curtains, a bag of coffee in one corner, and a guitar in the other.

The Battle of Natividad

Historically the Rancho Los Vergeles of Gomez will be most remembered for its place in the battle of Natividad during the Mexican War. It was the only battle fought in the North. Manuel Castro, who had been made commandant of the Northern California Forces, received word on his way north that two bands of Americans were moving 500 horses to deliver to Fremont at Monterey. The animals were scheduled to go to Los Angeles, where the Americans had suffered setbacks, to reinforce Stockton's supply. Castro was determined to intercept as many of the horses as he could.

The battle that ensued when the enemies met near the Lagunita (little lake), where the Vergeles and Natividad ranches join, was unlike anything a military strategist could have conceived. Captain Charles D. Burrass, who was bringing the horses from Sacramento with a miscellaneous company numbering 34, including ten Walla Walla Indians and two Delawares, arrived in San Juan Bautista the same day, November 15, 1846, as Captain Bluford K. Thompson. Thompson's group of 35 men was best described by one of its members, Edward C. Kemble, who later became a journalist of prominence:

The San Jose company was made of American rancheros, runaway sailors, Englishmen, Germans and Negroes—the most motley crew that ever fought under one flag (except a death's head and crossbones) and commanded by a Southern daredevil at once a desperado and a gentleman, if you can imagine such a commingling of opposite characters as B. K. Thompson, sometimes called red-haired Thompson, and also (let me not shock ears) as "H--- (infernal pit) roaring Thompson."

Neither company had been trained together and there was no unity of command. When the Americans learned they were to be under attack by Castro's men, Burrass corralled his horses in a hollow below the Gomez adobe. In the meantime Thompson sent for the men he had left in San Juan.

Under pressure from Thompson, Burrass issued an order to attack, against his better judgment. Considering that they were outnumbered two to one, and the importance of saving the horses, he was reluctant. Meanwhile the Walla Walla Indians on their Cayuse ponies were taunting the Californians and returning their fire with a shower of arrows. The Delawares, using their tomahawks, later scalped the dead among the Californians for trophies.

AVISO AL PUBLICO.

EL C. Joaquin Gomez pone en conocimiento del publico que se ha de venta su Rancho que se hall.

Se pone en conocimiento del publico que se halla de venta el Rancho de los Vergeles perteneciente a D'n. Joaquin Gomez, situado en las inmediaciones del Pueblo de San Juan Ba'g. distante nueve leguas de Monterey, cuyo Rancho tiene de extension sobre tres sitios de ganado mayor, con dos fincas bastante grandes y comodas, sobre quenientas reses y manadas que numeran entre yeguas potros y caballos de vienda. Esta Rancho es muy recommendable por su exquisita agua, abundancia de lana y pasturas asi como tambien por sus excelentes terenos de abrebadero y siembra.

La persona que se interesa a el puede occerrir con el esperado S. Gomez para convenio en precio.

JOSE JOAQUIN GOMEZ.

PUBLIC NOTICE.

JOAQUIN GOMEZ publishes herewith that he offers for sale his residence, or "Rancho Vergeles," situated in the neighborhood of the Mission or Pueblo San Juan, nine leagues distant from Monterey. The said Rancho here or consists of five miles of tillable ground, two pasture grounds sufficiently large for five hundred head of cattle and large herds of horses. This Rancho is very recommendable on account of its exquisite water, abundancy of wood, and rich pasture grounds; as also for its excellent soil which can be easily irrigated.

Persons inclined to buy, will apply to said Joaquin Gomez about conditions and price.

20-tf   JOSE JOAQUIN GOMEZ.

NAVY BREAD.

10,000 LBS. FINE NAVY BREAD just received and offered for sale by
WARD & SMITH.
Montgomery Street, San Francisco.   21-51

Advertisement in the California Star Weekly of May 29, 1847 announcing in both Spanish and English that Don Joaquin Gomez was offering for sale his Rancho Vergeles. Unfortunately Don Joaquin, who had given so generously of his hospitality to all who came, lost the ranch to James Stokes for bad debts.

Taking the lead, Burrass was mounted on Fremont's grey charger, "Sacramento," a gift to Fremont from Captain John Sutter. He was shot in the chest by the Californians and was buried with two other Americans who were killed in the action on the hill at the Gomez Rancho. Three volleys were fired over their grave. The wooden cross that marked their burial place is long gone. Joseph Foster, who was killed in the initial skirmish in the oak grove, was buried under the tree where he was killed. Carved on the tree was "Foster — 1846."

Tom Hill, a Delaware, and Charley McIntosh, a half-breed, were dispatched to Monterey with a message for Fremont while Thompson prepared for another attack from the Californians which never came. The forces reported by the lookout turned out to be the Americans, described by journalist Kemble:

...As the bugle played a lively march and the column began to ascend the hill the valiant chargers of the Salinas opened their ragged ranks like Joseph's coat, presented arms of all sorts, shapes and sizes and with Fremont at their head...the famous battalion of '46 marched through.

Fremont's batallion moved to San Juan Bautista to complete its plans. There he drilled his men in the plaza square before marching south in late November. Just where or what Gomez was doing during all this action is not clear. It is known that United States Consul Thomas O. Larkin (also a secret agent for the U.S.), with extremely bad timing, had stopped at the Gomez adobe on the night of November 15 on his way to Yerba Buena. He was captured and taken to Castro's camp as a hostage, but reported later that he was treated well.

The following year Gomez put his adobe and Rancho Vergeles up for sale. One advertisement in the *California Star* of July 31, 1847, refers to its location 30 miles from Monterey and near "St. John's" (San Juan). It said there were 500 head of cattle and 300 horses, but that it was capable of handling 5,000 head of cattle.

A previous advertisement in the same weekly San Francisco newspaper, on May 29, was published in both Spanish and English. Both refer to the advantages of the water (Mud Creek). Gomez was unable to sell, and the following year James Stokes picked up the ranch from him for bad debts and obtained the U.S. patent.

Gomez left the ranch in 1848. Had he been able to hold on for a short while longer, he could have gotten in on the Gold Rush boom in beef. Every day several hundred cattle and sheep went by his door over the Gabilans to San Juan. Mostly headed for the gold fields, they went over the Pacheco Pass to Sacramento by way of Stockton. Otherwise, their route was up the Santa Clara Valley to San Francisco.

It was a time of great cattle drives from Southern California. In 1856 S. Johnson reported that 36,000 cattle, 1,600 horses, 26,000 sheep, 1,345 hogs, and 800 mules crossed through the Vergeles Rancho over the Gabilans to San Juan. Johnson ran the post office listed at Natividad, although it was actually on Rancho Vergeles, granted to James Stokes. He and Stokes were also partners in a small hotel called the Gavilan House, in 1855. Later this was to become a stagecoach stop.

CHAPTER XII

Rancho San Antonio

1839 was a good year for Don Manuel Larios. He not only shared with his good friend, Don Juan Anzar, the 48,000-acre Rancho Santa Ana y Quien Sabe grant, but was the grantee of 4,493 acres of San Juan Bautista mission lands, known as Rancho San Antonio.

Manuel Larios was born in the Pueblo of San Jose de Guadalupe, near Mission Santa Clara in 1799, 22 years after the founding of this agricultural community by nine soldiers and their families for the King of Spain. He was the son of one of the first settlers, Jose Maria Larios. The family home was on Market Street.

At the age of 16 Manuel Larios joined the Spanish Army. He became an artilleryman and when he left the service at the end of the required term of seven years, he was a lieutenant. On his release from the army his sole possessions were five horses, two of his own and three that the government had given to him.

The same day that Larios left military service he was given a job by Don Juan Anzar, as overseer of his property. Anzar was a wealthy and prominent landowner whom Larios had gotten to know in Monterey.

Don Manuel was to be married three times. By his first wife, Maria Antonia Pacheco, he had 22 children, nine of whom lived. There were no children by his second marriage, to Guadalupe Castro, daughter of Angel Castro (uncle of General Castro), who had the Rancho Cienega de los Paicines as well as other lands.

His third wife was Rosario Armas y Higuera, a widow with seven children. Her first husband, known as Juan Temblor, the drummer boy, had been killed in a battle in the south with Castro's army. There was one child from the marriage of Don Manuel and Dona Rosario, named Estolano. Much of the story of Don Manuel has come from this youngest son, from two letters written by him to Bancroft in 1878, and from what he told historian Ralph Milliken during the time Estolano stayed at Milliken's house. Between the combined children of Rosario and Don Manuel, their husbands and wives and grandchildren, there were always comings and goings at the Rancho San Antonio which Don Manuel affectionately called "El Ranchito," meaning "Little Ranch"—a comparison with the spacious Santa Ana.

Manuel's 40-room adobe was built on a rise above the present San Juan-Hollister highway across from the cemetery. The location is marked by a yellow farmhouse and barn standing in the midst of a clump of trees by a hollow. This house is believed to have been built by one of the Larios

Don Manuel Larios, one of the last of the California dons in San Juan Bautista. He died at Rancho San Antonio in 1865.

Ranch house and barn believed to have been built by one of the sons of Don Manuel Larios. They are located on the site of the Larios adobe, which was destroyed in 1890. It had been the scene of many fiestas.

The Larios family cemetery. It adjoins the Protestant and Catholic cemeteries for which the generous Don Manuel donated the land.

heirs. It is on the part of the ranch now owned by Dorothy Avilla and Harvey Nyland, who inherited it from their father, Arthur Nyland. The most important room in the house, as it was with all the early-day adobes, was the enormous sala where the fiestas and family gatherings were held, sometimes for hundreds of guests.

The upper boundary of the San Antonio was the ridge in the Gabilans known as Los Pinecates. To the east was the Rancho Aromitas of Manuel's friend and partner, Don Juan Miguel Anzar. The El Camino Real en Medio that ran over the mountains from San Juan to Natividad bordered one side of the ranch. This was a route taken by horseback by those who wanted to cross the mountains in a hurry.

Life on the Ranchito was typical of that on most of the haciendas. When Don Manuel moved his family from the Santa Ana permanently he brought with him two Indians, Gasper and Chicala, who were an important part of the family. In fact, on one occasion he even took them to San Francisco with him.

One time Estolano was given a grizzly bear cub by his older brother, Dolores. He was named "Watch." (The letters were written in Spanish and no reason is given for this Anglicized name) and raised as a pet. One day a steer got loose and was headed for the children. Before anyone could act, Watch seized the steer by the head and with one paw on each horn forced the animal's head down and held him until the children were safe. Unfortunately, Watch later wore his chain loose, and with his first taste of freedom wandered over to a berry patch near the Vergeles Ranch and was shot.

The Larios family was close knit. One of the Larios girls, Guadalupe, was sent to Notre Dame convent in San Jose, where many of the Spanish families sent their daughters. She learned to play the serafina, to embroider, and especially to read aloud well. A ritual at night was for Guadalupe to read from one of the books in Don Manuel's large library. The children received an abundance of love, but they were taught obedience and respect for their elders and, at the age of two, were taught to cross themselves.

Their pleasures were simple. Along a level field in the foothills north of the house, oxen were used for planting and harvesting barley, corn and beans. A special treat for the children was to ride home at night on the oxen. One of the family's forms of diversion was swimming in the creek. During blackberry season they would go in the carreta on an outing to the river at Poso de Sanchez, a deep pool formed at the confluence of the Pajaro and the San Benito. While the children played in the water the women washed clothes and the men played cards.

Christmas Eve parties were a tradition, along with Midnight Mass. Don Manuel always went to San Francisco beforehand for presents and fruit. With his move over from Rancho Santa Ana, Larios brought with him the tradition of celebrating St. Ann's Day. Still visible near the existing yellow house is the flat area where the bullfights were held. Preparations were started well in advance at the plaza area, which was 80 feet wide and 100 feet long, on the south side of the house. While the Indians constructed a stockade the vaqueros were sent out to capture the fiercest bulls, found on the east side of the Gabilans, where the animals seldom saw a human. When they were lassoed and brought to the Ranchito, the sight of a person on foot made them almost frantic.

Members of the Larios family and guests came from all over for the fiesta. It is said that sometimes 200 guests would be on the balcony of the second floor of the adobe. The boys or young men would sit on the fence or on the side of the hill which formed a natural amphitheater. Many of the young women came on horseback, riding sidesaddle with silver-mounted bridles and martindales.

After the bullfight there was always a game of Monte. There was feasting—barbecues, empanadas, tortillas, and hot sauce—and music, usually consisting of violins, guitar and flute, for the dancing of the jota, the jarabe, and the fandango. These parties would go on for three days. Those who had come from a distance were put up at the adobe.

Among the relatives was Don Manuel's sister, Dona Pilar, the San Juan midwife, and her large family. Dona Pilar also was known for the cures resulting from the herb medicines she concocted.

Don Manuel's friends were many. Bishop Alemany, first Catholic Bishop of California, always visited the ranchito when going to Monterey. Jose Abrego, a prominent citizen of Monterey, was another friend. He always sent word to Don Manuel when an English ship was due to arrive. This would be the signal to start loading the carretas with soap, hides and tallow to be taken to Monterey for trade. This was how Don Manuel got his grandfather clock, books, and the furniture for his bedroom. The Abrego and Larios families visited back and forth, sometimes staying at each other's homes for a week. Abrego's daughter, Julia, married Joaquin Bolado, who bought the largest portion of Larios' Rancho Santa Ana.

During the Mexican War Larios reactivated his military career long enough at least to fight in the Battle of Natividad under Manuel Castro. After his death in 1865, the story of the rancho is a familiar one. The family started selling off land, and the Americans started buying it. One of the first was the ever-present Henry Miller, who by then was making heavy inroads into the Mexican grants, having bought part or all of Lomerias Muertas, Tequesquite, Las Animas, and the San Ysidro from John Gilroy. A young man who came from the

Dona Pilar, sister of Don Manuel Larios. She was highly regarded as a midwife and for her treatments with herbs. She lived in San Juan under the flags of Spain, Mexico, and the United States.

Azores and worked for Henry Miller, Joseph Machado de Avila, received help from Miller in buying 1,200 acres. One of his 12 children, a daughter named Ann Avilla, who lives in San Jose, said her father built a two-story ranch house on what became the San Juan grade, next to McAbees, in the 1890s, with five bedrooms upstairs for her eight brothers. She said they had it fixed up with the skins of animals such as wildcats, coyotes and raccoons, which they shot on the ranch.

Ann Avilla said, with a tone of disapproval, that after the boys were grown her father took the second story off. He didn't think they needed it any more. "My dad used to take his cattle to Watsonville to sell," she continued. "One night coming home he was held up at the Rocks. Dad whacked the robber over the head and he didn't get away with any of his money." She added that in those days there weren't any banks so her father used to leave his money with Thomas Flint.

When Ann was about eight years old, in 1904, the Avillas moved by spring wagon to Crow's Landing in the San Joaquin Valley, where her father started a dairy. Every summer they would come back in the surrey to the ranch to spend their vacations.

The San Antonio has seen many changes— Blanche Taix used to run sheep there—Colonel Griffen of Monterey owned the McAbee Ranch for

San Juan Bautista Cemetery. The land, originally part of the Rancho San Antonio, was given to the town by Don Manuel Larios. To read the names on the tombstones is to read the history of San Juan Bautista.

Former U.S. Congressman Jack Z. Anderson and Mrs. Anderson, whose home is at the far end of what was the Rancho San Antonio, on a knoll above the San Juan Valley. Anderson's sister, Betty, and her husband Ed Pearce have their home on the same knoll.

The famous "A" brand of the Anderson family pears. The orchards once covered the hillsides north of San Juan and fruit sheds are still standing on the flat.

a long time—Bill Caldera, who was Griffen's manager, now leases part of this ranch from Eugene Shumaker and lives in the old McAbee house—the Binghams own the Pinecate. Among the first to buy parcels of the San Antonio after Don Manuel's death were Thomas McMahon and Philip Dougherty. The latter was killed by being thrown from a wagon in Hollister. Jim Breen also owns a parcel. The Doughertys had a beautiful Victorian home, which was part of the Nyland ranch; it burned down a few years ago.

300 acres of the Avilla ranch are now owned by the Guggenberger-Edwards Charolais Ranch. Clyda and Gerhard Guggenberger own the ranch jointly with Congressman Don Edwards, and lease an additional 800 acres of the old McAbee Ranch. A private drive leads in off the San Juan Grade to the attractive white frame house that is set off by neat white board fences which mark off the corrals, stables and pasture. On the other side is the old Avilla house, where the foreman lives, and a windmill. Although modern in design and tastefully decorated with antiques, the Guggenberger house does share one thing in common with Don Manuel Larios' adobe, which was located directly below the back of their house to the right—it has a large sala, 36 by 54 feet. Larios' was probably twice that size, but by modern standards the Guggenbergers' is large.

The house rests on a hilltop with a 360-degree vista that has changed little since the early days. Out the kitchen window they see the picturesque Indian rocks. On one side is the village of San Juan, and on the other side are the rolling hills. In the spring their white Charolais cattle grazing on the green grass are worthy of a pastoral painting. Yet another modern note: their land was bought from a combine of actors—Danny Thomas, Vincent Price, Jim Nabors, and actress Elizabeth Montgomery.

The conversation piece on their ranch is the cave. Gerhard said it is quite a beautiful one and that a hermit lived there until recently. People wouldn't leave him alone, so he left. In earlier times the Indians came here once a year for a special ceremony. Gerhard also said there is a mountain lion wandering around and that the ranger told him it needs 30 square miles to survive.

At the farthest end of the San Antonio at Anzar Road are the homes of former U.S. Congressman and Mrs. Jack Z. Anderson, and his sister Betty

This house, located on Rancho San Antonio, was built in the 1890s by Joseph Machado de Avilla. The five bedrooms upstairs were for his eight sons.

Anderson Pearce and her husband, Ed. Their beautifully landscaped modern ranch houses are on a hill, separated by a reservoir, and look down on the San Juan Valley, on the fruit sheds where the famous "A" brand pears grown on this land were packed, directly across to the Lomerias Muertas hills. John Z. Anderson, grandfather of Jack and Betty, who started in the fruit business in 1863 after coming to California in 1852, was the first man to devise a method for shipping fruit by train east, and was the the first to hire women to do packing. George H. Anderson, his son, started buying land in San Juan in 1907. Ed Pearce knows San Juan Bautista, and expecially San Juan Canyon, where both he and his father were born, as do few other men. Both his father and grandfather were judges in San Juan Bautista, and both were also named Ed Pearce.

Just across Highway 156 from the Larios Adobe is the picturesque town cemetery. The names on the headstones and monuments tell the story of San Juan Bautista. The land for this cemetery was donated by Don Manuel Larios. Because in those days Catholics were buried only in consecrated ground, he thoughtfully donated an adjoining piece of land for the Protestants. There is also a Larios family plot. When Arch Hayes, a descendant of Manuel Larios, was asked if any of the Larios heirs still had property on the ranch, he said, "Yes, I do—in the Larios cemetery." Here the old Don, who was born in the pueblo of San Jose, served as soldier to the King of Spain, and was a bear and Indian fighter, is buried. It is rather sad to see that the grave of this man, who was so generous to all, has fallen into disrepair.

In his will, besides his ranch land, he listed as having on the San Antonio "50 to 60 head of cattle between tame and wild ones. About 20 horses between broken and unbroken. 70 sheep." The witnesses were Frederick MacDougall, Teodore Castellano and Luis German. Not too much of an estate, but more important, he left a legacy of love and affection and memories of a lifestyle that will never be known again.

Barbara Munson and her children riding in the Lomerias Muertas Hills. The name means "dead hills" and was given because of the sparseness of trees.

Fenton O'Connell at the front gate of his California style ranch house on the old Rancho Lomerias Muertas grant. The land was originally granted to Jose Antonio Castro and was once owned by Henry Miller.

CHAPTER XIII
Rancho Lomerias Muertas

According to the Fenton O'Connells there were no dramatic stories of bandits such as Joaquin Murietta or Tiburcio Vasquez hiding out on the Lomerias Muertas ranch, and no hidden treasure was ever found, although some people did come to dig. There is, however, a success story of cattle ranching. Fenton is a member of an old ranching family in San Benito and Santa Clara Counties. He and his wife, Pat, call their 10,500-acre spread "El Rancho San Benito." Made up mostly of the Lomerias Muertas Mexican land grant on the Bolsa Road, it also includes part of Rancho Llano del Tequesquite. The land was originally issued to Jose Antonio Castro of Sinaloa, Mexico in 1842, and patented to the heirs of Jose Maria Sanchez in 1866. It was through the efforts of Vicenta Sanchez and her husband, Dan Willson, that this was obtained.

The San Benito River runs through the ranch as does the Pajaro, which divides San Benito and Santa Clara Counties. The property was long a part of the Henry Miller empire. In 1924 J. L. Murphy from Colorado purchased it, and in 1940 O'Connell bought it from the Murphy estate. Before that it was known as the Ward Ranch. There are the Ward Hills on the ranch.

Choosing a site against the Lomerias Muertas Hills near a complex of pre-1900 ranch buildings, bunkhouses and shops, the O'Connells built their attractive Spanish-style house in 1940. They look down on farming land, part of which was once Spreckels' sugar beets, and across to San Felipe and the Dunne Ranch, in which Fenton shares ownership with his brother, James. On the Pacheco Pass he also has 8,500 acres which were bought from the Chauven estate and where he runs cattle. His youngest daughter, Madelyn, and her husband, John Bourdet, have recently remodeled one of the servants' quarters buildings of the James F.

Dunnes' Mountain House into a home for themselves. The O'Connells' daughter, Barbara Munson, and her family have a home on the Lomerias Muertas portion of the ranch, and another daughter, Karene (Mrs. James) Vernor, lives with her family in Moraga.

Fenton's grandfather, Thomas O'Connell, came in 1868 from New Haven, Connecticut, to California and farmed near Hollister for 26 years, during which time he bought part of the Rosa Morada grant. In 1895 he moved his family to San Jose, where he started a wood and coal business and later added a grocery store and butcher shop. By 1901 his four sons, George D. (Dan), Albert F. (Bert), Elmer S. (Cap), and Franklyn J. (Frank) had taken over the family business. Before long they branched out into cattle raising, leasing 12,000 acres and then purchasing the 20,000-acre Weber ranch, Canada de San Felipe y Las Animas, adding 3,000 acres to it. After they bought the Crowley stockyards at Coyote for a rail shipping point, like Henry Miller and others, they were integrated from calf to wholesale and retail meat distribution—a successful operation.

Charles Weber had come to Santa Clara County in the 1830s. He was a prosperous merchant in San Jose and married Ellen Murphy, one of Martin Murphy's daughters. During the war with Mexico he captained a mounted unit. Of this unit, Edwin Bryant wrote in his book *What I Saw in California*:

Left for the Pueblo in the afternoon with force commanded by Captain Weber. Made an ascension into the hills near rancho owned by Captian Weber. Ordered capture of two to three hundred public horses. It had been rumored that a party of Californians hovering about here were intending to capture and drive off these horses.

The accomplishment for which Weber is best known is the founding of the town of Stockton.

Franklyn O'Connell managed the ranch, and it was here that his three children, Fenton, James, and Ruth O'Connell Berry, who were born in San Jose, moved when they were young children in 1918. By the time they were five or six years old, Fenton and James were helping their father work cattle on horseback in the rough hill country. About 1925 Franklyn sold his interest in O'Connell Brothers and leased the Dunne Ranch from James Dunne's widow, Viola, later buying it.

One of the O'Connells' prized possessions is a large painting, three by four feet, which hangs over the fireplace, of a cattle drive on the Pacheco Pass. It was done by Andrew Hill, noted San Jose artist and photographer of the early part of the century. Easily distinguished in it are Jimmy Dunne and his wife, Viola.

Having received his indoctrination in the cattle business early, in 1927 Fenton started working in the summers on the Quinto Ranch next to the Fatjos, which his father and a man named Lansdale were leasing. In 1930 he dropped out of Santa Clara University and went to live there, receiving $35 a month, lodging and groceries. In 1932 his father leased the San Luis Gonzaga ranch owned by the Fatjo family. By the time Fenton was 20 he was managing 100,000 acres of land, running 8,000 head of cattle, employing 22 cowboys, and working 125 horses. Having learned from his father, who was regarded as one of the west's finest cattle judges, Fenton traveled from Mexico to Canada to buy, sell, and ship cattle.

Although he said he earned practically nothing in 1932, 1933, and 1934, between December 2, 1934 and April, 1935, he shipped 12,000 head of cattle from Texas, Mexico, Arizona, and New Mexico, and made $50,000. This made possible the accomplishment of what he had thought was an impossible dream, the purchase of the 10,500 acres of hills and valleys of the Ward Ranch, composed of the Lomerias Muertas and part of the Llano del Tequesquite.

CHAPTER XIV

Rancho Llano del Tequesquite

Best remembered for its San Felipe Lake, still called Soap Lake by old timers, is Rancho Llano del Tequesquite. Granted to Don Jose Maria Sanchez in 1835, this 16,000-acre rancho, situated in both San Benito and Santa Clara Counties, was first noted in 1772 by the Pedro Fages party and recorded by Padre Crespi, who told of passing through Tequesquite Slough and San Felipe Lake. The name came from the Mexican Aztec Indians: *tetl* (rock) and *quixquitl* (efflorescent) — in other words "saltpeter." A more common translation was "Lake of the Alkali."

Sanchez and Thomas Oliver Larkin, who had his finger in many pies, had a soap-making business going here. They enlarged an iron kettle from an old sailing vessel with boards up the sides and an adobe foundation around it to increase its capacity for boiling the soap. The process involved scraping the alkali off the ground to use in the soap, which was then shipped to Monterey to be sold to the sailing vessels. The kettle is now in front of the old City Hall in Gilroy.

Before his death in 1852, Sanchez, who married Encarnacion de Ortega, applied for the patent from the United States Land Commission. After his death, through the persistent efforts of Vicenta Sanchez and her husband, Dan Willson, as recorded in his diary, they obtained the patent for Vicenta and her brothers and sisters, Refugio, Candelaria, Gregorio, and Guadalupe. Vicenta sold 500 acres of her share of the Tequesquite, or Soap Ranch, as it was better known, to Dan's brother, Albert, the youngest of the Willson brothers. He had come to California from New England by way of the Isthmus of Panama, which he crossed by foot. After spending four years in the gold country at Shaw's Flat, he moved south to San Ysidro, following the example of his brothers.

Most of the Tequesquite today is cut up into small farms. According to the Thompson and West *Atlas of 1876,* Henry Miller owned most of the ranch at that time. Fenton O'Connell's El Rancho San Benito, however, does include part of this grant adjoining the Lomerias Muertas. Spreckels also owned 2,000 acres, near the lake, which he had planted in sugar beets. John Brendt, who had been manager for Henry Miller at Cottonwood and Canal Farm ranches, came here in the latter part of the 1890s to be superintendent of the ranch. A widower, he and four children, Georgia, Walter,

House on Pacheco Pass built by Spreckels Sugar Co. near San Felipe Lake. Jose Maria Sanchez, the grantee, and Thomas Oliver Larkin had a soap business at the lake. Always referred to as Soap Lake by old-timers, it was a part of Rancho Llano del Tequesquite grant to Sanchez.

Albert Willson came to southern Santa Clara County in 1856 after four years at Shaw's Flat. Through his brother, Dan Willson, he purchased 500 acres on Pacheco Pass above Soap Lake. Dan Willson's wife, Vicenta, was one of the heirs to Rancho Llano del Tesquesquite.

John Brendt came to Soap Lake in the 1890s with his four children, including Georgia, seen with him in this picture. He managed the Spreckels property. 2,000 acres were planted in sugar beets.

Frank, and Lee, lived in the big house on Pacheco Pass which sits on a rise above the road now owned by Mrs. John Bettencourt.

Georgia Brendt Bell (Mrs. Elbert) of Walnut Creek recalled that the house was surrounded by orchards, that the vast heart-shaped lawn extended from the house down to the road and that it was bordered by two rows of rose bushes with a path between. She said that her father planted the large tree that is still growing in the center of the lawn. Across the front between the two gates were red roses along the fence. The house had six bedrooms, she said, and a dining room off the kitchen for the help, and one for the family, a parlor, a living room, an office, and only one bathroom.

The chief vaquero for the ranch, Georgia recalled, was Juan Coscia; the bookkeeper was Daniel Burr, the cooks were Chinese, and the Japanese were employed for thinning the sugar beets. So big was the sugar beet growing business that in 1895 the railroad ran a little spur from the ranch across the valley. A special feature of the ranch, Mrs. Bell said, were the seven or eight artesian wells at the far end.

There were two dairies, a winter and a summer dairy, and cheese was produced which was shipped up to San Francisco. Georgia remembered that the cheese factory was between the ranchhouse and the Prunedale School, where she and her brothers attended classes. For the earlier grades there was a Spreckels school on the ranch.

The Brendts left the ranch in 1906. The sugar beets have long been gone, but there is a dairy of 370 cows operated by Louis Bettencourt and his brother, Joe. Another Bettencourt lives in the big old house.

Heading grain on the Tequesquite Ranch in the late 1890s.

CHAPTER XV

ℋ Rancho Bolsa de San Felipe

After 1870 the story of Rancho Bolsa de San Felipe is the story of the Hudner family. Since that date four generations of Hudners have continuously farmed or ranched the land.

James Hudner of County Cork, Ireland, as so many of his countrymen did at that period, came to the United States seeking freedom of opportunity and of religion. In 1856, leaving his wife and two children in Mill River, Massachusetts, he set out for California to find the golden egg. He evidently found one large enough to buy a farm in Saratoga, in the Santa Clara Valley, and to bring his wife and sons to California by way of the Isthmus of Panama.

After a stay of some years in Saratoga, James heard about the San Justo Homestead Association and the new town of Hollister being founded. He went down to investigate and stayed to join. He bought a parcel of the San Justo land north of Hollister and was a partner with James Herbert in some land purchases. Herbert homesteaded 160 acres. Rosemary Hudner Herbert (Mrs. Philip), whose mother, Agnes, was the daughter of James Hudner, lives at the old homestead in the first house that James Hudner built on the ranch. Her sons, Phil and Pat Herbert, are the fourth generation to farm this land.

The adjoining Bolsa Ranch, part of Rancho Bolsa de San Felipe, which Mrs. Paul Hudner, the former Mary Dooling, owns, together with her sons, Stephen and Philip, and where she lives, was purchased by James Hudner in 1870 from Mariano Malarin. Malarin was married to Lola Pacheco, daughter of Don Francisco Pacheco, and the Bolsa was part of her father's vast land holdings, acquired when the mission lands were dispersed. It was a Mexican grant by Governor Alvarado in 1840. In fact, it is believed that the padres at the mission gave him permission to take this land even before the secularization in 1834. They were not

using it, and Pacheco had been instrumental in quelling Indian uprisings at La Purisima Mission. Pacheco built an adobe brick house on the land and for a time his neighbor, Jose Maria Sanchez of the Llano del Tequesquite rancho, shared the house with him.

Following the pattern of many other ranchers of that period, Hudner sent his son, John, to Santa Clara College. John then studied law in the office of the well-known Judge Archer in San Jose. Returning to Hollister to practice law, he married Mary Breen (always known as Molly), daughter of Patrick Breen, Jr. of the San Juan Breens. He became district attorney and then Superior Court Judge of San Benito County.

Mary Hudner said the ranch house was where she and her husband, Paul, came when they were married 50 years ago. It is one of a complex of buildings making up the ranch headquarters—barns, corrals, houses for employees, and an old white concrete granary nestled against the

Phil Hudner and the foreman, Irv Carreira, of Bolsa de San Felipe Ranch, part of the original land grant to Francisco Pacheco. Phil is the fourth generation of Hudners on the ranch. He practices law in San Francisco. Sancho, his pet longhorned steer, is in foreground.

89

Paul Hudner II straddling a fence by the barn on Bolsa Ranch.

Main house at Bolsa Ranch headquarters. Mary Hudner, who manages the ranch, moved here 50 years ago with her late husband, Paul Hudner.

foothills. The house, which has been remodeled and redecorated many times over the years (the dining room, formerly part of the kitchen, has several ceiling levels), has a nice country feeling. The well-cared-for flower garden in front is a pleasant contrast to the green trees surrounding the house and the golden brown hills. Stretching out in front down to Bolsa Road are the flatlands which have been leased for agriculture, while the cattle roam the hills.

Mary Hudner said that her husband increased the Bolsa's acreage by purchasing parcels of the San Justo and Cienega del Gabilan ranches, that the Bolsa is a large part of the Paul Hudner estate which she manages.

Helen Hudner, a sister of Paul Hudner, said that she lives in the original Judge John Hudner home in Hollister, built in the 1880s, where she and her brothers, Paul and Charles, were raised. Charles followed neither ranching nor law, but became president of the Federal Intermediate Credit Bank and always lived at the Pacific Union Club in San Francisco. She also told of the little Southern Pacific station on the ranch and how her father used to catch a ride on the train from Tres Pinos to Gilroy and get off at the ranch. As a matter of fact this station was mentioned in *Historic Spots in California* by Hoover, Rensch, and Abeloe, in telling of Pedro Fages' inland trip from Monterey with Padre Juan Crespi as his diarist. The authors wrote that after crossing the San Juan Valley, the Fages party "entered the Santa Clara Valley north of Hudner (a Southern Pacific flag stop in San Benito County), passed the Tequesquite Slough and San Felipe Lake..."

Mary Hudner's son, Phil, practices law in San Francisco and comes down on weekends with his

Three Mutsun Indians photographed by Paul Hudner. They were called "Vinegar, Salt, and Pepper."

wife, Carla, and their three children, from Marin. In talking about the Hudners, Breens, and Doolings, Phil noted that not only did these families have a penchant for ranching but a talent for law as well, especially the judicial branch of the law. James P. Breen, brother of Patrick Breen, Jr., was San Benito County's first Superior Court Judge. He was followed by Judge M. T. Dooling, Sr., who was appointed to the Federal Bench. Phil said his grandfather, John L. Hudner, was appointed to the Superior Court bench and re-elected until his death. He was succeeded by Superior Judge M. T. Dooling, Jr., who later served on the California Supreme Court. A later Superior Court Judge was Thomas P. O'Connell, whose mother, Amy Breen O'Connell, was a daughter of Patrick Breen, Jr. and a sister of Molly (Mrs. John L.) Hudner. Also in the practice of law are Philip's two cousins, Thomas and John Breen, sons of Jack Breen.

Paul Hudner, who did not study law, but became a highly successful rancher, also acquired the Rosa Morada Ranch, but that is another story—the story of the Doolings.

CHAPTER XVI

Rancho San Joaquin o Rosa Morada

The story of Rancho San Joaquin o Rosa Morada is not laced with drama or intrigue, but its cast of characters features well-known old San Benito County names, and it is set in a scenic background that seems to have a certain tranquility. There may well have been Indian raids, however, at the time the original Mexican grant of two square leagues was made by Governor Gutierrez to Cruz Cervantes in 1836. During this period Indians from the San Joaquin Valley were crossing over the mountains and raiding the San Juan ranches. Many of the grants on this side of the valley, including those of Cervantes' next-door neighbors, Juan Anzar and Manuel Larios, were made to provide a buffer against Indian attacks. All that seems to be known about Cervantes is that he had horses, cattle and sheep on his land, with corrals, and four or five acres under cultivation.

After the United States patent was issued to Cervantes in 1874, it was transferred to Flint-Bixby and pre-dated 1863. When the Flint property was divided, Thomas Flint received the San Justo ranch, and Benjamin Flint the San Joaquin o Rosa Morada. The Flints always referred to this ranch as the "Little San Joaquin" because Flint-Bixby had the immense San Joaquin ranch in Orange County in partnership with James Irvine. The Doolings have always called it the Rosa Morada. In 1879 Thomas O'Connell, grandfather of Fenton and James O'Connell, bought a small parcel of the ranch off Fairview Road. It was always referred to as the O'Connell Place. When the O'Connells moved to San Jose in 1899 with their four sons, William Dooling and his bride, Molly McAuliffe, moved into the house located at the corner of Rosa Morada and Dooling Road. The Doolings had come to San Benito County in 1868.

There were three Dooling brothers, Timothy, Maurice, and Daniel, father of Will, who came to

the United States from Ireland. In 1852 they came to California by way of the Isthmus. For many years they worked the mines in Nevada City, where Will Dooling was born in 1862.

All three brothers came to San Benito County and acquired ranches. Two characteristics have dominated the Dooling progeny: a love of the land and a love of scholarship. Timothy's son, Maurice T. Dooling, was a Greek and Latin scholar at St. Mary's college, spoke a number of languages, and was appointed by President Wilson as U.S. District Judge. His son, Justice Maurice T. Dooling, was appointed to the California Supreme Court by Governor Edmund G. Brown in 1960. He married Mary Devlin, the daughter of noted attorney Francis J. Devlin, in 1916. Although their judicial appointments took them away from Hollister and the land, neither of the Judge Doolings ever severed his connections with the ranches.

John Erkman and his mother, Elizabeth Dooling Erkman, at the old homestead, which John is restoring, on the Rosa Morada Ranch.

Entrance to Rancho Rosa Morada.

FOR STATE SENATOR

WILLIAM R. FLINT

REPUBLICAN CANDIDATE

11th Senatorial District Counties of San Benito, Santa Cruz, San Mateo

Senator William Flint, son of Ben Flint of Flint & Bixby Co.

Through a confusion of some sort Rosa Morada was listed on the maps and on the signpost as O'Rosa Morada. In Spanish the letter "o" means "or," but some supervisor apparently thought because of so many Irish in the Fairview district that it was an Irish name, and inserted the apostrophe. This proved to be a touchy subject for a long time.

Will Dooling and his brother, Jeff, were partners in cattle raising. After Will's death in 1928 the property was divided between the two families. Jeff Dooling's widow, Anna, still lives on the Fairview ranch, and her sons, Jeff, Jr. and Willis, and daughter, Mrs. Charles Hall, run the family's Lone Tree Ranch. Paul Hudner purchased the Will Dooling and the Walter Flint ranches in 1944 and 1945. They are now owned by the Paul Hudner Estate which Mary Hudner operates and owns jointly with her sons Stephen and Philip Hudner. Five of these acres, including the old Dooling house, were deeded by Mary Hudner to her nephew, John Erkman. John, a school teacher in Hollister, is in the midst of restoring the house where his mother, Elizabeth Erkman (Mrs. John) and her three sisters, Kathryn Dooling, Marjorie Snyder (Mrs. Calvert) of Stockton, and Mary Hudner were born.

Taking an active interest in the work being done to the old family homestead, Mary and Elizabeth pointed out where there had been a row of old buildings across the back, including a bunkhouse, a granary, and a Chinese cook's house. Remaining are the tank house, the old smoke house, and most important, the mellow weathered old fences. From the window of the family kitchen, where John has his grandmother's old oak table, one views a rustic scene of the Dos Picachos Creek, which runs by the house, and a graceful grouping of oak trees. The McMahon Hills are directly ahead. They were named for Thomas McMahon, who owned a part of the ranch. He was a successful Hollister businessman, originally from San Juan, whose holdings included the Hotel Hollister, formerly the McMahon House, now owned by the Hollingberry family. He donated the present site of Sacred Heart Church and School to the church. His wife, Isabel, was the only daughter of Margaret and Patrick Breen of the Donner Party.

Against the hills is the house built by William Flint, son of Benjamin, in about 1900, after he returned from a year in the Philippine Islands for the government. He co-owned the ranch with his brothers, George C. and Walter P. Flint, and had 1,000 acres under cultivation and 3,000 being used as range. In 1908 William was elected to the State Assembly and was one of the Flints to serve (during the so-called Flint dynasty) as master of Texas Lodge No. 46 F. & A.M. of San Juan.

His white house, built on the side of the hill, is surrounded by large trees and has a bay window in front looking down on the valley. Next door, across a ravine and connected by a footbridge, is an attractive red house with red roof and pepper trees in front and back, which was built by his brother,

Walter Flint, an architect, when he moved down from Oakland. After Senator Flint and his wife, the former Mary Louise Kemp of San Juan, left, Walter and his wife moved into the white house and used the red house as a party house. Elizabeth Erkman remembered going to parties there. In back of the two houses is a large old barn and smaller buildings once used for farm implements. John Erkman said that on a clear day he can see the Flint-Bixby house (now the St. Francis Retreat House) in the San Juan Hills. Elizabeth and Mary Hudner looked back on the days when they used to ride horseback through these hills, herding cattle for their father.

In between John Erkman's house and the Flint places is a stretch of land which formerly belonged to Joe Ayer of Gilroy who at one time worked the Sargent Ranch. On it is a pastoral scene that would be pleasing to the eye of a landscape painter. There is a large pond in a hollow, called Catfish Lake, where cattle were grazing along the shore, ducks flying over and making perfect landings on the water, and oak trees on the gentle rise of the hills around it reflected in the water. As a matter of fact, a photographer did capture this scene for the cover of the Hollister telephone book a couple of years ago.

Home of Walter Flint on San Joaquin o Rosa Morada Ranch. The Flints always referred to this as the "Little San Joaquin" because they owned the expansive San Joaquin Ranch in Southern California. When William Flint left the Victorian house next door, Walter Flint and his wife moved into it and converted this into their "party house."

Home of State Senator William Flint, on San Joaquin o Rosa Morada Ranch. Original grant was to Cruz Cervantes. It was later owned by Flint & Bixby and is now part of the Paul Hudner estate.

James Dunne home on San Felipe. Early accounts described its beautiful gardens.

James Dunne, who purchased 25,000 acres of Rancho Ausaymas y San Felipe in 1857 from Francisco Pacheco. During his early days on the ranch Dunne had problems with squatters. He frequently slept beneath the trees, a brace of pistols at his side.

James F. Dunne (Jimmy) with his wife, the former Viola Lowery of San Jose, in one of their early automobiles.

San Felipe residence of James F. Dunne and his wife, Viola. It was described as the finest home south of San Jose. Built in 1907 and sometimes known as "Casa del Rancho," it was elegantly appointed. It is now occupied by Mr. and Mrs. James O'Connell, Jr.

CHAPTER XVII
James Dunne Ranch

The Dunne Ranch, which is bordered by the Tequesquite and the San Luis Gonzaga ranches, straddling San Benito and Santa Clara Counties, is still called by that name even though it has been in the hands of the O'Connell family for the past 50 years. The late Franklyn O'Connell purchased it from Viola Dunne, widow of James F. Dunne, after leasing it for a number of years. Jimmy Dunne, as he was always called, had owned the picturesque ranch through which the Pacheco Creek runs, for 50 years before that, having inherited it from his father, James Dunne.

James, with his brother, Peter Dunne, and Gustave Touchard, purchased four square leagues of El Rancho Ausaymas y San Felipe for $20,000 from Francisco Pacheco in 1857. That same year they also acquired from Pacheco two square leagues of the Bolsa San Felipe. Translated to acreage this would be more than 25,000 acres. The senior James Dunne always called his ranch the "San Felipe."

Dunne apparently bought out his partners, because at his death in 1874 the entire ranch, along with his part of "El Topo" in San Benito and Monterey Counties, went to James F. Dunne. The settling of this will, by the way, set off a fierce legal contest in Probate Court between the executor of the estate, A. J. Donnelly, and C. T. Ryland, who held power of attorney for James Dunne's widow, Catherine, and her three minor children. Ryland, on behalf of his client, accused Donnelly of mismanagement of the estate. The decision of Judge Payne was overturned by the Supreme Court in favor of Donnelly. The press gave it complete coverage and was extremely critical of C. T. Ryland and Judge Payne. Under a heading "Dishonor and Dishonesty," they wrote, "As a public journalist we condemn the conduct of Ryland and Rankin in the Dunne estate, and it devolves upon all good citizens to comment. For rascality in connection with dead men's estates must be discouraged." The press at the same time defended Catherine Dunne as an innocent victim.

James Dunne came to California in 1848 from Queen's County, Ireland, by way of New Orleans, where he worked as a clerk in the mercantile business. He became a successful businessman in San Francisco, but his interest in land grew, and after acquiring the San Felipe ranch, he sold his San Francisco business. He was married first to Catherine McDonald, the mother of Jimmy Dunne, who died in 1855. In 1862 he married Catherine O'Toole Murphy, widow of Bernard Murphy of the well-known Martin Murphy clan, who had large land holdings in her own name. Although he was to live only 12 years after their marriage, the couple had three children: Peter J., Catherine, who married R. W. Hersey, and Mary Phileta, who married Joseph Rucker. When the house was being remodeled, James O'Connell found a prayer book inscribed by James Murphy (son of Martin), "To James Dunne, March 1, 1854." He also found a gold ring decorated with three gold nuggets and engraved on the inside, "James Dunne to Catherine Dunne - 1850," and the original patent for El Topo Ranch (San Lorenzo), signed by President Ulysses S. Grant.

During the early days on the ranch Dunne had problems with squatters. "At night," wrote the *San Jose Mercury* for a special Gilroy edition in 1892, "he frequently slept beneath the trees on the place, a brace of pistols at his side and fully prepared for any emergency." There was also a strong feeling against the Americans at that time on the part of the Californians, many of whom had lost their land. The story went on to say, "...but these problems have passed and thousands of cattle have grazed on these oak covered hillsides and moved off to market." It went on to describe the fine home (later replaced by the present house) built by his son,

Fenton O'Connell, Ruth O'Connell Berry, and James O'Connell on Dunne Ranch which their father, Franklyn O'Connell purchased from Mrs. James F. Dunne.

James F. Dunne, the extensive gardens, and the great stables surrounded by a large corral for his purebred horses.

James F. Dunne (Jimmy) was a blend of cattleman and urbanite. Although he kept a suite of rooms at the Palace Hotel in San Francisco and traveled extensively with his wife, Viola, he equally enjoyed life on the ranch. Charlie Maggini, the well-known cowboy who was U.S. Champion Roper in 1929, recalled that Jimmy Dunne always wore a large white handkerchief around his neck. He would often say to the cowboys, "Fellows, let's go down to the Corners for a drink," and they would lope four or so abreast down to Dunnesville, where he would buy them a drink or two or three. This intersection at San Felipe and Shore Roads was originally known as "Chase's Corners" for a man by that name who had the bar there.

Another story about Jimmy Dunne was told by Consuelo Roca Laurent. When she was a little girl she went with her father, Dr. Ramon Roca, from their home on the adjoining ranch (Ausaymas) to see Dunne about some property. As they were walking around Dunne said to her father, "Let's have a little drink." With that he walked over to an oak tree and took out a bottle of whiskey. He had bottles spotted around the ranch in case he got thirsty.

The James F. Dunnes

In 1883 James Francis Dunne and Viola Lowery were married in the home of her parents, Mr. and Mrs. G. W. Lowery in San Jose. A newspaper report of the wedding described "the elegant lace curtains trimmed with smilax and long graceful sprays of Lady Bankshire roses...the wedding bell of white rosebuds hanging from the arch...the tout ensemble softened by the gaslight...as Father Bixio pronounced the solemn words and the young couple plighted the vows that made them one."

In 1906–07 the Dunnes built a magnificent new home of Colonial style architecture, said to be the finest home south of San Jose. In a 1907 issue of the *Gilroy Advocate* the house and a reception given by the Dunnes were described at length. The report told of the orchestra playing on the veranda which surrounds three sides of the house, of Mrs. Dunne's appearance in "an imported Parisian gown of ivory white battenberg lace and wavy silk, made entraine with which she wore a necklace of diamonds and amethysts."

Describing the second floor, which unfortunately has since been removed, the writer said:

There are seven well ventilated bed chambers—each in a different color—a portico and rear porch off the bedchambers where the ladies may enjoy an early sunbath or afternoon siesta. Altogether we know of no finer home in the country—and old time hospitality that has made the Dunnes famous the past half century in this neighborhood still reigns supreme at 'Casa del Rancho.' "

James O'Connell, Jr. and his wife Cheryle, the present occupants, are restoring the house. They have put many of the original pieces of furniture and lamps back in the living room, which has a high baronial ceiling and an enormous English walk-in fireplace with cozy seats covered in velvet on each side. To the left of the entrance hall is an ornate carved teak archway leading to the oriental room. The teak chairs inlaid with mother-of-pearl are from the Dunnes' travels, as is the light fixture.

Through the lower portion of three handsome

James O'Connell, Sr., in front of home on Dunne Ranch, which he owns jointly with his brother, Fenton O'Connell. Note second floor has been removed.

Water tower from original Dunne Ranch. Ranch offices were in part of this structure.

James O'Connell, Jr., in front of shed, oldest building on Dunne Ranch.

arched stained-glass windows can be seen open fields of cows grazing and the mountains of the Pacheco Pass rising up in the background.

On the walls are portraits of the senior James Dunne, and of Viola and Jimmy Dunne on their travels around the world. There is a photograph album showing their fine thoroughbred horses and their early-day automobiles, which they seemed to like almost as much as the horses. It contains pictures of the elaborate furnishings and the beautiful gardens and newspaper clippings of trips taken in their Pierce Arrow car to the Topo Ranch. One of the clippings says of the car:

It is equipped with every convenience and attachment known to the motor world and is a thing of beauty, power and speed. Driven by engines of 60 horse power it negotiates heavy grades with the speed of a bird....On the return trip the Arrow crossed the Pajaro river under a full head of steam and parted the waters on either side like a beautiful clipper ship.

In 1925, upon returning from a trip to Europe with Viola, Dunne took ill and died several weeks later at his San Felipe Ranch. He is buried in Gilroy.

The O'Connells

After the death of Jimmy Dunne the era of the O'Connells began. The 17,500-acre spread is now owned by Franklyn O'Connell's sons, Fenton and James O'Connell. Their sister, Ruth Berry (Mrs. Chandler), has since disposed of her portion.

Viola Dunne had run an advertisement for the sale of the ranch, which read, "Most beautiful ranch in the state—20 room residence—guest cot-

tage, superintendent's cottage, chauffeur's cottage, ample garage with or without Pierce Arrow cars — a thoroughly equipped ranch in every detail — ready to step in June 1, 1925." Step in the O'Connells did, and it appears O'Connells will be there for some time to come.

Their lifestyle has been a little different from that of the Dunnes. Franklyn O'Connell often entertained with informal barbecues. He was a friend of U.S. Supreme Court Justice Warren, who used to come to the ranch when he was governor, as did Lieutenant Governor Powers, who was a good friend, and Governor Goodwin Knight. Will Rogers also was a guest at the ranch, and Herbert Hoover was there when Hitler moved into Poland, the start of World War II. O'Connell was an honorary member of the Santa Clara football team and used to entertain the team every year.

The grounds are no longer maintained by a crew of gardeners, but Jim and Cheryle are working on them. Many of the lovely old trees and shrubs acquired by the Dunnes on their travels are doing well. Still standing are the original greenhouse, the old water tower, and the gazebo, in addition to the ranch buildings.

James O'Connell, Sr. and his wife, Sylvia, live in a modern ranch house on the hill above. They look out over the ranch. Pointing to a hill across the Pass, Jim said that was where the Dunnes had a fine summer house.

On the other side of the ranch border he pointed to the former J. D. Culp property, where 135 acres were planted in tobacco. So excellent was the product that it won a silver award in the San Francisco Exposition of 1915.

Left and above: Creating a dramatic entrance to the Rancho Ausaymas y San Felipe headquarters of the Hawkins Cattle Company on Viboras Creek is the lane of eucalyptus trees three-quarters of a mile long. They were planted by Jimmy Raimondi for Dr. Ramon Roca in the late 1890s. Jimmy hand-watered the 750 trees with a wagon and tank.

Debbie Hawkins and Juan Bautista Heguy, vaquero, at Rancho Ausaymas y San Felipe.

This house built in the 1890s by Dr. Ramon Roca near Pacheco Pass was cut in three parts and moved by wagon to a site on Viboras Creek. Dr. Roca sold his share of Rancho Ausaymas y San Felipe to Charles N. Hawkins.

CHAPTER XVIII

Rancho Ausaymas y San Felipe

The two-story adobe built by Don Francisco Pacheco on his rancho Ausaymas y San Felipe has been described as a "feudal estate." The land was composed of two Mexican grants of two square leagues each, one from Governor Figueroa in 1833 and the other from Governor Gutierrez in 1836. According to records of 1852, the house was valued at between $15,000 and $20,000. There were ten cabins for laborers, and thousands of horses, cattle and hogs, with pens and corrals, and enough of the land was in cultivation to provide for all who lived upon it. It was located off present Highway 156 near Pacheco Creek, on the right-hand side going from Pacheco Pass to Hollister. This piece of property, with some of the original buildings still standing, is now owned by Frank Smith.

Sometime around 1852 the Pacheco family suffered an unnerving incident. After the "undesirables" were driven out of San Francisco by the vigilantes, they headed south. One of the places they hit was the Pacheco Rancho. They bound up Pacheco and his wife and daughter, and according to one version of the story, made off with $18,000 in gold dust. Consuelo Roca Laurent, whose mother, Mariana Malarin Roca, was Pacheco's granddaughter and inherited this ranch, said that when the robbers came they pulled down the top of the desk and took all the silver, little knowing that they were missing the big cache, the gold which was underneath.

Don Francisco moved his wife and daughter, Lola (Isadora), to his large adobe home at Monterey. A few years later Lola was married to Mariano Malarin in the San Carlos Cathedral. His father, Don Juan Malarin, was a wealthy and highly esteemed Peruvian trader who came to California in 1820 as master of the "Senoriano." He married Josefa Estrada, of a prominent family, and received the Mexican grant "Llanitos de los Correos," which stretched for 8,859 acres on the west side of Salinas River opposite Chualar and Gonzales. He sent his son to Peru to study law, but this did not keep Mariano from running into financial problems with David Jacks, well known in Monterey as an opportunist and a manipulator who became a large landowner.

Thomas B. Hawkins, William Hawkins, and Thomas W. (Tommy) Hawkins, members of the Hawkins Cattle Company (with others). Charles N. Hawkins, father of Thomas B., bought Rancho Ausaymas y San Felipe from Dr. Ramon Roca in 1906.

99

A vivid description of the adobe and life on the landed estates was given some years ago to the *Evening Freelance* by a Chester Gillespie who had lived there with his parents from 1889 to 1904. He and his mother cherished the unusual life there and had at one time made notes and drawings of the adobe. He said it was a long narrow building with broad verandas that ran the length and breadth of the house, with a 15-foot passage running crossways through the center. This connected the two verandas and opened to rooms on either side. The walls were three feet thick and heavily whitewashed. The roof was of redwood shingles from the Santa Cruz Mountains instead of tile. He said that there were 22 rooms including 11 bedrooms, but only a single bathroom, and two kitchens, one facing north for summer use and the other facing south for the sun in the winter. In between was a 35-foot long dining room, and upstairs was a 50-foot long parlor, the scene of many fiestas.

Gillespie said that the ranch was a grand baronial affair, with 70 to 80 miles of fencing because of its unusual length, and that in back of the adobe were barns, storage sheds, storerooms, a blacksmith shop, winery, swimming pool, and race track. Almost completely self-sustaining, the ranch had fruit orchards, vegetable gardens, and a vineyard. There was a row of olive trees along the country road for olive oil, meat from the cattle, chickens for eating and eggs, and cows for milk, butter and cheese. During the Gillespies' stay his father, Samuel, was superintendent, and a nephew of Mariano, Ignacio Malarin, was the manager. A maiden aunt, Dona Maria Malarin, also lived at the adobe, and Gillespie recalled her long black braids that reached to her knees.

There was large acreage of hay and grain and what must have been one of the earliest of harvester machines pulled by 20 horses, and also a hay baler. Most important to a young boy was the cookhouse that followed the harvesting crews, and the pies made by the Chinese cook. They made their own wine, and he described Felipe, the Portuguese winemaker, in the vat in his bare feet, crushing the juice from the grapes. Occasionally he would stand poised on one foot, with the arm on the other side upraised for balance. With his free hand he held a tiny wine glass under the big toe of the upraised foot to let the juice run off into the wine glass.

After the family drove to mass in Hollister on Sunday mornings there would be barbecues out in the hills in huge earthen pits, with dancing, horse racing, and swimming.

Lola and Mariano Malarin, who also acquired a house in Santa Clara, had two daughters, Paula, who married Dr. Luis Fatjo, and Mariana, who married Dr. Ramon Roca. When the property was divided Mariana and Dr. Roca received the Ausaymas ranch with the adobe, and Paula and Dr. Fatjo received the San Luis Gonzaga. After the earthquake of 1896 the Rocas built a large frame house on the bench between the creek and the adobe. They had three daughters, Consuelo Laurent (Mrs. Andre) of Los Gatos, Monserrat Roca of San Jose, and Lolita Roca Rose of San Francisco. Consuelo said her mother didn't like the new location and the house was cut in three sections and moved by wagon to a more pleasant site about three miles away, on the Viboras Creek. Consuelo has many memories of her childhood on the ranch. It was a big occasion to go visit their cousins, the Fatjos, on the San Luis ranch, almost a day's trip in the phaeton along a creek road that Pacheco had made. Along the way they would stop and rest the horses and have a picnic beside a stream.

In the summers, however, the Fatjos and their three children would move over to the Rocas' ranch because of the extreme heat at the San Luis. Christmases were always spent together, a happy time for the six cousins.

On Sundays they would go to mass, she said, in Hollister.

We would start out in the Pierce Arrow or whatever car Father would have. The cars in those days weren't very dependable, so we would be followed by the phaeton and the horses. Sometimes we would have to resort to the buggy if the car broke down. As we got a little older the two families rented a big house in San Francisco around 1904 called the Casey House. We all lived there for a year and then each family got its own house.

When the earthquake hit in 1906 the two families moved to Spain. Dr. Fatjo died in Spain, and Paula Fatjo returned to California with her three children. Dr. Roca and Mariana, however, stayed on until 1920. Their daughters attended convent schools in Ireland and England.

♘ *The Hawkins Cattle Company*

The approach to the Rancho de las Ausaymas is dramatic. Planted at the time the Rocas moved the house there, about 80 years ago, is a lane of eucalyptus trees three-quarters of a mile long. The trees were planted by Jimmy Raimondi, who worked on the ranch. He not only hand-planted the 750 trees, but also hand-watered them with a wagon and tank.

For the past 70 years the Ausaymas has been owned by the Hawkins family of Hollister. "Charles N. Hawkins had sold the Rancho Cienega de los Paicines to an easterner by the name of Kingsley Macomber (this is now the Law ranch), and wanted to reinvest his money," said his grandson, William Hawkins, who lives on the southwest border of the ranch. "Many people had tried to buy the Ausaymas, but Dr. Roca had refused. This was about the time Dr. Roca had taken his three daughters to Spain. Grandfather cabled him there and, to his surprise, received an answer accepting his offer. Dr. Roca came over from Spain to finalize the arrangements."

"The amazing thing," said Marion Hawkins, "Dr. Roca didn't take a thing out of that big 17-room house. He left his completely stocked wine cellar, his medical books printed in Spanish in the 1870s, and the furniture. He didn't even take his clothes."

Bill and Marion Hawkins lived in the Roca house which, incidentally, was scheduled to be taken down in 1976, when they were first married. They pointed out where Dr. Roca had his swimming pool and another building where the dressing rooms were. When Bill and Marion built their modern house on a knoll above Comstock Road with a 360-degree view, they had Dr. Roca's meat house moved over. It is used as a gazebo with white wicker furniture, but the old meat hooks are still in place.

Built along the Viboras Road are the homes of Bill's father, Thomas B. Hawkins, son of Charles, who bought the property from Dr. Roca, and of his

Gazebo on Bill and Marion Hawkins' property on Comstock Road. Formerly the meat house, they moved it over from ranch headquarters when they built their modern home. The meat hooks are still in place.

brother, Thomas W. (Tommy) Hawkins. Thomas B. Hawkins' brother, C. J. Hawkins, a member of the Hawkins Cattle Company, lives on Orchard Road. Their sister, Pearl Hawkins Schulze, sold her part of the ranch to Fenton O'Connell and Louis Bourdet. Tommy Hawkins said his house was built on an Indian burial ground and that they have found many artifacts. The houses face Las Viboras (Snake) Creek, and in the back is a meadow from which rises up almost perpendicularly a high hill on which the cattle graze.

The Hawkins family has a long history in San Benito County. Thomas B. Hawkins told about his grandfather, Thomas S. Hawkins, who came to California overland in 1861 and was a leader in the founding of Hollister.

Above, the Hodges house on the south side of Fourth Street, between Monterey and West, where jail is now located. Hodges bought the block between Monterey and West and William and Ann Streets. This building was used by the Methodist Church for a time.

Above, Fourth Street in early Hollister.

Colonel William Welles Hollister, for whom the town of Hollister is named. He sold his half of the San Justo Rancho to the San Justo Homestead Association for $370,000. He had paid Flint & Bixby $12,500 for the same land 10 or 12 years earlier.

Below, Colonel Hollister's home as it appeared before the founding of the town. Located at the corner of Monterey and Fourth Streets, it later became the Montgomery House.

Below, the Granger's Union on San Benito Street in Hollister.

CHAPTER XIX

The Hollister Story

With the organization of the San Justo Homestead Association and the purchase of 21,000 acres of Rancho San Justo from Colonel William Welles Hollister in 1868, a new town was born. Instead of calling it San Justo, however, the founding fathers said they were tired of all those Spanish names, so they decided to name it Hollister after the man who sold them the property. The town was divided into 50 homestead lots for which 50 farmers paid $2,000 each. 100 acres were reserved in the center for the town, which was laid out into blocks and lots. The Association paid Hollister $370,000 for the same property for which he had paid only $12,500, less than a dozen years before.

A board of directors was organized with Samuel S. Swope elected its first president, Henry W. Briggs, secretary, J. R. Weller, Thomas S. Hawkins, C. Wentz, William T. Brown and William N. Furlong, additional board members. Their names were given to alleys in the new town. Colonel Hollister and his wife were the only persons to have streets named for them, William and Ann. The couple had been married in 1862 in San Francisco by Thomas Starr King. Ann (Hannah) was the daughter of the famous vigilante leader, Samuel James.

With the new town launched, Hollister sold his mansion on Fourth Street to J. I. Hodges, who also bought a large tract adjoining the West Street boundary of the town. This house later became the Montgomery Hotel. With the sale of the property and his enormous profits from his sheep enterprise, Hollister lost no time in heading south with his sheep to Santa Barbara. Before leaving he also purchased a piece of property included in the San Justo sale which he had previously sold to Jasper Twitchell, to give him clear title.

He had already bought up several Spanish and Mexican land grant ranches in the vicinity of the Santa Barbara area, in partnership with Albert and Thomas Dibblee, including the old Francisco Ortega rancho, Nuestra Senora del Refugio. The land he most coveted, however, was in the Tecolotito Canyon in the Dos Pueblos area, which he had seen on his first trip north with Auntie Lucy Brown. He bought 5,000 acres bordering Tecolotito Creek at ten dollars in gold per acre, even though Judge J. F. Maguire of Santa Barbara had warned that it was an illegal transaction, that the property was protected by a trust for Nicolas Den's underage children. This later was to prove to be the one big mistake of Hollister's phenomenal business career.

He renamed the Tecolotito "Glen Annie" for his wife and set about to make it a showplace. His baronial mansion was surrounded by extensive landscaping, lawns, plantings, and a horticultural arboretum. Everything from orchids to redwoods grew at the Glen Annie, and it is said that it was comparable to a modern day country club. Hollister put in six miles of fencing, something new for Santa Barbara County, and built neat wooden barns of midwestern styling, no doubt reminiscent of his native Ohio. They somehow didn't seem compatible with the Hispanic background of the Goleta Valley. He planted groves of citrus trees, financed Stearns Wharf, built the Arlington House, a luxuriously furnished 90-room hotel, built the first library, and established the *Santa Barbara Morning Press*. Its editor, Harrison Gray Otis, was later to found the prestigious *Los Angeles Times*.

Hollister, however, was to meet his Waterloo. Kate Den Bell (Mrs. John) decided to take action on the Tecolotito transaction and enlisted the services of Thomas B. Bishop, San Francisco attorney. After years of litigation, the property was restored to the Dens, with Bishop taking his fee in a share of the property. In the meantime Hollister died and mysteriously, the day following his wife's eviction the house burned to the ground. Gone were all the mementoes and the story of Hollister's life.

Above, the home of Thomas S. Hawkins, which covered almost a block on South Street. Below, the Hazel Hawkins Hospital, built by Thomas in memory of his granddaughter, Hazel Hawkins.

Thomas S. Hawkins, one of the founders of Hollister and a prominent businessman.

Above, T. S. Hawkins built this house at the corner of Monterey and South Streets for his son Warren. Below, residence built for his daughter on South Street. Originally four rooms, it was enlarged over the years to ten.

Hazel Hawkins, called "Little Sunshine" by her adoring grandfather, died of appendicitis at the age of seven.

The Town of Hollister

Two members of the original board of the San Justo Homestead Association subsequently had streets named for them in the town of Hollister. One was Abraham Sally, who served as treasurer, secretary, and finally president. Another street was named for a man who contributed much to the town, Thomas S. Hawkins. He told the story of his life and times in his book, *Recollections of a Busy Life.* He had come overland in the early 1860s, farming first in Mountain View and then in Gilroy. From Gilroy he would take his wheat by wagon to Alviso and put it on a ship to go up the bay to San Francisco, sometimes driving through "bandit-infested" territory. Joining the San Justo Homestead Association in 1868, he chose a 172-acre plot on the south side of town, but business seemed to be his forte. He was chairman of the Bank of Hollister, the Hollister Water Company, the Hollister Warehouse Company, and the Hollister Gas Company.

Not only did he build a fine home and tennis court for himself on South Street, that covered all of one block except the two ends, but on the corner at Monterey Street he built a home for his son, Warren Hawkins, which is now occupied by Mrs. Marian Currie, and at the other corner a house for his daughter, Kathryn Hawkins Boyns, where Tom Sparling now lives. Kathryn designed the house, originally a four-room cottage of Queen Anne design. It has gradually been added onto, and now has ten rooms. Because of its distinctive architecture, it is referred to around Hollister as the Bird Cage house.

The Victorian house on the other corner is where T. S. Hawkins' beloved granddaughter died of appendicitis at the age of seven. He felt that had there been a hospital in Hollister she might have been saved. Consequently, in memory of "Little Sunshine," as he always called her, he built the Hazel Hawkins Memorial Hospital, which opened in 1907. Another daughter, who was named Jean, was born to the Warren Hawkinses. She married E. E. Sparling, and now lives on the Los Viboras ranch left to her by her grandfather, adjoining the Ausaymas ranch of her cousins, the Hawkinses. It is just below the French Ranch.

At the time of its birth, this new town of Hollister was still in Monterey County. It was a long trip to the county seat, with the Gabilans to cross. As soon as the San Justo Homestead Association was organized they started agitating for a division of the county, with the Gabilans considered a logical point of demarcation. Five years later, after many

Miss Marjorie Flint's home on South Street, built in 1871. It served for a time in the 1890s as the high school.

Fred Farnham had the San Felipe Market. He used this wagon to deliver meat. His sister, Mrs. Chester Bromley, still lives in the Hollister area.

Deer Camp near Chittenden. Front row: Charley Dowdy, Al Willson, CC Zanetta, Elmer Sherman, and Fred Kemp. Back row: Charley Plummer, Cory Briggs, Asula Castro, Mike Castro (relative of General Castro), Jim Butler, Billie Breen, and Tom Nyland.

The home of Superior Court Judge John Hudner, now occupied by his daughter, Helen Hudner.

editorials and political maneuvers, the divisionists were finally successful. Governor Booth signed legislation establishing San Benito County and appointed five commissioners to organize the county government. They were T. S. Hawkins, Jesse Whitton (J. C. Fremont's mapmaker and surveyor), Mark Pomeroy, John Breen, and H. M. Hayes. They met at the Baldwin House in Hollister and elected John Breen president and H. M. Hayes secretary. Despite opposition from Tres Pinos, mainly from the Arques brothers, Joaquin and Luis, Hollister was elected to be the county seat.

Hollister seemed to love a celebration in those early days. As reported in the *Hollister Advance* of February 7, 1874:

Within an hour after the news was received [of the formation of San Benito County] bonfires spreading with close intervals, along the line of San Benito Street from the Eagle Hotel at the southern end to Beach and Farish's store at the northern end, illuminated the town with a brilliancy that was noticed at a distance of 30 miles, and by many distant persons who were un-

Signatures of prominent early San Benito County citizens affixed to official map.

conscious of the cause, it was believed the whole town was sinking under the ravages of a general conflagration.

As might naturally be predicted, whiskey flowed freely throughout all available channels.

Revolvers were used in the general tumult and we regret to say that in one case a revolver burst, seriously injuring the hand of a young man named Schwabacher.

In another, a woman was shot in the knee at a disreputable house on Fourth Street. This, however, is also reported as an accident, and the woman is not dangerously hurt.

By midnight all was calm and the bonfires had dimmed.

Another occasion celebrated with equal exuberance was the coming of the railroad to Hollister. When news was received in 1871 that the Southern Pacific would extend its railroad through Hollister, the *Central Californian* reported:

It was worth a jollification. Quite a number of people gave vent to their joy by repairing to Hollister Hill and burning up quite an amount of gunpowder. The flag was also run up—not up the heights but up the pole—and citizens felt jubilant generally.

The grade stakes were set and graders started working from both the Hollister and the Gilroy ends. An editorial comment was:

However thick the clouds that have hung over Hollister since its conversion from a sheep pasture some two and a half years since, to a well laid out country town, they have all been dispelled by the cunning hand of progress and the timely visitation of abundant rains.

A later edition, reporting on the progress, said, "The iron horse will resound through the valley of the San Benito within two months." In July the railroad ran an excursion train from Gilroy to Hollister with 800 to 900 residents taking the 20-mile ride.

While Hollister was hoisting its flag, over at San Juan theirs was at half-mast, at least figuratively. This was the death knell for the mission town, as far as progress was concerned.

CHAPTER XX

Y *Rancho San Luis y Gonzaga*

A visit with Paula Fatjo on her Rancho San Luis Gonzaga on the Pacheco Pass was like reliving a century and a half of California history. Paula is a direct descendant of Francisco Perez Pacheco, a carriage maker who came to California as an artillery soldier in the Mexican Army to defend the missions. That was in 1819. He stayed to become one of the state's largest landowners, owning over 100,000 acres and controlling many more. The San Luis covered 48,000 acres on both sides of the pass. In fact, as owner of the contiguous Rancho Ausaymas y San Felipe, covering 35,000 acres, he could ride horseback from just east of Gilroy almost to Los Banos on his own property. He also received the Bolsa de San Felipe grant of 7,000 acres and purchased the Rancho San Justo of 35,000 acres from General Jose Castro. The San Justo, half of which later became Hollister, he sold to Flint & Bixby in 1855.

Paula and her cousin, Bunny Fatjo Kalend, who lives on another part of the ranch (across from Bell's Station) with her husband, Michael Kalend, and family, are believed to be the only descendants of a Mexican land grantee in direct blood line still living on the family land, in California. Paula's father, Clemente Fatjo, and Bunny's father, Luis Fatjo, were brothers. Bunny moved back to the San Luis just a few years ago after raising her children in Burlingame. She used to come down in the summers as a child, she said, to stay on the part of the ranch leased by John Somavia, where the Glenn Mathis ranch house is now, built on a hill above the pass. Bunny also is "early California" on the side of her mother, who was a Temple and a descendant of Francisco Temple of Rancho La Puente in Southern California, encompassing Temple City and the beach areas such as Newport. In 1943 the San Luis Ranch was divided between the three children of Dr. Luis Fatjo: Mary Judge Fatjo (Mrs. Clemente), her sister-in-law, Lolita Fatjo Judge (Mrs. Austen), and Luis Fatjo.

As Paula explained the history of the Pacheco Pass, a 25-mile gap which links the Santa Clara and San Joaquin Valleys, she said that the Yokut Indians had a trail from the San Joaquin Valley to the coast where they would go for fish. The first white men to use it were the Franciscan friars and the Spanish explorers. In 1846, after their retreat from Gabilan Peak above San Juan, Fremont and his men crossed the pass on their way to Sutter's Fort and Sacramento. Three years later it was to become the route of the gold seekers on their way to Kern County. Then from 1858 to 1861 it was the route of the Butterfield Overland Stage. A. D. Firebaugh put a toll road over the pass in 1856, which Paula said went by the present location of her house to two miles west of the summit in Santa Clara County, and a mile from where another Pacheco adobe was built. Firebaugh sold it to Bell of Bell's Station.

Although Paula was raised in San Francisco, went east to a Miss Finch's finishing school, and was once described by Walter Winchell in his column as one of the great beauties, her heart was always at the San Luis Gonzaga. In 1949 she moved to the ranch permanently. Bing Crosby had leased 16,000 acres from the estate in 1947, but she and her mother had reserved a part of it. With her feeling for history she chose the piece of land on the other side of the pass in Merced County on the *llano* (flat) and remodeled her home, an old adobe built in 1843 by Juan Perez Pacheco, brother of her great-grandmother, Lola Pacheco Malarin. Subsequently, Don Francisco built a large two-story adobe nearby which was destroyed by an earthquake in 1868. There is a painting of this adobe in the Oakland Museum which Dr. Albert Shumate received permission to have copied for Paula.

Paula'a grandfather, Dr. Luis Fatjo, also built a large home on the ranch with walls two to three feet thick, and tremendous stables for his thoroughbred horses. The grant had been made by the Mexican government to Juan Perez Pacheco, son of Don

Left, Feliciana Gonzalez Pacheco, wife of Don Francisco Pacheco. Right, Ysadora Pacheco (known as Lola), who married Mariano Malarin, son of a prominent Monterey family. Barbieri portrait.

Portrait of Don Francisco Perez Pacheco, by Leonardo Barbieri, an Italian painter who came to California in 1847 and painted many prominent citizens, including members of the Constitutional Convention of 1849. He painted members of the Pacheco family in 1852.

A marble bust of Mariano Malarin.

Juan Perez Pacheco, painted by Leonardo Barbieri. He received the San Luis Gonzaga, but died young and the ranch was inherited by his father. It is still in the family.

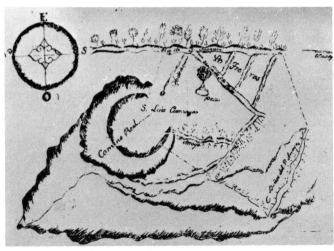

Above, a painting of the second Pacheco house on the flat where San Luis Dam is now located. Right, early Spanish map of Rancho San Luis Gonzaga.

The children of Mariana Roca and Paula Fatjo, at the San Luis Gonzaga Ranch. They were the grandchildren of Lola Pacheco Malarin.

Francisco, as a protective measure against the San Joaquin Valley Indians who were crossing the pass and raiding the ranches in the San Juan Valley. This accounted for the loop holes for guns in the thick walls of Paula's adobe. Juan Perez Pacheco was not to have the property for long, however, for he died the following year, and it reverted to his father.

The adobe was built on an ancient *aguaje* or water hole where herds of antelope came to drink and which was the locale of a prehistoric Indian village called Lis-nay-yuk. Tribes of Indians would stop here to rest before or after moving across the Pacheco Pass. Its name, San Luis Gonzaga, however, was given by a man known as the "greatest pathfinder and Indian fighter of his day," Gabriel Moraga, and his companion, Father Pedro Munoz, who camped here after crossing the pass from Mission San Juan Bautista. It was June 21, 1805, the feast day of the noted Spanish Jesuit, Luis de Gonzaga, patron saint of scholars, and following the custom of that time, Moraga named the site for him.

About 150 years later the United States Department of the Interior selected this property as the location of a new dam. This was disturbing news to Paula, but when it became evident that in spite of all her efforts there was no way that she could stop the government from appropriating 7,000 acres of this part of the ranch for the San Luis dam, Paula says she was determined to try to save the adobe from being covered with several hundred feet of water.

"I made arrangements to have it moved the ten miles up the Pacheco Pass by truck," she said. "As it inched up the grade, it was within a mile of its destination when the side walls collapsed." The two end walls were saved, and she had them set up on a foundation behind her house. Although she tried to

preserve the adobe bricks, she said they have disintegrated. Paula, however, has bricks from another Pacheco house which she hopes to have laid for the side walls.

Not only is San Luis Gonzaga an operating cattle ranch, but its mistress inherited a love for fine horses from her grandfather. She breeds Arabians and has about 30 of these fine animals on the ranch. "I fell in love with Arabs the first time I saw them when I was a girl and my mother took me to visit the Gabilan ranch up near Fremont Peak," she said. "Jessie Carr Bryan was one of the original breeders in the area." Paula has shown her Arabs in the big shows and ridden them in the Santa Barbara Fiesta, and they have given creditable performances in the big endurance contest, the Tevis Cup 100 Mile Ride that takes place from the Lake Tahoe area to Auburn every July.

Paula Fatjo, fifth generation Pacheco, on family land grant, San Luis Gonzaga, with one of her prize Arabian horses.

109

Above: Corrals and oak-dotted hills on the San Luis Gonzaga on Pacheco Pass, near the home of Paula Fatjo, great-great-granddaughter of Francisco Pacheco, grantee of the ranch. Left: Adobe built by Juan Pacheco in the early 1840s on the San Joaquin side of Pacheco Pass near an ancient water hole. Note the loop holes in the walls for guns—a protective measure against marauding Indians.

In addition to her horses and polled Hereford cattle, she has an assortment of pets ranging from Sophie, the Great Pyrenees dog, and white peacocks, to a little guinea hen named "Solo," who followed Paula wherever she went.

The house, with its vista of rolling hills and oak trees, old cabins, barns and fences, has the early California feeling of her old adobe. The Indian-style fireplace with a niche for the "Tree of Life" from Mexico, large blacksmith bellows, old bottles of hand-blown glass, some antique furniture, and the front door made from an old water tank on the ranch — all contribute to this feeling. The house is located near the site of another adobe on the old Pacheco Pass. Parts of the pass can be seen in front of Paula's place.

In the family album and scrapbook there are pictures of Paula's father, Clemente, of his brother and sister, and his cousins and their father, Dr. Ramon Roca.

Included in her memorabilia were the famous Bull's Head checks, "as good as gold," signed by Henry Miller, who used to run his cattle across the ranch from the San Joaquin Valley to San Francisco before the railroads. He had feeding corrals along the way, and for many years he leased the ranch.

Asked about this man Pacheco, her great-great-grandfather, whose name lives on, in her direct and to-the-point manner, Paula said:

The classic story is that his wife, my great-great-grandmother, was the descendant of an Aztec princess, not an American Indian as many thought. After losing a son and daughter they had only one daughter left. Her name was Ysadora, but she was always called Lola. After California went into the Union, Pacheco realized it meant deep trouble ahead for the Californians who were trying to hold onto the land, and he had concerns for Lola's future. In those days, you know, girls married at

15. Lola was already 30. He supposedly went up and down the state to find a husband for her.

About this time the Malarins, a prominent family in Monterey (she was an Estrada) were deeply in debt to Jacks, paying interest of 24 percent. The father, Juan Malarin, had died, and his son, Mariano, who had been educated as a lawyer in Peru, was trying to hold onto the land. Pacheco arranged a marriage between Lola and Mariano Malarin. It turned out to be a very good marriage, fortunately, and they were very much in love.

Paula said that after their wedding at the San Carlos Cathedral in Monterey in 1858, Lola and Mariano moved to the large adobe house Pacheco had built on the adjoining Rancho Ausaymas y San Felipe beside Pacheco Creek about eight miles from Hollister. They also had a home in Santa Clara which occupied a block at the corner of Washington and Santa Clara Streets. Their neighbors on the other corners were the Arguellos (descendants of two governors of California, one under Spain and the other under Mexico); the Antonio Fatjos (Refugio Fatjo was the sister of Mariano Malarin), and the Notre Dame sisters, on the fourth corner.

Two daughters were born to the couple, Paula at the San Felipe adobe, and Mariana in Monterey. The two girls were both married to doctors, Mariana to Dr. Ramon Roca and Paula to Dr. Luis Fatjo. It was a mere coincidence that Paula married a man with the same name as her father's brother-in-law, Antonio Fatjo, although there was a distant relationship. In time the two family ranches were divided between the daughters, the Fatjos (Paula's grandparents) receiving the part on the Pacheco Pass extending to the San Luis Dam. The remainder of the Ausaymas y San Felipe portion went to the Rocas. A portion of the Ausaymas y San Felipe and of the Bolsa de San Felipe had already been sold by Pacheco to James Dunne in 1857 before his daughter's marriage. Lola and Mariano meanwhile were spending more and more of their time at the Pacheco home in Monterey, built by Don Pacheco in 1840 at the corner of Abrego and Webster Streets. At that time Pacheco was already a well-to-do citizen and the house, with 25 rooms, was the largest in Monterey. It is now a private Men's Club, but has had its ups and downs. It was a rooming house for a while, a dance hall, a private hospital, and even a brothel whose clients are said to have paid their fees with silver spurs.

The Pacheco Pass

The story of Pacheco Pass is a panorama of drama in its two-century history from Indian trail to modern freeway. A story is told about Joaquin Murietta, the famous bandit who seems to have been everywhere, that a posse followed him up the Camino Real on the coast to the Pacheco Pass, where they learned he was hiding out at the San Luis Gonzaga Rancho, and that just before they arrived he cut his way out of the tent house at the rancho to escape.

On the aesthetic side is the experience of John Muir, California's great naturalist, who described the scenery on his visit to the ranch:

It's folly to try to translate into words the splendor of nature. The scenery and all of nature in the Pass is fairly enchanting. Strange and beautiful mountain ferns are there, low in dark canyons and high upon rocky sunlit peaks; banks of blooming shrubs, and sprinklings and gatherings of garment flowers, precious and pure as ever enjoyed the sweets of a mountain home.

Stamp used by the Bicycle Mail Route from Fresno to San Francisco, a unique version of the Pony Express in 1894 during the railroad strike. Note the change in the spelling of San Francisco—the "c" was printed first as an "s."

111

As Muir descended, he wrote of the Valley, "The floweriest piece of world I ever walked, one vast, level, even flower bed, a sheet of flowers, a smooth sea."

"Grizzly Bear" Adams' experiences on the San Luis Ranch in the early 1850s were described by Hittell in his *History of California*. Captain George Derby, the famous "John Phoenix," crossed the Pass in 1849, accompanied by Halleck and Canby. The latter was later murdered by the Modoc Indians. Derby wrote that the Pass was "...found to be of easy practicability for mules, but exceedingly difficult for wagons."

Andrew S. Hallidie, later to become famous as inventor of the San Francisco cable cars, wrote of his trip from San Francisco to the Kern River Mines in 1853, "For the entire distance with the exception of the Pueblo of San Jose there were neither towns, villages or settlements and but one ranch where there was any activity, the St. Luis Ranch on the southeast side of the coast range after passing over the Pacheco Pass."

On the first westbound stage of the Butterfield Mail from St. Louis to San Francisco in 1858, a 2,800-mile ride, W. L. Ormsby of the *New York Herald* told of arriving at the San Luis Rancho, entrance to the Pacheco Pass, two weeks after fording the Rio Grande River. Ormsby wrote:

It is the only house within thirty miles...the owner's hospitable table is always open to all who pass that way. It is a great rendezvous for drovers going down into the valleys after cattle seen dotting the plains for miles around. The owner keeps 1,400 head of fine cattle himself.

The trip, which required 23 days, was suspended in 1861 at the outbreak of the Civil War.

Plans were proposed but never carried out for a railroad line from the coast counties through the Pacheco Pass into the San Joaquin Valley and on to the Colorado River near Fort Mojave. Stanford's Central Pacific Railroad to Oakland precluded that.

Most unusual use of the Pass, however, was probably the bicycle version of the Pony Express. In the summer of 1894, trainmen in Fresno, protesting the new Pullman cars, went out on strike. This meant retrogressing back to the horse for delivery of the mail—a week's trip over rutted dirt roads to cover the 200 miles.

The problem was solved by John Nourse, grocer in Fresno, as told by Thomas J. Acheson. Bicycles were coming into popularity. Why not set up a bicycle relay. Arthur Banta, who had a "going" business in "The Victory Cyclery" agreed en-thusiastically to take on the assignment. The routes were studied for relay stops and riders selected with care. Advertisements were placed in newspapers. Circulars declared:

Bicycle messenger route to San Francisco. The undersigned [Banta] begs to announce to the public that he will establish a Messenger Route to San Francisco on bicycles via White's Bridge, Pacheco Pass, Gilroy and San Jose. A daily service will be established beginning Saturday morning, July 7, 1894. The rate of letters to San Francisco and all intermediate points will be twenty-five cents...

As preposterous as the idea may have seemed to many, three days after start of the operation, the service was running smoothly on an 18-hour schedule, the riders passing Rancho San Luis before going over the Pass. Supplementing the mail service, the riders started carrying merchandise, such as compressed yeast to a bakery, quinine to a druggist, a set of false teeth to a dentist, and a shipment of nitrate of silver to a photographer.

A special stamp was designed by J. C. Duelle, a retired United States engraver living near Fresno. 800 were run off before it was discovered that the city was spelled "San Fransisco." A thousand corrected stamps were issued before the end of the railroad strike and the end of the bicycle service.

The man for whom this Pass was named, as well as the creek and canyon and Pacheco Peak, which can be seen from Mission San Juan Bautista, died in Monterey in 1860. The life of Don Francisco Perez Pacheco in California is a success story. Contrary to the image of the Californian as an easy-going, fun-loving fiesta goer, Pacheco was an industrious, hard-working man. He was not the ranchero Gertrude Atherton wrote about in *The Splendid Forties*. He rose from a sub-lieutenant in the Mexican Army to Captain of Defensores in 1844, and tithe collector in 1848, to become the richest man in Monterey County. In those days a man's wealth was recorded.

In his will Pacheco left "...the larger amount to my daughter, Ysadora (Lola)...with kind care and attention." He was apparently disillusioned with her in-laws' free-spending ways, for he left a sum to each with the provision that they could not sue for more. In this document he refers, rather sadly it seems, to his "ceaseless toil" and to being "weary of life."

Don Francisco Perez was buried in front of the main altar of San Carlos Cathedral in Monterey next to his wife, who preceded him in death by three years, and another daughter. The marble vault is marked "Pacheco Family - 1858."

CHAPTER XXI

The French Ranch

It was a long trail a-winding — six miles of steady grade through the wooded hills below the Mt. Diablo Range — to reach the French Ranch, but it was worth every turn and curve. At the ranch headquarters we found hospitable Jim Indart, grandson of Juan Indart, a French Basque rancher who came to California during the Gold Rush, and of Theodore H. French, who homesteaded the property in the 1870s. Jim lives with his wife, Hazel, in a modern ranch house. Set in a basin as a protection from the breezes, it is joined by a complex of old ranch buildings and surrounded by oak, laurel and buckeye. Hazel Indart said that when it snows in the winter they can't see anything but snow because of the position of their house.

Starting with 160 acres, T. H. French and his heirs have increased the size of the ranch a hundred-fold, Jim said. French, a native of Williamsburg, Missouri, ran away from home at the age of 15 and joined the Missouri regiment. He was injured several times and had his horse shot from under him on one occasion. After the war, instead of returning home, he set out for California. During his eventful five-month journey across the plains, he encountered Indians numerous times and once had hand-to-hand combat.

After arriving in California, he worked in several places, starting in San Leandro, while looking for a place to settle permanently. His search ended in 1871 when he found this property 16 miles from Hollister, extending up into the Diablo Range. In 1879 he married a girl from London, England, Jemima Gardner, who was always called Jimmy. They had seven children, including Lucy, who married Jean Pierre Indart, son of Juan Indart. Jack, as he was always called, died when his son Jim was a small boy.

Near Hazel and Jim's house is a little white building which they said was part of T. H. French's original home. It is now a bunkhouse with Frank Barielles its occupant until last year. Past 80 years of age, Barielles worked actively as a cowboy, roping and branding along with the Indarts' cousin, 19-year-old Mitt French, who comes up on weekends and summer vacations from Gavilan College. Another member of the ranch staff is Tommy, the Australian shepherd, who not only functions as a cowboy, according to his mistress, but flushes out birds for shooting. His only problem is that he has lost most of his teeth from killing wild pigs.

There are several handsome old barns on the ranch, one a testimonial to the art of the woodpecker in free form design. Jim Indart said the acorns would soon fall and that the woodpeckers would be filling the holes with acorns for the winter. "My cousins and I always used to wonder when we were kids," Indart said, "whether the woodpecker made the hole first and found the acorn to fit, or if they made the holes to fit the acorns." Across the canyon is one of the prettiest and the oldest barns of all on a hilltop.

Theodore H. French, who homesteaded property in the San Diablo Range in the 1870s. The ranch started with 160 acres and now covers 16,000 acres.

113

Lucy French Indart was born on the French ranch, one of seven children. An expert horsewoman, Lucy won her spurs in the fiesta of 1908 in San Juan, as the most expert woman rider and lariat thrower. Her husband, Jack Indart, died young, leaving her with one son, Jim Indart, who runs the French ranch. Note the little dog on her saddle.

The Indarts' low California style house is very western in feeling, as they themselves are. The design of the French brand, a "+", is set in the brick fireplace wall. Jim said that this is the oldest brand in continuous use, since 1876, in the state of California. The irons in the fireplace have the original brand of Grandfather Indart. Both Jim and Hazel have been winning trophies at horse shows since they were very young, and they have a trophy room to prove it. There are many trophies from team roping at Bolado Park, the Grand National, and other shows. Among Jim's collection of guns is his grandfather's Remington 44, from the Civil War.

A gallery of pictures tells the story of both sides of the family. Violet Gooch (Mrs. Dave), who was over from Capitola visiting, said she and her sister, Gladys Harris (Mrs. Tom), of Carmel, are the only two of the seven French children living. They share ownership of the ranch with the Indarts, as do Gladys Harris's daughters, Molly McMahon (Mrs. Joe) of Menlo Park, and Joan Irvin (Mrs. Martin) of Carmel, and Mitt's father, Hugh French. Violet pointed out a picture of her sister, Lucy French Indart (Jim's mother), wearing leather chaps and seated on a horse. She said Lucy often rode horseback over to Capitola to visit her. She would stop overnight at Hollister enroute and make it the rest of the way in one day. Lucy won her spurs for being the most expert rider and lariat thrower in the San Juan Fiesta of 1908.

Inheriting his mother's love for horses and a propensity for ranching from both sides of the family, Jim said all he ever wanted to be was a rancher. When his grandfather French died in 1933 he took over. In 1935 he married his childhood sweetheart, Hazel Caldera. Their ranch was something to see as we drove over it in a four-wheel drive pickup. "We have a preserve of 1,000 acres around the ranch house," Hazel said, as we passed a buck along the way, "so the deer won't be touched." They had gone out hunting in the jeep the night before and had seen a coyote heading for the house and shot him. Later they saw six bucks. From Chapparal Peak the view was spectacular. Looking over to Mariposa Peak, which can be seen from Hollister, Jim said it is a watershed, that the rain runs down to Pacheco Creek. Three counties, San Benito, Santa Clara, and Merced, come together on the ranch and fall together like pieces of pie.

On the property there are 20 reservoirs — all springs and running troughs — no wells or windmills. Geographically, the ranch parallels Pacheco Pass and is bordered on the north by Rancho San Luis Gonzaga, operated by Paula Fatjo, one of Francisco Pacheco's descendants, and on the south by the Quien Sabe Ranch of the Somavia family. The Indarts used to go to Hollister by horseback, but times have changed and now they take the jeep. Their closest neighbors, they said, are the Earl Sparlings at Las Viboras, six miles to the west where they ship their cattle.

On a serious note Jim Indart said, "My grandfather spent his lifetime putting this ranch together. We have spent most of our lifetime holding it together." Looking toward his cousin, Mitt, he added, "Our hope is that the next generation will be able to carry on."

Mitt French and Hazel and Jim Indart fence-sitting on the French ranch.

CHAPTER XXII

QS *Rancho Santa Ana y Quien Sabe*

One of the largest and most modernly equipped ranches in the state, as well as bountifully endowed with natural beauty, is the Rancho Quien Sabe of Juanita and Ramon Somavia. Located in the Diablo Range high above Santa Ana Valley, the Quien Sabe covers 42,000 acres of rolling hills, accented by the dark green California live oak, and with picturesque landmarks such as Castle Rock and School House Ridge standing out against the skyline.

The Quien Sabe was originally part of a Mexican Grant, Rancho Santa Ana y Quien Sabe, consisting of eleven square leagues (the maximum amount permitted for a grant), to Juan Miguel Anzar and Manuel Larios in 1839. The land had first been granted to Francisco J. C. Negrete, an Hijar colonist who applied for it in 1834. He had served in the *ayuntamiento* in Monterey. After receiving the

Map of Santa Ana y Quien Sabe Rancho showing location of the house of Don Manuel Larios on Santa Ana (lower portion), and the house and corral of Don Juan Miguel Anzar in the Quien Sabe hills. Roads led from the Larios house to San Juan Bautista and to the Angel Castro house. (Courtesy of Huntington Library)

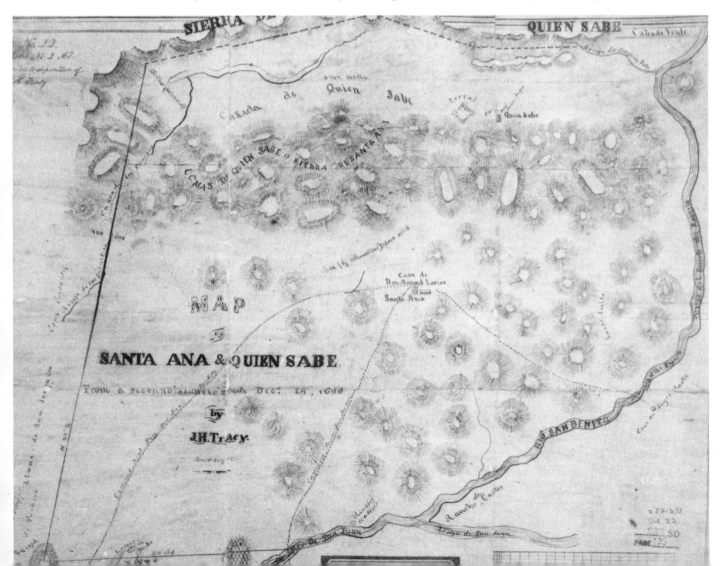

Road leading to headquarters of Quien Sabe Ranch. Schoolhouse Ridge is a landmark.

Below left: Corral on Quien Sabe Ranch.

grant in 1836, Negrete went to Mexico as secretary to Governor Chico and never came back, thus losing his claim. Anzar and Larios held the ranch in partnership until 1848, when they decided to divide it.

Don Juan Anzar came from Mexico in 1833 with his brother, Padre Jose Antonio Anzar, the last of the Franciscan priests at Mission San Juan Bautista. Both were regarded as men of means when they arrived. Larios had been employed by Anzar to manage his properties from the day he completed his army service. Don Juan had 800 head of cattle on the upper reaches of the ranch, and, according to a map of 1856, a *casa* where some of his help lived, and corrals. He was, however, an absentee owner and paid Don Manuel Larios to oversee his part of the rancho. When they decided to divide the property in 1848, Larios took the lower portion in the Santa Ana Valley, and Anzar the upper portion.

Standing out against the horizon above Little Quien Sabe Valley is the Somavias' spacious home, with its tiled bell tower, reminiscent of a castle in Spain. This somehow seems fitting because Juanita Somavia's family, the De Laveagas, who bought the property in the early 1870s, came from Spain.

The house is built at an elevation of 1,800 feet on a site previously chosen by Juanita's father, Jose Vicente De Laveaga, for a home for himself. His estate in San Mateo was considered one of the showplaces of the San Francisco Peninsula. Also of estate proportions was his place in Cupertino, Deep Cliff, built on a promontory overlooking what is now Deep Cliff golf course. The land has been subdivided and the only building still standing is the old barn which is said to have cost $20,000 and where his first wife, Florence Callaghan De Laveaga, kept her thoroughbred horses. One of the neighbors at that time, Ralph Rambo of San Jose, remembered that as a boy he was fascinated with the De Laveagas' fleet of seven Pierce Arrow cars lined up in the drive, one for each day of the week. Another long-time Cupertino resident and town historian, Ernest Stocklmeir, recalled with interest De Laveaga's collection of rare waterfowl. Although they were valued at $100,000 at the time of his death, Mrs. Somavia had a difficult time giving them away.

The story of the Quien Sabe in the De Laveaga family dates back to the early 1870s when Juanita Somavia's great-grandfather, Jose Vicente De Laveaga, who came from Spain by way of Mexico

116

and married Dolores Aguirre of San Jose, purchased the Quien Sabe and Las Aguilas ranches from Frederick MacDougall for $180,000. MacDougall had married the widow of Don Juan Anzar, Maria Antonia Castro de Anzar, who lived only a year after the marriage. Thus he inherited the vast properties of Anzar, together with Anzar's three sons, Guadalupe, Anatolio, and Juan. Anatolio and Juan died in their early twenties. Apparently MacDougall made some sort of arrangement with Lupe Anzar, because the records of the sale in 1875 in Hollister name the co-owners as Frederick and Francesca MacDougall, A. Calderon, Mercedes Calderon, Pedro Baca, and Joseph Estrem. MacDougall, by the way, had in the meantime served as Mayor of Los Angeles from 1872 to 1874.

After the death of Jose Vicente De Laveaga and Dona Dolores, their son, Miguel (Juanita Somavia's grandfather), bought out the interests in the Quien Sabe of his three sisters: Maria Concepcion, Maria Ignacia, and Josefa, who married Juan Cebrian. The family was later to become involved in a lawsuit over the will and property management of the estate of Maria Concepcion De Laveaga, after her death in 1909. The suit was brought by Miguel against Juan and Josefa Cebrian, who had taken charge of her sister's affairs. Miguel eventually lost the bitterly fought suit, which was the longest trial in the history of the state at that time.

Upon the death of Miguel De Laveaga, the Quien Sabe was inherited by his three children: Jose Vicente, Juanita Somavia's father; Edward, who successfully subdivided his Orinda ranch; and Julie, who married Andrew Welch and became a society leader. Jose Vicente then bought out his brother's and sisters' interests. His only daughter, Juanita, was married on April 27, 1930, to Jose Ramon Somavia in an elaborate ceremony in St. Matthew's Catholic Church, San Mateo. Thomas Work of Monterey was best man, and Robert Fatjo, Jr. of Santa Clara, cousin of the groom, was an usher. Ramon Somavia's family dates back to Jose Arguello, Spanish Governor of California. His grandmother was a Malarin.

The House on the Hill

The house Juanita and Ramon built for themselves in 1931, after the death of her father, and where they raised their five children—Jose Ramon II, Jose Vicente, Florence Russo, Valerie Ebright, and Ramona Hageman—has 35 rooms, including six bedrooms. There are 20-foot-high ceilings in the living areas. In the basement are recreation rooms, a chapel, space to seat 100 for a banquet, a gun room stocked with equipment to reload shotgun shells and repair gun equipment, and an indoor swimming pool. There is a cook house, a bunk house, a machine shop equipped to handle repairs from small to large, a butcher shop, and freezers.

Over in the Big Quien Sabe Valley, Jerry Whitaker, ranch manager, took pride in showing the feed lot. He said it is a complete feeding operation. The feed lot with its concrete floor is the largest covered feed lot in California. Explaining the operation, Whitaker said the normal procedure is to raise the cattle on grass until they weigh 600 to 700 pounds. They are then brought in to be conditioned. There is a mill that converts hay, barley, molasses, vitamins and minerals into pellets, and a granary that takes a million dollars to fill with grain for feed. He said that when built 13 years ago the feed lots and mill cost $2,500,000. The ranch used to have its own dairy, he said, for milk and butter.

Geographically, according to Whitaker, the ranch is well located near Highway 5 for shipping, but he added that the Bay Area can consume the product of the ranch. He also said that a map was found showing that back in 1879 there were plans to build a town with homesites on the hilltops, but, of course, the railroad didn't go through to the San Joaquin. The Quien Sabe has become increasingly private; requests from motion picture companies to come in to photograph western films have been refused.

How the Santa Ana y Quien Sabe got its name has long been a subject of interest. Literally translated it means "Saint Ann and Who Knows." Ramona Somavia Hageman of Carmel, daughter of Juanita and Ramon, said that the story she heard was that when wild horses and cattle roamed freely the Californians herded them into the valleys where they could not be seen. When the Americans would ask the Indians where the horses were, the natives, who had been Christianized and taught not to tell a lie, would reply with a shrug and that marvelous Spanish all-purpose phrase, "Quien sabe?" (who knows?). This incident may well be true, but the name goes back much further. There was a canyon and a mountain recorded by Sebastian Rodriguez in 1828 called Quien Sabe. Whether the name referred to a particular incident or was a jest will probably never be known.

Regardless of its name, there is beauty everywhere on the Quien Sabe. There are springs all over the ranch. One doesn't have to walk a mile

Spacious home of Ramon and Juanita Somavia above Little Quien Sabe Valley.

to get a drink of water, according to Whitaker, and it has a large reservoir stocked with fish. "One of the secrets of a good ranch is water and from the factor of water going down to the streams, it's one of the finest ranches in the United States," said Whitaker. "The ranch also has more fencing and cross-fencing than any other ranch. The entire 42,000 acres are surrounded by fences. Besides that, it has its own landing strip."

The Quien Sabe is a bit awesome.

Rancho Santa Ana

When Don Manuel Larios received the grant for Rancho Santa Ana y Quien Sabe with his friend, Don Juan Anzar, from Governor Juan Bautista Alvarado, he built a large adobe house with a chapel and fortress along the Santa Ana River just above what is now called Santa Anita Road. A large old barn now marks the site. Dominating the skyline was Santa Ana Peak on the Quien Sabe. The fortress was to serve its purpose well. One of the reasons for the grant was to prevent the Indians from crossing over to San Juan Bautista. The rancho was a self-contained community with weaving shops, shoemakers, saddlers, silversmiths, and blacksmiths.

An old map of the rancho dated 1856 shows the camino for San Juan leading from the adobe in one direction and in another a road leading to the "casa of Angel Castro" on the Rancho Cienega de los Paicines (now the ranch of Mrs. Robert Law), with the San Benito River running through. Bordering the Santa Ana y Quien Sabe on one side was the Arroyo de Los Picachos, and the name of Cruz Cervantes appears with a reference to the Llano de San Joaquin (the Rancho San Joaquin o Rosa Morada). Next to it the map shows the "San Felipe de Pacheco" (Bolsa de San Felipe) and to the east

El Rancho de Las Aguilas (Real de Aguilas).

Don Manuel was well-prepared to handle the Indians, having been an Indian fighter and a bear hunter like his father. He was married three times: first to Maria Antonia Pacheco; then to Guadalupe Castro, daughter of Angel Castro, his neighbor; and finally to Dona Rosario de Armas at the Mission San Juan, with Patrick and Margaret Breen as witnesses.

With his marriage to Dona Rosario he acquired a family of seven children in addition to his own nine. One more child, Estolano, was born to Dona Rosario when her husband was 56 years of age. Much of what is known of the popular Don was passed on by Estolano, who lived until 1941. Besides the combined children of Don Manuel and Dona Rosario, there were husbands and wives and grandchildren so that sometimes there would be 50 people living at the rancho at one time.

The biggest celebration of the year was always on July 26, the feast day of St. Ann, patron saint of the rancho. Mass was celebrated first, followed by a great fiesta, California style, that would usually go on for three days. Horse racing was foremost. As every early visitor to California has written, the Californians were the finest horsemen in the world. Horses in California had multiplied at such a rate, they were easily available. From a gallop these men could literally stop their horses on a dime. The bear and bull fights were another form of entertainment—and there were certainly plenty of bears in the Quien Sabe hills. Climaxing the day would be the barbecue. A whole steer would be cooked in the ground and then hung up, so they could help themselves. After this came the singing and dancing. Again, as at all the California fiestas, there would be someone who could play the violin and others the guitar.

Although Estolano was not born until after the

118

Rancho Santa Ana of Don Manuel Larios.

Hauling grain on Quien Sabe Ranch.

family moved to the San Antonio, he was young enough at the time the letters to Bancroft were written to remember in detail the stories he had heard of the bear and Indian fights. The Larios and Higuera families were fun-loving and easy-going people, but there always lurked the threat of an Indian attack. One night Rosario had gotten her youngest to sleep in a hammock on the veranda. Larios, who always retired early, was in his bed upstairs, and the other women were making bread for a holy day at Mission San Juan Bautista in the ovens outside, when they heard the sounds of coyotes barking. At first they were not concerned, but when arrows of the Yokut Indians started raining in, they rushed into the house.

The commotion awakened Don Manuel, who immediately ordered the young Larios and Higuera men to man the turrets on the four sides of the house upstairs, just as the Indians were letting the horses out of the adobe corral nearby. Suddenly Dona Rosario realized that the baby was outside. The other women prevented her from going out in the heat of the attack—then Angelita Higuera ran out and rescued her baby brother.

Going to mass in San Juan Bautista was always an important event of the week. The women and children would ride in the ox-drawn carreta with an Indian driver walking alongside to prod the animals. Sheep and goat skins put on the bottom of the carreta were soft and eased the bumps over the rough camino to San Juan. When they completed the trip they would find the mission plaza filled with carretas and saddle horses from the surrounding ranchos, horses hitched to every available tree. Here they would be joined by Don Manuel and the rest of the family, who came by horseback.

After mass they usually visited Dona Alta Gracia Ursua, sister of Padre Anzar and Don Juan Anzar, at her house across the plaza which had been the monjerio and later was converted into the Zanetta house. Frequently there would be bear and bull fights in the plaza in the afternoons, which they would watch from the balcony of Dona Alta Gracia's adobe.

The family always spent the summers at Don Manuel's Rancho San Antonio in San Juan, where he had a large adobe home. In 1853 he decided to move his family permanently to "El Ranchito," as he called his smaller ranch. He had been *juez* in San Juan in 1840, and had many friends in the town, and his sister, Dona Pilar, a well-known midwife, also lived there with her large family.

Soon after leaving the Santa Ana he started selling off parcels of the ranch. One entry in the title search indicates:

Manuel Larios to Horace Hawes — Deed 21 August 1857 in consideration of professional service rendered by Horace Hawes counselor at law in support of the claim of said Larios for the Rancho of Santa Ana y Quien Sabe...1/10 of said rancho pertaining to said Larios is known by the name of Santa Ana.

This apparently was for services in partition of the ranch by Anzar and Larios, and was the equivalent of 2,300 acres. On page 41 of the deed there is a notation of Hawes receiving $55,888.60 worth of Santa Ana y Quien Sabe, apparently for legal services.

A San Franciscan named Frank Lynch leased the adobe and the name "Lynch" appears in the transaction of the sale of several parcels.

In 1881 the ravages of weather and time had taken their toll, and the old Larios adobe was destroyed.

Left, Joaquin Bolado, who acquired a large share of Santa Ana Rancho from Don Manuel Larios and his heirs. Bolado called his ranch the Santa Anita. A native of Spain, he came to Monterey by way of Mexico in 1849 and married Julia Abrego, daughter of a well-known Monterey merchant.

Right, Julia Bolado Ashe Davis, the daughter of Joaquin Bolado. She was always called Dulce and, by her family, "Mama Dulce." She donated land for Bolado Park in memory of her father.

Joaquin Bolado house on Rancho Santa Anita, built by a fine carpenter Bolado imported from Mexico.

Casa Grande, built by Julia Bolado Ashe Davis.

Below, Rancho Santa Anita, now owned by Jack Schwabacher.

5 CHAPTER XXIII
Rancho Santa Anita

After the death of Don Manuel Larios in 1865 the largest portion of Rancho Santa Ana was acquired by a Spaniard named Joaquin Bolado, who had come to California in 1849. He named his rancho "Santa Anita, " which means "Little Santa Ana." This was a relative term, however, because the Santa Anita extended all the way from Tres Pinos across the Santa Ana Valley up to the crest of the Quien Sabe Hills.

The Santa Anita ranch remained in the Bolado family and was operated by his heirs until about ten years ago when his grandson Farragut Ashe died. Only Bolado's great-grandson, David Farragut Ashe, still lives on the ranch. He has about 40 acres and a beautiful homesite, with a view overlooking the valley. Dave Ashe's father, Farragut, and his brother, Gaston, were sons of Julia Bolado Ashe Davis.

Jack Schwabacher is the present owner of the Santa Anita. He first leased it for five years, then bought it with a combine. About two years ago he bought out the other owners. They included such theatrical names as Art and Jack Linkletter, Pat Boone, and Jack Wrather, husband of Bonita Granville. Schwabacher, who raises stocker and feeder cattle, said he is developing new waters and replacing fencing. In love with this land with its green hills in the spring and golden grasses in the summer, Schwabacher added that he has an architect working on plans to remodel the "Casa Grande," the house built by the daughter of Joaquin Bolado, Julia Bolado Ashe Davis, in 1919, and that he plans to move his family over from Carmel Valley. Convenient to the house, on a plateau and hidden from the road, is a landing strip where he can fly in from his other properties.

The story of how Joaquin Bolado bought two of the parcels of the Santa Anita is rather an unusual one — even for those days. It seems that Dr. Frederick A. MacDougall became guardian of Don Manuel Larios' two minor children, Patrocinio and Estolano. Inasmuch as the children were without resources, MacDougall petitioned the court for permission to sell their interest in the Santa Ana for their support and education. Following due process of law, he posted in three public places in Monterey County the announcement of the auction of this land. One of the notices was at the Plaza Hotel in the town of San Juan, one at Kemp's Bola de Oro Saloon, and the third at a location which was not defined in the legal search.

The public auction was held August 9, 1867, at 12 o'clock in front of the Plaza Hotel. One of the favorite stories that Mark Regan, the stagecoach driver, used to tell his passengers, as he drove them in his Concord coach to or from San Juan Bautista and Gilroy, was of driving Joaquin Bolado from Tres Pinos to San Juan, carrying six sacks of gold. The story evidently grew with the telling, because the records show that Bolado actually had only two sacks of gold coin worth $3,350 each, for the Larios boys, and was the highest bidder.

Originally Bolado had a partner, another Spaniard named Jose Arques, who owned one-third interest which was later bought by Bolado.

The original house, which Joaquin Bolado built in the 1860s near Santa Anita Road, at the entrance to the ranch headquarters, is still standing. Unpretentious in appearance, it has always been called the "little house." Patsy Ashe Newman of Hillsborough, a great-granddaughter of Bolado, said, however, that it was quite a house in its day—that Bolado brought a carpenter up from Mexico to do the construction. His name was Delgado and he was considered quite a craftsman. She said that the house had lovely paneling, a ballroom, and many sitting rooms as well as bedrooms. When guests came to a party in those days it was from long distances by horse and buggy. The nearest ranch was miles away, so guests always stayed the night.

Joaquin Bolado and his wife, Julia, lived in San

Francisco. They did move to the ranch during a drought period of the sixties, when he suffered severe losses on the San Luis Obispo Ranch as well as the Santa Anita. One year he lost 14,000 head of cattle at San Luis and 3,000 on the Santa Anita, besides a thousand horses. Bolado's only daughter, Julia, who was always called "Dulce," meaning sweet, and in later years "Mama Dulce," used to have many houseguests when she and Gaston Mears Ashe were married and stayed in this house. Prince Poniatowsky, who founded Tanforan Racetrack with Ashe, was a frequent visitor, and the room where he stayed was always called the "Prince's Room." There were many parties at the Santa Anita during this era.

Gaston Ashe had an interesting background. His father, Dr. Richard P. Ashe, came to California from Asheville, North Carolina (the town was named for a forebear in the 18th century) in 1856 to be naval officer of the Port of San Francisco. It was a sort of governorship, and the first such official appointment after the United States had taken over California. His wife's sister, Caroline Loyall, married Admiral David Farragut, who became famous during the Civil War for his phrase, "Damn the torpedoes, full speed ahead!" Dr. Richard Ashe was also captain of the Vigilante Committee's Company A. Gaston's brother, Porter Ashe, married one of the Crockers and his sister, Elizabeth Ashe, was one of the founders of the Settlement House and an ambulance driver in World War I.

Unfortunately, Gaston Ashe spent his wife's money freely but not wisely. She knew nothing about finances and had no one to advise her. Finally, she realized that all she had left was the ranch. Dulce had had enough. She secured a divorce in 1908. Years later, in 1922, she married Francis H. Davis, a socially prominent San Franciscan who designed and built the Portland Cement plant at Davenport. They lived in Santa Cruz, and after he retired, in San Francisco and at the ranch. Meanwhile Mama Dulce had built the Casa Grande (big house) at the ranch on the top of a hill above the ranch property. It has a Spanish-Moorish style of architecture, and is built of stucco with tile roof, archways, balconies on the back side to take advantage of the view of the Santa Ana Valley, and large rooms with high ceilings. It was here that Farragut and Kathleen Ashe came for their honeymoon, and where Mama Dulce's granddaughter, Patsy, and her husband, Pete Newman, were married in the garden in 1949, with busses bringing down guests from San Francisco.

The house, decorated by Gump's, had a country feeling with English chintzes in bright colors, Chinese cloisonne lamps and art objects she had collected from all over the world. She had a Steinway piano, but the conversation piece was the little spinet which had been in the Casa Abrego adobe of Mama Dulce's grandfather, Don Jose Abrego, in Monterey. A successful merchant, he had it brought to Monterey by a sea captain named Stephen Smith. It is said to have enlivened many a party at the Abrego adobe, particularly during the first state convention in 1849, when the residents opened their homes and entertained the delegates. One of the unusual features of this house were the timbers used in the ballroom which had come from the shipwrecked smugglers' ship, the *Natalie,* on which Napoleon was said to have escaped from Elba. As the guests danced the quadrille and the polka to the music of this piano, the Abrego parties rivaled those of Jessie Fremont, wife of John C. Fremont, who was noted as a hostess. The Fremonts had taken part of the Castro adobe for the convention.

Presiding at these parties was Dona Josefa Estrada de Abrego, Mama Dulce's grandmother, who was a half sister of Juan Bautista Alvarado, governor of California during the Mexican period. It was this same governor, incidentally, who granted the Rancho Santa Ana y Quien Sabe to Larios and Anzar. Mama Dulce wrote down the story of the Bolados, the Abregos, and the Estradas for her grandchildren, some time before her death in the 1950s, as it had been told to her by her mother and grandmother. She said that her great-grandmother was Dona Maria Vallejo de Alvarado y Estrada. Her first husband, Jose Alvarado, died when she was 18, in 1811, and her son, Juan Bautista Alvarado, was raised by her father, Don Ygnacio Vallejo. The Vallejos, Mama Dulce said, had come to Santa Barbara with pathfinder Francisco Ortega in 1774. Dona Maria later married Don Jose Estrada. Her daughter, Julia Josefa Estrada, married Jose Abrego. Mama Dulce wrote:

My grandmother, Julia Josefa Estrada Abrego, gave birth to 18 children. Only nine lived, six of whom were boys. My mother Julia married Joaquin Bolado. She was only 14 when they met. Joaquin pretended he was courting Panchita Alvarado, and so it was a complete surprise when he told Don Jose Abrego of his intentions for the 14-year-old Julia. She was a tomboy and played with her brothers. Abrego said she was too young, that he would have to wait six months.

At the end of that time, the narration continued, Julia was dressed in a silk gown from the City of Paris, and, on this never-to-be-forgotten evening, danced. Don Jose, by the way, not only had the first piano in Monterey, but he had the first full-length mirror. When Julia came down the stairs and saw her reflection in this mirror, she said, "Who is that lovely girl?" She did, on occasion, revert back to putting on her old clothes and playing with her brothers. She and Bolado were married in 1857.

In 1862 Joaquin and Julia took a trip to Europe with friends by the name of Baron, who chartered a boat from San Francisco to Panama. After crossing the Isthmus, they took another boat to Europe, where they spent two years. During this time they visited relatives in Santander, Spain, Bolado's birthplace. After their return from Europe, their only child to live, Julia, was born in 1864. In her recorded memories she also told of the family home on Sutter Street in San Francisco. From her bedroom window she could see Union Square where she liked to play. Her parents were highly protective of her and never allowed her to ride a horse.

Mama Dulce's father, Joaquin Bolado, had quite a different background. He had come to California in 1849 by way of Zacatecas, Mexico, where he had an uncle. At that time many families in Spain sent their sons to Mexico and South America, to avoid their being drafted and sent to Africa, where there was a good chance that they might contract yellow fever. Bolado was working for a shipping firm during the Mexican War and had huge sums of bullion in his charge. On one occasion his escort was Captain Lewis, the commander of the Texas Rangers. After a trip to Monterey, where he learned of the discovery of gold, Bolado organized an expedition of about 50 Mexicans to return to California. On their arrival in Monterey they proceeded to what is now Watsonville, where they secured six carretas, and from there went to the Tuolumne River. They met with little success in their diggings, however, and most of them went on to Sonora.

Bolado went instead to San Jose, where he got into the general merchandising business. His friend, Jose Arques, was in the mercantile business in neighboring Santa Clara, but this business was not where the money was. Having been to the gold fields, Bolado knew the demand for meat and the prices paid for it. Consequently, he contracted to lease Pacheco's Rancho San Luis Gonzaga on the Pacheco Pass from Mariano Malarin, Pacheco's son-in-law, to run livestock in partnership with a pair of Spaniards named Ripa Pagaza and Castanos. This was a highly successful enterprise, with butchers coming to the ranch from such places as Sonora and Angels Camp. There was also a market for meat in other parts of California, including San Francisco, so that within six years their profits reached $200,000.

For a short time in 1860, Bolado took a ranch near Nicolaus between Sacramento and Marysville, before going to San Francisco and into trade with Mexico and Central America. He had banking interests in San Francisco and Hollister as well as being president of the Farmers Warehouse Company at Tres Pinos.

Bolado is credited with having done much for the little community of Tres Pinos after the railroad came. Grain, hay, dairy products, poultry, wool, and hides were shipped out from the terminal, and from there big teams hauled supplies to the New Idria Mines which were then flourishing.

These were troubled years, however. Many of the miners were disillusioned over the fortunes they had not found at the gold fields, and many of the Spaniards who had lost their land through legalities or, in some cases illegalities, were angry. As a result many defied the law. Tiburcio Vasquez, the noted bandit, was an example. He had friends in Tres Pinos and often passed through on his way to Arroyo Cantua or on his way across the hills to the San Joaquin Valley. During these trips he would stop at the Santa Anita and change horses with Bolado.

During her years at the Casa Grande on the Santa Anita, Julia Bolado Ashe Davis (Mama Dulce) was known for her philanthropies. Several times she brought young boys with a counselor from San Francisco, giving them an opportunity to get out of the city which they might never have had otherwise. They camped along the Tres Pinos Creek.

In the late 1920s, together with her two sons, Farragut and Gaston Ashe, she donated 28 acres of beautiful land along the San Benito River to the 23rd District Agricultural Association. It was developed with picnic and barbecue areas, a swimming pool, and a golf course, and is the site of the annual San Benito County Saddle Horse Show and Rodeo. The late Farragut Ashe and his wife, Kathleen, who now lives in Hollister, had a home on the ridge above this park. To perpetuate the name of the Spaniard who did and cared so much for Tres Pinos and his Santa Anita Rancho, it is called Bolado Park.

View of Tres Pinos. Etcheverry house is on the right. Note the large grain warehouses.

Main block in Tres Pinos when it was a thriving shipping town for hay, grain and cattle. Left to right, a meat market, ice cream parlor, harness maker's shop, and a two-story hall with a restaurant and bar. There were five saloons in town.

The Leonard Store on main street of Tres Pinos sold groceries and general merchandise. It is still standing.

Above, the Southern Pacific train arriving at Tres Pinos. With the coming of the railroad, the little town developed into a thriving community.

Right, harvester being pulled by early-day Caterpillar in Tres Pinos area. Arthur Fruits is on horseback.

CHAPTER XXIV

Tres Pinos

A mere shadow of its former self is the little town of Tres Pinos, five miles south of Hollister. Once a prosperous center of trade for hay, grain, and cattle, it had the distinctive flavor of the old west. Gone are the wooden sidewalks, most of the old store buildings with their false fronts, the hitching posts, and the wooden watering troughs for horses. Some of the enormous grain storehouses (there were once seven) are still standing, however, as is the old scale house. One of the warehouses was opened by Jeremiah (Jerry) Croxon in partnership with A. H. Fredson. Croxon had been head bookkeeper at the New Idria Mines, and later became sheriff of San Benito County.

The May Day parades, horse races down the center of the main street, and trick riding events are now but childhood memories of people like Lola Galli, Hazel Indart, and George Kincaid, who grew up in Tres Pinos. In those days, they said, the town consisted of one main block. There were six bars (one that was illegal); now there are only two. Kincaid remembers seeing the cowboys riding their horses right up to the bar. He said that there were always four or five fist fights over the weekend, and that whoever started one would be thrown into the watering trough to cool off.

George Kincaid remembers being taken to a bullfight in 1909 by Lonnie Fredson. The bullfight was held in the cattle corrals across the road from the Pinnacles Garage, which George started in 1928 and still operates. He said a special train brought people down from San Francisco for the bullfight. Kincaid's father, William Kincaid, the town blacksmith, was also constable, and later judge. William's wife, Marie, was the mother of 15 children and was also judge for many years. George said that at the same time she was judge he was constable, and that they really had law and order then. In 1958 Kincaid entered politics and still serves as county supervisor.

As one enters the little town from the north, on the right can be seen the little red firehouse, still in good repair, where the ladder truck of the Tres Pinos Bucket Brigade was based. Kincaid said that the vehicle had wagon wheels with rubber tires and a large tank containing a Boston-type chemical, and that there were buckets on the side. At the sound of the bell the townsmen would come running and four or six men in harness would pull it to the scene of the fire.

At the other end of town is the little white frame Church of the Immaculate Conception, an artist's dream of a country church, with tall slender lines and a bell tower topped with a cross. On the side walls are beautifully crafted stained-glass panels, arched at the top, and dedicated to the memory of

Tres Pinos firehouse which stands at the north end of town and is still in use.

Ben Sepulveda with an early-day gas buggy.

The Church of the Immaculate Conception built in 1894 on land donated by Juan Etcheverry.

early residents of Tres Pinos, including Juan Etcheverry and Juan Indart. Father Morgan, the present pastor, said that at one time the parish extended to the New Idria Mines and to King City, and that people came from all over to attend mass there. Built in 1894, the church was moved to its present site on land given by Jack Etcheverry. Part of the surrounding area is still owned by Etcheverry heirs. This was the church to which Elena Sayers said her grandfather Sebastian Garcia brought his kidnapped bride on horseback to be married.

This part of San Benito County was all ranching and farming, and was noted for the quality of its grain, when the Southern Pacific put the railroad through in 1873. They built a station and stole the name for it from a community called Tres Pinos, which was five miles farther south and which had also hoped to get the railroad. As it turned out, that settlement not only lost the railroad but settled on a new name, Paicines, for the ranch on which it was located. It was, nevertheless, a sore point and cause for considerable confusion over the names. Tres Pinos had originally been chosen in the first place, it was said, because of three pine trees that grew on a hillside nearby.

As the town grew around the railroad station the new Tres Pinos became a prosperous shipping center. Emerging as one of its leading citizens was the

French-Basque rancher, Juan Etcheverry, on whose land the town was built and whose ranch surrounded the town. He took over the Southern Pacific Hotel, which was called the "S P" or the Etcheverry Hotel. It was on the corner at the entrance to the town. Next door was the livery stable which Etcheverry built and operated. On the same side of the street, at the end, was the Etcheverry home, and adjoining that, the rolling hills where his cattle and sheep grazed.

When Juan died in 1897, his son, John Felix (Jack), at the age of 17, took over his father's complete operation, including the large ranch holdings. Three years later Juan's wife, Marie Amastoy Etcheverry, followed Juan in death. When Jack Etcheverry married Nellie Judge, they first lived in the hotel and then moved to Hollister. Their children, Margaret Etcheverry Reese (Mrs. David), now of Woodside, Mary Etcheverry Noble of Menlo Park, and the late John Felix Etcheverry, Jr., were raised in the house in Hollister.

Before the arrival of the railroad, wagons piled high with hay, pulled by double teams of horses, would depart from Tres Pinos for various parts of the country. When the railroad came Tres Pinos became a shipping point for central and southern San Benito County for cattle from the Quien Sabe, the Santa Anita, Cienega de Los Paicines, the Los Muertos (Las Aguilas), and others. The railroad was also the terminal for the stage line and express owned by A. G. Fruitts from the New Idria Mines. In 1944 the railroad discontinued its run to Tres Pinos and dismantled the station. Some years later, the hotel that had been the scene of so much activity was also taken down.

Juan Etcheverry, who owned the land on which Tres Pinos was built, as well as the land from Ridgemark Golf Course beyond the church. He operated the S P or Etcheverry hotel and the livery stables next door, and his home was at the end of the street.

The Etcheverry-Grunnagle House

A couple of years ago, when the late George Grunnagle and his wife, Mary, of Hollister, old family friends of the Etcheverrys, learned that the

The Etcheverry Hotel, built by the Southern Pacific when the railroad came in 1873. It was run by Juan Etcheverry and later by his son, Jack.

The Etcheverry home in Tres Pinos in the 1880s. Jack Etcheverry is at the left. He took over the hotel, ranch and livery stables after the death of his father, Juan, in 1897. Next is Mary Indart, who married a Navelet of San Jose; then Maria Etcheverry and an unidentified neighbor. The house was recently restored by Mary Grunnagle.

John Felix (Jack) Etcheverry, who at the age of 17 took over the operation of the ranch, hotel and stables, after the death of his father, Juan. Jack was a much-loved figure in Tres Pinos.

Above, the Grunnagle house, front view. When the Etcheverry house was about to be torn down, the Grunnagles had it turned around and moved across the street, and restored it with great charm. Below, the back view of the house. Margaret Etcheverry Reese, the daughter of Jack Etcheverry, and Mary Grunnagle are in the picture.

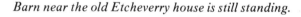

Barn near the old Etcheverry house is still standing.

100-year-old Etcheverry family home was to be torn down, they couldn't hear of it. Mary Grunnagle said, "We owned the lot across the street and decided we could move the Etcheverry house onto our property and restore it. We had already decided we wanted to retire in Tres Pinos."

Every little detail, such as moving the original picket fence and painting it white, was given attention, and the results are delightful. Margaret Etcheverry Reese, who was visiting her family's old home, said that of course they were pleased to have it saved. The Grunnagles added a little house on the back of the lot for entertaining, and Margaret's mother's piano, one of the few upright models built by Steinway, is there. Her mother didn't have room in the house for a grand piano, Margaret said.

The only basic changes the Grunnagles made in the house were the removal of a wall or two to make rooms larger, and the lowering of the ceilings from 15 feet to 12 feet in height. All the original doors and hardware were kept. Mary Grunnagle has furnished the house with her wonderful antiques—an organ and a mirror from Virginia City, an octagonal-shaped clock in the kitchen that Supreme Court Justice Maurice T. Dooling's family had in Nevada City, and antique carved chairs. An appropriate touch in the white tiled kitchen is the insertion of three tiles with a pine tree design—for Tres Pinos, of course.

Telling about Tres Pinos in its heyday, Margaret said the hotel was a bustling place. It was to Tres Pinos what the Plaza Hotel was to San Juan. Hay and grain buyers and stockmen would come and stay. The train would stop overnight before going back so the railroad men also were guests. The station was across from the hotel and the turntable was a short distance away. In the kitchen there were three Chinese cooks to handle the busy dining room. There was a pool room, a public room with a fireplace and poker tables, and a bar which was

probably called a saloon in those days. Margaret said she has the barber pole from the town barber shop.

Her father, who had his finger in many pies, was, at the age of 21, the youngest supervisor to be elected in San Benito County. He helped to organize the Bolado Park Horse Show and Rodeo, and for years was the announcer. The Etcheverry Ranch extended along Airline Highway from just beyond the Ridgemark golf course down past the church. George Medeiros was always foreman of the ranch for Etcheverry, and it seems fitting that his son, George Medeiros, Jr. is foreman for the present owner of the ranch, James Richardson.

4 *The Four Juans*

Once upon a time there were four young men, all named Juan, who left their homes in the Basque country of France to go to South America. They were not there very long before they heard fabulous

Jean Pierre Indart, twin brother of Domie Indart and father of Jim Indart, with an unidentified woman.

Right, Miss Domenica Indart, daughter of Juan Indart. After her father's death, Domie, as she was always known, took over the management of Rancho Indart. Well known for her skill as a horsewoman and her knowledge of the cattle business, she was much admired and loved. Left, Lucy French Indart and Domie on Rancho Indart.

Hauling grain to the New Idria Mines. The grain in the Tres Pinos area was of such excellent quality that it was hauled all over the country.

stories about the gold in California. They decided that was the place to go. After a short time in the gold fields, however, like so many others, they decided there was more money to be made in the meat business, so they started driving cattle from Southern California to Copperopolis near Sonora in the gold country. That was in the early 1850s.

Eventually two of the Juans, Juan Grande (Big John) Etcheverry and Juan Chico (Little John) Indart, came to Tres Pinos. Juan Primo (Cousin John) went back to the home country, and Juan Flaco (Slim John) decided to go over to the San Joaquin Valley. Etcheverry and Indart bought ranching land on the Santa Anita ranch from Joaquin Bolado, who had acquired a large part of the Santa Ana rancho from Manuel Larios and his estate.

Juan Chico and Juan Grande were good friends and very successful with their ranch. One day, however, they decided to divide the property. Juan Indart was being married in San Francisco to Miss Mary Errica, a native of France. The division of the land was solved very simply in a single day when they rode out and designated the boundaries by streams, valleys and ridges. Each one was happy with the arrangement, and there was never any trouble over it. The family friendship has carried through to their grandchildren.

Five children were born to Juan and Mary Indart at their Tres Pinos ranch. They were Peter John, Tillie, Domenica, Jean Pierre, and Mary. Tillie married John Garat and spent most of her married

Mules carrying fuel for the New Idria Mines.

life on the Indart-Garat Ranch, 100 miles out of Elko. Garat was the manager of this ranch, which is now owned by Pete Jackson of the Alisal Guest Ranch. Domenica and Jean Pierre were twins. Jean Pierre, who was known as Jack, married Lucy French. Mary married into the Navelet florist family of San Jose and spent her last years living with her sister Domie.

✶ *Miss Domie*

With the death of her twin brother at a young age, Domenica Indart, who was always called Domie, took over the management of the Rancho Indart. A cattleman's cattlewoman, she knew her business, and increased the herd and the size of the ranch by purchasing the adjoining property of Jose Arques. Not only was she respected for her knowledge of the cattle business, but she was greatly admired for her gentle qualities. She was described by old-timers as petite, quick, having a French accent, and very much alive. An expert horsewoman, but extremely modest, when her uncle gave her a beautiful saddle encrusted with silver, she took off the silver and gave it to members of the family and used the saddle plain. Lola Galli, who has no peer as a western horsewoman, said, "Domie was my ideal." Actually, she seemed to be everyone's ideal.

In her book, *California Missions and Their Romances,* Mrs. Fremont Older described the fiesta at Mission San Juan Bautista which she and her husband helped to put on in 1908, to raise funds to repair damage done to the mission by the earthquake of 1906. She wrote that "Miss Indart was judged the 'most graceful equestrienne' " and also that she was among the young ladies doing the Virginia Reel on horseback. A member of the board of directors of the San Benito County Horse Show and Rodeo at Bolado Park, Domie worked actively on its behalf from its beginning in 1929.

On Sunday afternoons she was always at home at

Rancho Indart on the Santa Anita Road. Everyone came to call either in a horse and buggy or on horseback. Mary Grunnagle said that one of the first things her husband did after they were married was to take her to meet Domie.

"Domie built up one of the best Hereford herds that you could find in California," said her nephew, Jim Indart—a man who should know, having been in ranching all his life. "She reserved the right to pick the best bulls from Arthur Nyland at his San Juan Bautista Ranch." During her illness, Jim said, he took this over for her.

Domie never married. She had a sweetheart, Thede French, who died. Apparently there was no one else. Her mother, whom she cared for, was 98 years of age when she died in 1937. Domie's last days were spent at Wheeler Hospital in Gilroy. She was joined there by her sister, Mary Navelet, who had a room near her so they could visit back and forth. She never gave up, but at the age of 88 her life was over.

Rancho Indart was bought by Quentin Tobias, who has given it its original name, "Santa Ana." To accommodate his happy household of nine children, Tobias has made additions to the house and to the ranch. Domie would have liked that.

Bolado Park

The San Benito County Horse Show and Rodeo was probably best described by the late Honorable Maxwell McNutt, breeder and trainer of horses as well as California historian, when he wrote:

San Benito County typifies what remains of Spanish California. Bolado Park is its playground and there, as nowhere else, are the arts of the vaquero kept alive and old California again comes into its own.

This show has been held continuously since 1929, except for the war years. It is really an extension of the early California period and the preservation of the Spanish tradition of a rodeo, or roundup, held once a year by the *haciendados* for dividing and branding the cattle. It also served as a means of acquainting the Mexican longhorns with humans, to keep them from going completely wild. Word would be sent out to all the ranchos, and on the appointed day the vaqueros would bring their wives and children so they could enjoy the celebration afterwards.

When the Americans came the roundups continued, with the neighboring ranchers coming to help with the branding and marking of the beef cattle. Afterwards, to have a little fun, the riders would

Copy of the first program for the San Benito County Saddle Horse Show. There was no program for the first show the previous year.

show off their ability as expert ropers. It was his memory of these occasions that inspired Jake Leonard to join a meeting of a group at the Tres Pinos School to talk about organizing a horse show that would feature cowboy and cow-horse contests and would be home-grown. The group also included Jessie Bryan, Jack Etcheverry, Bill Butts, Dick Nolte, and John Baumgartner. They decided to give it a try. The first show, in 1929, was put on in conjunction with the County Fair and didn't even have a program, but the enthusiasm for and the success of this venture established a tradition which has continued for 46 years.

Jim Indart and Lola Galli following bucking bronco. Neither has missed a Bolado Park Horse Show and Rodeo since the first in 1929. Indart was chairman of the track for the 1976 show.

Above, Louie Cabral doing the Roman ride, jumping three teams of horses in tandem, at Bolado. He has appeared at rodeos all over the country and in Canada performing trick riding.

Lola Galli carrying the flag at Bolado Park on Peanuts, a horse brought down from Nevada for the Wild Horse Race. Lola broke and trained Peanuts and he became a high point winner.

Corrals, chutes, fences and grandstands had to be built. For the most part, this was underwritten by the late W. I. Hawkins, who was active in Farm Bureau activities and in the building of the Bolado Park pavillion and swimming pool. It was Hawkins who originally influenced Julia Bolado Davis and her sons, Gaston and Farragut Ashe, to give the land for Bolado Park. The Horse Show and Rodeo became a community effort, with the ranchers volunteering their time for much of the labor necessary to put up the structures.

Elected to the board of directors in 1930 were: Jake Leonard, president (he also served in the State Assembly later); Bill Butts, show manager; H. T. Liliencrantz, parade; R. R. Root and Al Parker (he now lives in Santa Maria), track; Ed Butts and Gilbert Brown, arena; Art Fruits and John Indart, police; and Claude Sharp, housing, barns, grounds, and programs. Sharp is still a member of the board but unable to take active part. As of 1976 John Baumgartner, chairman of the board, was the only original member still active. He also has the distinction of being on the Cowboy Hall of Fame board of directors. Hazel Cromie, secretary of the board for many years, now lives in Le Grand, California.

From the first show there has been a continuity of families and participants. Jim Indart, a nephew of both Domie Indart and Bill Butts, members of the first board of directors, is now chairman of the track. His wife, Hazel, with whom he competed in team roping for years, helps with the moving of the cattle, as does Lola Galli, who was also in that first show. Hazel Indart's brother, Bill Caldera, is chairman of the arena and runs the rodeo. Hugh French, who won the prize for "Best Little Outfit for Boys" in that first show, is still participating, and his son, Mitt, now enters the bronc riding. Memories of the early days are many—of Sheriff Jerry Croxon, with his white beard and frock coat, riding in the parade on Jessie Bryan's black horse—of Charles Maggini, who rode both broncs and bulls in that first show and was United States Roping Champion the same year, and is still active as foreman of Henry Coe's Rancho San Felipe—and of Louis Cabral who delighted showgoers for years with his sensational trick riding. He was the original driver of the Wells Fargo coach for the television commercial, and still provides oxen that are trained and cattle for television and movie productions. He did such tricks as jumping three horses abreast over fire and Roman Rider team-jumping tandem horses, standing on the back of the last two.

In the early days they didn't truck the horses to Bolado Park. The ranchers and vaqueros rode there on horseback, and came distances of 40 or more miles by *caballata*. The bells of the lead horse could be heard for miles as they arrived from the Panoche, Peach Tree, and Priest's Valley. George Frusetta would bring 20 horses from his San Benito ranch, so that all the children in Tres Pinos would have a horse to ride, and drive them down the middle of the main street, the bell ringing. The origin of the caballata was in the days before fencing. The ranchers would tie a sheep bell around the neck of a mare or gelding, and when they wanted to gather up the horses, the others would follow the horse with the bell.

The problem of stabling the horses that first year of the Horse Show was solved by some, including the Butts Brothers, Jake Leonard, and John Baumgartner, by building small corrals among the willows in back of the arena, each with a makeshift saddle shed boarded with a few willow branches for a roof and enough room for a bed of straw for the groom. For water Jake Leonard dug a well three feet deep and brought over an old Douglas pump from his ranch. For a trough he used a washtub. Some of the contestants tied their horses to a willow tree, brought their blankets, grub and cooking utensils, and camped. Others used Jack Etcheverry's livery stables next to his hotel. Frank and Lola Galli used the old Etcheverry barn that is still standing at the end of 5th Street. Another empty old barn, where the golf course is now, was used by some, and for still others, Wiley Garner furnished a stable and corrals across the river. Some of the wives and children came by wagon and camped along the river. In fact, some families still camp out when they come for the show.

The present steel and concrete grandstand was completed in 1950. In the entrance, through the efforts of Harry Breen, descendant of the first American family to live in San Juan, imprinted in concrete are 224 livestock brands of San Benito County ranches. Also on display in the lobby, in specially built cabinets on the wall, are more than 200 original horse and cattle brands on leather and rawhide, all of which had been filed as original brands.

The Saddle Horse Show and Rodeo, featuring bull and bronc riding, calf roping, bulldogging, wild cow-milking contests, and ending with the wild horse race, one of the few such races in the country, is always staged the last weekend in June. The activities start at noon on Friday with a parade, and whether they are participants or not, most ranch families ride in it just for the fun of hearing their names announced over the microphone by the emcee as they pass the grandstand, and wave to the crowd. Beforehand, many have a picnic under the trees on the lawn that stretches along the front of the stadium.

Lola Galli

The late Will Rogers wrote in his syndicated column of May 17, 1934, after taking part in a branding at the Quien Sabe ranch, "Didn't mind all the men beating me roping, but when a girl did, it looks like golf will be coming up pretty soon." The dateline was Hollister, and the girl was Lola Galli. Rogers later told her that he used Hollister because he figured if he wrote "Tres Pinos"

Above, Will Rogers, closest to camera, during a branding on the Quien Sabe Ranch. Behind him are Bill Butts and Mrs. Juanita Somavia. On the calf is Del Owens, a friend of Rogers who was on the Santa Anita Ranch at the time. Lola Galli is on the white horse to the right and Shorty Williamson from King City is on the horse by the barn. Right, Will Rogers column of May 17, 1934.

Will Rogers Says:

HOLLISTER, May 17—Editor The Chronicle: Sure had a good time today, been out to a calf branding at the "Quien Sabe" ranch. Forty thousand acres and one of the prettiest in California. Didn't mind all the men beating me roping but when a girl did, it looks like golf will be coming on me pretty soon.

This is a real old cow-town, but prunes and Easterners are getting a hold in here and they are both hard to eradicate. There is not a better day in the world to be spent than with a lot of wise old cowmen around, barbecued beef, black coffee and good free holy beans.

Cattlemen have lost more in the last few years than anybody and say less about it. When you ever have any doubt as to what might happen in these U. S. go to the country and talk with them and you will come back reassured. Yours,
WILL ROGERS.

everybody would be getting out their maps and trying to find it.

Lola Galli started showing horses when she was 16 years old, at the Salinas Rodeo in 1923. Within a couple of years she was breaking horses. Her admirers in San Benito County say that no other woman has broken as many horses that could go out and win. She has probably received more honors than any other western horsewoman, if one judges by her houseful of trophies. When asked how many she has won, she said, "I have no idea. I never counted them . . . and I have given so many of them away." In 1973 she was presented a beautiful trophy by the Salinas Rodeo Association for 50 years of participation. She first carried the

Lola Galli on right with her husband, the late Frank Galli, team roping at Bolado Park.

The 105-year-old house on Panoche-New Idria Road where Hugh Mathews took his bride, Laura Call, to live. Lola lives next door on the old Mathews ranch.

flag leading the parade in 1926 and then continuously from 1928 through 1947. In 1974 the Directors of the California Rodeo Association awarded her a large silver trophy for 51 years of competition.

Born and raised in Tres Pinos, Lola's mother was a Shore of the family for whom Shore Road was named. Her father, Arthur Fruits, ran the stage and freight between Tres Pinos and the New Idria Mines in the southwest part of the county. He later was sheriff of San Benito County for many years. After Lola graduated from high school, she lived at the Willie Butts' ranch. Before she married Frank Galli she also went up to the Ashurst Ranch about five miles from the New Idria Mines to help run cattle from Firebaugh to be butchered for the people at New Idria. This was a trip of about 25 miles each way, she said, and they camped along the way.

The New Idria Mines, among the richest quicksilver mines in the world, are believed to have been discovered in 1851 by Spanish missionaries who did assay tests and found that the ore was cinnabar. In Bret Harte's *Story of a Mine,* he tells the story a little differently. Three prospectors were burning some rock as a test to see if there was silver and instead found a pool of liquid silver. Records for the working of the mine date back to 1854. Before the coming of the railroad to Tres Pinos in 1874, the quicksilver was transported by way of San Juan Bautista. After 120 years of operation New Idria was closed forever in June of 1974.

Following Lola's marriage to Frank Galli, the couple lived for many years on the Quien Sabe, which Frank managed. Not only is Lola's house on the Panoche-New Idria Road full of trophies, but her walls are covered with pictures. There is one of

her father's stage being pulled by a team of four horses, and another of the freight being pulled by ten horses. The old stage route was along the creek in back of her house, she said, and the first stop from Tres Pinos on the way to New Idria was Elkhorn, about a mile up the road, where they changed horses.

"One of those horses," she said, speaking of the team, "was my first horse. When I was a little girl I used to ride the 'off-wheel' horse up this road to meet the stage and then ride back to town." She also told a story of the problems they encountered in the rainy weather and of the time the freight overturned between her present house and Elkhorn, while crossing the creek, resulting in the loss of valuable vials of quicksilver which were never recovered.

This picture of the stage served as a model for Ed Borein, the famous Western artist, for his Christmas card one year. Lola has it framed, along with other Christmas cards of his. The Boreins were friends of Lola and Frank Galli and when Lola would go down to ride in the Santa Barbara Fiesta Parade she always stayed with them. "He used to come up to the Bolado Park shows with Charlie Thompson, a writer."

On the wall in the hallway is a grouping of old Charles Russell prints. Lola said that they once hung in the bar of the old Etcheverry Hotel and when the hotel was taken down, the prints were given to her. Of all the pictures of horses, she singled out one of a horse called "Peanuts." He was a wild horse, she said, brought from Nevada by Harry Rowell for the wild horse race at Bolado. "I bought him for 55 dollars. He did well for me—was high point hackamore the year after I got him, high

The stage from New Idria Mines to Tres Pinos on the Panoche-New Idria Road. It was owned by Arthur Fruits, father of Lola, who was sheriff of San Benito County for many years.

point rein horse, and always in the money in the stock horse class."

Also in Lola's gallery is a picture taken of Will Rogers in the corral during a branding on the Quien Sabe Ranch. In the picture is Mrs. Ramon Somavia (Juanita De Laveaga), whose family has owned the Quien Sabe since the 1870s, Willie Butts, Del Owens, a friend of Rogers, who was on the Davis ranch (Santa Anita) at that time, Shorty Williamson from King City, and Lola. In telling how she and Frank met Will Rogers, she said:

He came to the ring one morning at Salinas while we were working the stock. Later he came to see us several times at the Quien Sabe. One time he came for a branding. Frank gave him a good horse and told him he would have to dally (take turns). This is what Will wanted—to be just like the rest. He didn't want a fuss made over him.

Asked if he was a good roper, she said, "Yes. He was always spinning a rope like he did on the stage. One thing he could never do though, was make a figure eight." In the column Rogers wrote on Tres Pinos, with his effective way of expressing himself,

he said, "There is no better day in the world to be spent than with a lot of wise old cow men around barbecuing beef, black coffee and good free holy beans [Rogers-ese for the Spanish word *frijoles*, meaning beans]."

He wound up the column saying, "Cattlemen have lost more in the last few years than anybody and say less about it. When you ever have doubt as to what might happen in these U.S. go to the country and talk with them and you will come back reassured. Yours, Will Rogers." Lola said that Will wanted to come up to the ranch before he went to Alaska, but couldn't make it. Unfortunately, he never had another chance.

Lola's house on the Panoche-New Idria Road is on the old Mathews Ranch next door to the white clapboard house where Hugh Mathews took his bride, the former Laura Call, to live in 1871. In back of the house are water troughs where travelers to the New Idria Mines used to stop to water their horses. Mathews came to California on the first train from New York in 1869, and built the house and barn which are both still standing and which the late Josephine McCreery bought in 1969. The Call Ranch, just up the road from the Mathews Ranch, is now owned by the John Apels. Call Mountain in the southern part of the county was named for George Washington Call, who crossed overland by way of the Oregon Trail in 1865.

One of Call's daughters married John B. Miller, whose family ranch is still being actively operated on the Panoche Road. The property was homesteaded by John Henry Miller, who came to California in 1877, settled first in Brown's Valley, and then bought the Panoche Road ranch in 1881. John Henry's grandson, John R. Miller, and his wife, the former Barbara Moore, are the present owners of the ranch. Their son, Martin, carrying on the ranching tradition, is managing the Las Aguilas Ranch for John Irwin II.

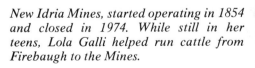

New Idria Mines, started operating in 1854 and closed in 1974. While still in her teens, Lola Galli helped run cattle from Firebaugh to the Mines.

Seated are Deborah and Henry Melendy in front of their house on Bear Valley Ranch. Standing, left to right, Daniel, Deborah Melendy Joice, George, Ella Melendy Burns, Tom, Lue Melendy Meyers, and Henry, Jr. Henry and Deborah were married at Mission San Juan Bautista in 1868 and homesteaded land in Bear Valley.

George Melendy Ranch

A pair of former school teachers, Charlotte Berberich (Mrs. Kingsley) and Lila Elliott (Mrs. Ralph) run the 22,000-acre George Melendy Ranch of their family in Bear Valley. A brother , Martin Melendy, shares a third ownership of the land, but the sisters own and handle the stock. Their grandfather, Henry Melendy, came to California in the early 1860s. His brother had gone off to the Civil War as a drummer boy and their mother urged Henry to join his uncle, Aaron Rockwood, in bringing horses to California. During an Indian attack, however, all the horses were stolen. Somehow they managed to get some mules to make the rest of the trip.

In California Henry became the friend of a young man named John Shell, whose uncle, Dr. Powers, owned land at a place called Bear Valley near the Pinnacles. They decided to go there together. Dr. Powers later met a tragic end—his body was found hanging from a tree on the property in 1885.

One day in 1865, to their surprise, John Shell's mother arrived by covered wagon with his step-father and sisters, Deborah and Susan, who were driving the Durham cows. Henry and Deborah fell in love. In order to receive homestead property it was necessary to be either 21 or married. They solved this by going to San Juan Bautista to be married on April 7, 1868, and thus were able to get the piece of land across the road, which they had wanted. For their cattle brand they combined the initials of their first names, HD, and later registered it. The youngest son of their youngest son, named Walter Melendy, now has the ranch and is using this brand.

The oldest of the Melendys' nine children, George, who always seemed to be needed on the ranch, didn't marry until he was 35. His wife, Elizabeth Kelly (always known as Lizzie), of the Martin Kelly family in La Gloria Valley, was a school teacher. George and Lizzie started with a small rented ranch on the San Benito River (Willow Creek also runs through this ranch and joins the San Benito) just over the hill east of his father's ranch in Bear Valley. As neighboring homesteads were offered for sale, they borrowed money and bought all available land until they owned 14,000 acres and were renting an additional 8,000— making it an operating ranch of a total of 22,000 acres.

They had started married life with one horse and two milk cows which belonged to Elizabeth and two horses that were George's. First they tried raising sheep, but coyotes caught and killed them all. They had a small dairy for a few years, and then got beef cattle started, as well as pigs and turkeys. Some of the cattle they bought were from James Dunne and had a "D" brand. Inasmuch as Dunne said he was not going to use the brand any longer, they registered it and it is still in use today by their daughters. Beef cattle in those days were driven by men on horseback to Tres Pinos to be shipped. The pigs, however, had to be driven on foot the 20 miles.

On a hill near the site of the old Willow Creek School, where the Melendy children attended classes, is the Willow Creek Cemetery. About 30 members of the family are buried there. Every year on Memorial Day Melendy family descendants gather for a reunion and to decorate the graves.

Unknown to those early settlers in the 1860s was the existence of the San Andreas Fault. This geophysical phenomenon runs between the house and barn of the George Melendy Ranch. The west side of the house is moving north about one inch a year and is under study by about 15 agencies which have instruments hooked up to the telephone lines to take the information directly to Menlo Park.

The Kelly Ranch

Charlotte and Lila's maternal grandparents had the Martin P. Kelly Ranch, which dates back to the 1870s and has remained in the family. Martin came from New York after rejecting the offer of his friend, John D. Rockefeller, to become a partner in the oil business. On the way by ship he became desperately ill and was given up for dead. Fortunately, a Catholic nun discovered that a mirror fogged when put to his face, and nursed him back to health.

Martin married Sarah Belle Cole from Minnesota, who came to California on the first train. A progressive farmer, he enlarged a natural lake and irrigated some of the land, terracing to distribute the water. Besides raising cattle he had fine draft horses, keeping a stallion so he could raise his own. He also raised thoroughbred horses which Elizabeth (Melendy) and her sister, Helena, broke so they could be sold to the track. In addition to this he had a dairy of Ayershire cows on which he used his old mission brand, a quarter circle and a cross on the left hip.

Following the deaths of Martin Kelly in 1923 and his wife in 1935, two of their sons, Superior Court Judge Henry C. Kelly of Yuma, Arizona, and Charles, together with a sister, Helena Kelly De Paquette, bought the cattle interest from the other four members of the family. After Henry died in 1958, Charles and Helena (always called Lena) continued to operate the ranch until her death in 1972.

THE PINNACLES

The location of the ranch in La Gloria Valley, with the Pinnacles close by, inspired Lena to write an account of this national monument's history for the *Evening Free Lance* of July 14, 1915. She said:

It is safe to say that nowhere on the face of the earth has nature worked such a profound upheaval as here. The subterranean passages with mushroom forms, the huge underground pools of water, the dark caverns, twin and balancing rocks and innumerable other weird phenomena are advocates in themselves and need but to be seen to make the Pinnacles along with Yellowstone and Yosemite, rank among the wonders of the world.

Lena quoted George Vancouver, the British sea captain who, on an exploring mission, visited Monterey three times in the early 1790s, and on an inland exploration by horseback crossed the Salinas Valley to, it is believed, the southern end of the Gabilans. In the report to His Majesty in London in 1798, Vancouver wrote:

I was able to join the party [he had been ill] to the valley through which the Monterey River flows and there was gratified with the sight of the most extraordinary mountain I ever beheld. One side presented the appearance of a sumptuous edifice falling into decay: the columns, which looked as if raised with much labor and

Tiburcio Vasquez, who was tried and convicted of killing two of three victims in the Snyder's Store robbery and shootout in Paicines. He was hanged in the Santa Clara County Courthouse jail yard in San Jose on March 19, 1875. Despite his exploits, most of the ranchers never believed he killed a man.

industry, were of great magnitude, seemed to be of elegant form and to be composed of the same cream-colored stone of which I have made mention.

Between these magnificent columns are deep excavations, resembling different passages into the interior parts of the supposed buildings, whose roof, being the summit of the mountain, appeared to be wholly supported by these columns rising perpendicularly with the most mathematical exactness.

Lena Kelly De Paquette advised that the Pinnacles could be reached by Hollister or Gonzales, and that those traveling by way of Gonzales would pass through La Gloria Valley, "a far-famed, dainty, lovely dimple in the cheek of nature, 1,735 feet above sea level."

Tiburcio Vasquez

In spite of all the tales that have been told about the notorious bandit, Tiburcio Vasquez, the general feeling of the families of ranchers in and around Tres Pinos, Bear Valley and San Juan, is that Vasquez never killed a man.

Juanita Joseph of Tres Pinos, whose great-great-uncle, Leander Davidson, was a victim of the gunfire in the famous shootout at Snyder's store, said that no one in her family or any of the other families she knew believed that Vasquez ever killed a person. Davidson had given up the sea and with his wife had ranched in Bear Valley before moving to Tres Pinos (now Paicines) to manage the hotel, which was directly across the street from Snyder's store. Hearing the commotion, he opened the door just enough to see what was going on and a bullet came through the door, killing him instantly as he fell into his wife's arms. Ironically, while all this was happening, his wife's brother, Ebenezer Burton, great-grandfather of Juanita Joseph, was in Snyder's store lying flat on the floor; he escaped unscathed.

Another story told by Juanita Joseph concerned her great-grandmother, Susan Shell, and took place at the Bear Valley ranch across from the Pinnacles. She said Vasquez roamed through the country freely. He never hid out as some believed. Riding into the ranch yard, he saw Susan at the well drawing water and asked her for a drink. As she was lifting the dipper of water to hand it to him he tickled her under the chin, and she flipped the dipper of water in his face. Although Susan was nervous as to what his reaction would be, he only laughed. Her brothers, in the house, were aware of what was going on and had their guns ready, but as far as Vasquez was concerned it was a joke, and he continued on his way.

This was Vasquez territory. Susan's sister, Deborah, who married Henry Melendy and lived at Bear Valley, also knew Vasquez. The bandit and his men used to stop at the Henry Melendy ranch and Deborah would feed them. One time she had some washing to do and one of Vasquez's men watched her baby while she did it.

Henry Lawn, an elder in the Mormon Church who lived in the Cienega Valley, according to his grandson, Lloyd Waters, knew Vasquez in San Juan Bautista. This was probably during the time Vasquez's mother had a tamale parlor on Third Street, between 1863 and 1866. Lawn said that while traveling at night he would meet Vasquez and his men from time to time and that Vasquez was always friendly. Waters said his grandfather always felt that Vasquez wasn't the atrocious bandit many of his followers were.

Many of the old ranching families have stories to tell of Vasquez stopping to exchange horses and to spend the night. John Marentis of San Juan said his parents told him that Vasquez sometimes stopped at the Aromitas Ranch when Pedro Marentis was manager and that it was said he was always very nice.

That he was a bandit, robbed stagecoaches, waylaid travelers, stole horses, and carried a gun, cannot be denied. He was daring and audacious. One time he sued the sheriff in Los Angeles County for repossession of rifles which had been confiscated by the sheriff after a robbery which Vasquez had committed. In appearance Vasquez was slight, five feet six inches tall, neatly dressed in the Early California style, and soft spoken, all of which belied his daring exploits which extended from Sonoma to Los Angeles and included a network of lady loves along the way who hid him when necessary.

Born in 1835 in Monterey, of good family, he seemed always to be different from the rest of the children. At 16 he quit school and set up a dance house which was said to be his ruin. The women who came to these fandangoes had a strange fascination for the youth. It was here he became acquainted with Anastacio Garcia, a vicious bandit who taught him all his tricks and probably also the deep-rooted hatred for Gringos that so many of the Californians had at that time. Vasquez's passion was a love for women, and this was often his undoing. In San Juan he made off with the wife of Abelardo Salazar, which resulted in a shootout on Main Street between the two men, almost causing Vasquez's demise. With a gunshot wound in his neck, he barely made it to his hideout at Cantua Canyon on the other side of the New Idria Mines. Another amour, Rosaria Leiva, was the wife of one of his men. When her husband discovered what was going on, he not only tipped off the authorities as to Vasquez's whereabouts on one occasion, but testified against him at the trial.

Ironically, the robbery at Snyder's store was to have been the farewell appearance for this man, who, with his sense of the dramatic, would have gone far on the stage had he chosen that profession. Deciding that his pattern for action and his hideouts were becoming too well known, he had concluded that he should move south. Snyder's was chosen because it was a stagecoach stop and the only store serving a large area.

He was tried and convicted, on circumstantial evidence, for the killing of two of the three victims in Snyder's store, in Santa Clara County Courthouse in San Jose. Tickets to attend his hanging were at a premium. 400 invitations were issued by Sheriff J. H. Adams, all that could be accommodated in the small jail courtyard where the hanging took place on "the 19th day of March, A.D. 1875 at 1:30 o'clock P.M."

CHAPTER XXV

K *Rancho Cienega de los Paicines*

Another fine old rancho that escaped the push of progress and resisted the pocketbook pressure is the 8,000-acre Rancho Cienega de los Paicines. Still an operating cattle ranch, it is owned by Mrs. Robert Law and managed by her son, Robert Law, Jr.

Enhancing the natural beauty of the setting is the lane of overhanging pepper trees leading back to the house and ranch buildings, which include an unusually artistic barn which dates back to the period of Alexander B. Grogan, owner of the ranch between 1867 and 1886. At the entrance to the house is the old brass bell that once hung from the gingerbread-trimmed eave of the house and was rung to call workmen to meals. When Katherine Law and her late husband bought the place in 1943, they had to update the white frame house that Grogan had built in 1867. They actually had a choice of two houses—one a larger and more elaborate place of Moorish design where the previous owner, Walter Murphy, had lived, and this smaller frame house with its magnificent view.

The remodeling job was a big one. At first they had to burn wood to heat water, and lighting was provided by gas jets. They knocked out walls to convert the parlor into a spacious living room, remodeled the bathrooms, most of which had outside entrances, and modernized the kitchen, among other things. Both the dining and living room have large bay windows through which one looks down on acres of meadow dotted with oak trees, where cattle graze. On the other side are the Gabilan mountains which are frequently covered with snow in the winter.

Just below the house was the two-story adobe built by Angel Castro for his wife, Ysabel Butron, and their family. Castro received the grant of 8,918 acres in 1842 jointly with Jose Rodriguez, who married his daughter, Hilaria. According to Abeloe's *Historic Spots in California,* the sala in this adobe was reproduced on stage in San Francisco for the David Belasco production, "Rose of the Rancho" in 1906. Most of the Mexican grants were issued to those who had done service to the government—Castro was mayordomo of Mission San Juan Bautista in 1835 during the period of secularization by Mexico. He had received another grant in 1836 called San Francisco del Rosario, probably the land he had in San Juan Canyon. Very little is known about that grant.

At the time Castro received the Paicines grant, he was commander of a militia company at San Jose and Branciforte (near what is now Santa Cruz). This name, Cienega de los Paicines, according to *California Place Names* by Gudde, "refers to a Costanoan village Paisin on the San Benito River." "Cienega," of course, means marsh. The grant covered that land extending from Tres Pinos Creek on the east to the Cienega Valley at the foot of the Gabilans on the west. The San Benito River and its tributary, Pescadero Creek, run through part of the ranch. The southeastern boundary is near where the old Paicines School stood on the old stage road to San Benito. One of Angel Castro's daughters, Guadalupe, was the second wife of Don Manuel Larios, who owned the neighboring Rancho Santa Ana y Quien Sabe. On a *diseno* (hand-sketched map) of Larios' ranch only two roads are shown. One led to the casa of Angel Castro across the San Benito River, the other to San Juan Bautista.

When the Kingsley Macombers lived in the big house in the early part of the century, the Chinese cooks lived in the adobe and did the cooking there. During the Walter Murphys' occupation, the adobe had deteriorated and was taken down.

The first owner of the Paicines Rancho after the Castros and the Rodriguezes was Francisco Villegas, who sold it to Alexander B. Grogan in 1867 for $17,000 in gold coin. Grogan also bought 2,000 acres from Theophile Vache, who planted

Left: Entrance to Rancho Cienega de los Paicines. The grape vines were planted by Almaden Wines who lease part of the land. Above: Cheese house on Cienega de los Paicines Ranch. Alexander Grogan had a dairy.

The late Robert Law and his wife, Katherine, beside the house built by Grogan in 1867.

This picturesque barn on Cienega de los Paicines ranch was built during the era of Alexander Grogan.

grapes and started a winery on La Cienega Road in the 1850s. This winery is now owned by Almaden.

Grogan was a native of Belfast, Ireland, who went first to Valparaiso, Chile and came to San Francisco in 1848 with a letter of credit from Faxon D. Atherton. Atherton had been in California from 1836–1839 and later returned with his family to stay permanently. In addition to building the Law house, Grogan built many of the ranch buildings, including the milk house near where the old adobe was, and the cheese house, a charming little building, part of his dairy operation. In 1874 he imported Ayrshire cows to introduce to the local dairy industry. Before Paicines became the permanent name of the little town that had been called Tres Pinos, it was known for three months in 1874 as Grogan.

Upon Grogan's death in 1886 his sister, Emily Grogan of Belfast, inherited the ranch. Isaac Thexton served as manager for her. During this time she sold 1,000 acres for Willow Grove School for $1. When she died in 1900 three nephews inherited the estate and in turn sold the ranch to Richard Sudden and T. F. Brown. Charles B. Hawkins was the next owner and in 1906 he sold to Kingsley Macomber and Colonel George Sykes.

Sykes, a prominent woolen manufacturer, took 2,000 acres across the road from the Macombers. They planted orchards and ran cattle on the upper portion. After Colonel Sykes' death his wife stayed on for several years and finally sold to the Almaden Winery. The late Luis Benoist and his wife redecorated the house in the superb way they did all of their houses, and used it for a summer home.

Paicines Hotel, where Leander Davidson was killed by a bullet that passed through the front door during the shootout at Snyder's Store across the street. Tiburcio Vasquez was convicted of two of the three deaths in this gunfight, and was hanged in San Jose. The hotel is now gone, as is the little church seen to the left. Snyder's store was turned around and moved across the street. At that time the town was called Tres Pinos. Its name was changed to Grogan for a while and finally to Paicines, for the ranch.

The Almaden Vineyards planted grapes and leased 1,000 acres from the Law ranch on which to grow varietal grapes.

The Macombers were from Long Island. Mrs. Macomber was a Harkness. Her father was head of Standard Oil of New Jersey and used to come out in his private railroad car which he kept in a barn in Tres Pinos. When he was ready to go back the old engine would push the car up to Gilroy where it would hook on to a train for Los Angeles and then the East. In the *Monterey Counties Biographical Sketches* by Guinn, printed in 1910, there is a piece on the Rancho Cienega de los Paicines which says that "fifty persons reside at the ranch, and for their benefit a post office, store and a blacksmith shop are maintained. There is also a hotel on the ranch." The store referred to was Snyder's, in which the famous shootout by Vasquez and his men occurred. The store has been moved across the street and turned around. The hotel is gone and as of this writing, the post office is fighting for its existence and probably won't make it. The Guinn account also refers to 1,000 head of high grade Durham cattle and 100 head of registered blooded imported cattle, forming a "herd of unrivalled

Pepper tree lane leading back to ranch headquarters. The trees were planted during the era of Alexander B. Grogan, who purchased the ranch in 1867.

quality and wide reputation." In the Macomber stable of fine horses, Guinn lists 150 head, including Percherons and Belgians imported from Europe and thoroughbred trotters of American strain.

Macomber had a race track on the site of what is now the Santa Clara County Fairgrounds, and Lilla Renshaw Hunter, a neighbor, recalled that as a child a special treat was to go with her father and Mr. Macomber to see the horses work out there.

The big house on the ranch was built by the Macombers in 1912. It was patterned after one they had seen when staying in Nice. One wing has since been removed by the Laws so as not to hide the view of the valley. Josephine Grant McCreery purchased this house and completely redecorated it just before her death in 1972. Kingsley Macomber had a brother, Dr. H. J. Macomber, who had practiced medicine in Pasadena, who lived in the smaller house at one time.

Kingsley Macomber, a dashing, handsome man, played polo at Pebble Beach, where he had another large home. Bob Law was also a polo player. Another equestrian activity of Macomber was hunting. He didn't hunt the fox, however, and he didn't use the standard hunting hounds. Instead he had greyhounds and hunted the coyote. In the old stable over the stall of the winning horse would be hung the brush or tail. Today the ranch is used by the Los Altos Hunt, who rent the property for the traditional hunt. Although it doesn't seem quite in character in this very western background, their presence with the sound of the hunting horn and the yipping of the hounds, adds color as the riders gallop across the fields, jumping creeks and natural hazards, their red tailcoats flying.

In 1927 the Macombers sold the ranch to a multi-millionaire from Chicago by the name of Walter Murphy. By a coincidence, Bob Law met Murphy at the Arizona Biltmore one time and Murphy told him about his ranch at Paicines. Little did Law suspect that he would one day own the ranch. Murphy was a friend of the Roosevelts, and in the late thirties or early forties Jimmy Roosevelt spent a year at the ranch recuperating from an illness. Murphy gave a luncheon for Roosevelt which Bob Law attended, as did Murphy's neighbor, Lilla Hunter, with her parents, the Howard Renshaws.

Although he was not a Catholic, Murphy was very generous to Mission San Juan Bautista. He built new living quarters for the priests and later a recreational center, which is now the popular Cademartori's Santa Maria Restaurant. After Murphy's death the Laws purchased the ranch from his estate.

OH CHAPTER XXVI
The Oak Hill Ranch

Located in the Live Oak area, adjoining the southern end of Rancho Cienega de los Paicines, the Oak Hill Ranch of Bruce and Martha Hill. It was originally homesteaded in 1867 by Jasper Henry Lawn of San Juan Bautista, before Hollister was founded. Lawn chose a pretty site for his ranch against the Gabilans, with the San Benito River slicing through the property. The Hills now have 700 acres.

From Old Airline Highway to the Hills' house, three-quarters of a mile, the road is bordered by lichen-covered picket fences, orchards on one side and the Gabilan Mountains rising up on the other. Just before reaching the ranch headquarters, the road circles a little lake bordered by willows that is used as a swimming hole in the summer. Dominating the scene, however, is a majestic high-pitched old barn, one side of which is covered with brilliant green moss in the spring.

Dick Hill, son of Bruce and Martha, who manages the ranch and lives there in the original Lawn house with his wife Kathryn and two sons, pointed out the construction of the barn. "You can tell if a barn is old by the way it is built," he said, pointing out the tremendous pine poles inside that hold up the roof with no cross bracing. They are bolted at the ground to short poles. The roof, he said, is the original one, put on in 1867, made of three-foot shakes. He noted that it doesn't sag, and added that the roof of the main section of his house has the same kind of shakes.

The old buildings, including a bunkhouse, water tower, and blacksmith shop that is now used as a garage, blend with the countryside and merge with the mountains. A nostalgic note for old-timers is the flagpole from the old Paicines school set in an island surrounded by the driveway in front of the house. Next to it is a row of old pepper trees. The Hills' house, built, they said, in about 1900, was two cabins tied together. Since moving to the ranch in

1937, they have enclosed porches and added onto the house, making it into a comfortable home. From a pioneer family, Bruce Hill's people were Oakland-based. Martha Hill, however, is deep-rooted in San Benito County on both sides. Her mother was a Bonnel; her uncle, Frank Bonnel, was one of Hollister's first dentists; and her mother's sister, Elizabeth, married Robert G. Einfalt, publisher of the *Telegram* in Gilroy. Benjamin Franklin Bonnel came overland in a party with the famous Captain Yount, Indian Wars fighter and mountain man, for whom Yountville was named, and married Parthinia Petray, who had come by way of the Isthmus.

They gradually moved south to the Gilroy-Hollister area. Their daughter, Martha Bonnel, married Frank Shore, son of Richard E. Shore, who had come to California in 1849 with a companion on horseback after fighting in the Mexican War. Dick Hill, who is a California history buff and president of the San Benito County Historical Society, said:

I suppose the fact that the family home in Missouri was close to the main road going west and seeing the wagon trains going by must have stirred their imaginations. They didn't follow the wagon trains, however. They rode horseback and came through New Mexico and Arizona. Acquainted with the territory, having fought in the Mexican war, they knew that the Indians stuck to camp at night, so they would tie up by a stand of cottonwoods and sleep during the day. After dark they traveled.

Richard E. Shore settled first in Mountain View after a fling at gold digging. He had relatives there, such well-known families as the Bubbs, the Springers and, Martha thinks, the Appersons—at least they were good friends. They had all come out from Washington County, Missouri, including George Hearst who married Phoebe Apperson.

Continuing the story, Martha Hill said her great-

Left, Bruce Hill and son Richard look down from the loft of the old barn. Right, Lloyd Waters, whose grandfather Jasper Henry Lawn homesteaded the Oak Hill Ranch in 1867, and Martha Hill, one of the present owners.

Old picket fences covered with lichen line the road up to the ranch.

grandfather Richard Shore came to San Benito County and bought a part of the Ausaymas y San Felipe along Tequesquite Creek. He built a large two-story home on Shore Road (named for him) near the intersection of Lovers Lane. "When my father, Frank Shore, was married to my mother, Martha Bonnel, he gave them half the property. They built the house next door where I was born. It, too, is still standing."

Jasper Henry Lawn

Lloyd Waters, a neighbor and grandson of Jasper Henry Lawn (always known as Henry), who lives nearby, came over to the Hills'. He brought his grandfather's diary and a picture of his mother, Marianne Lawn, taken at Live Oaks School in 1888. In the diary Lawn wrote of bringing his wife and three children over from San Juan to see their new house (probably a one-room cabin, Waters said) and of the children jumping up and down. This was the first house they had ever lived in with a floor.

Henry was only nine years old when his widowed mother decided to come West with her parents, the Joshua Twitchells (who are buried in San Juan), and other relatives in a wagon train. Young Henry drove three yoke of oxen all the way. They had the not-unusual encounters with Indians; one member of the party was killed by an Indian, as was "Old Buck," an ox, by an arrow that just missed Henry. After stopping over the winter of 1848–49 at Ogden Creek, they reached Sutter's Fort in June of 1849. There they found a settlement of tents, building frames covered with cloth or canvas. With the wagon train was a man named Silas Beckwith. Two days after their arrival, Silas and Eunice Twitchell Lawn, Henry's mother, were married.

Going into the hotel business, Beckwith rented Captain John Sutter's large old adobe, for which he paid $800 a month. Young Henry, ten years old, was general bartender and assistant receiver of monies, which included gold nuggets and gold dust. They ran three large monte banks, roulette tables and all kinds of games of chance with cards. Unfortunately, Silas took in a partner and he "took" them for almost everything.

In 1851 the family moved to San Juan Bautista. Henry learned the carpenter trade and when he was 14 years old he went to school for six months. The Sisters held school in the wing of the mission. "But they taught all Spanish," Waters said. "No one insisted that English be taught. He learned to read and write in Spanish." After the family had moved to the ranch, where their family increased to eleven children, they joined the Reorganized Church of Jesus Christ of Latter Day Saints, and Henry was a traveling minister for 35 years.

Lloyd Waters' mother was born on this ranch. He told a story about one time the family was going to Nevada near Carson City to start a new church. They stopped at a farm near their destination. "The farmer told them to help themselves—that garden over there was planted by number one wife—that one by number two wife, etc. It developed he had five wives. That was the first my family knew about polygamy. They turned around and went back to San Juan Bautista."

CHAPTER XXVII

Ϙ *Rancho Real de Aguilas*

After driving through the Santa Ana Valley from Tres Pinos, at the end of Santa Anita Road, one comes to the entrance to the old Selby McCreery Ranch. Over the gates is a signpost reading, "Rancho Real de Aguilas 1844 AD" (Royal Ranch of the Eagles), with a ranch brand at either end. The new owner of this 33,000-acre ranch, John N. Irwin II, is using the original name of the grant, given to it by Saturnino Carriaga and Francisco Arias, who received seven square leagues from Governor Micheltorena in 1844.

John Irwin is a lawyer in New York who served as Ambassador to France under Nixon and Ford, returning to New York in late 1974. He previously had served in various capacities under Presidents Truman, Eisenhower and Johnson, and was Deputy Secretary of State under William Rogers.

From the gates the drive back to the ranch headquarters was on five miles of narrow winding road, sometimes alongside a deep drop where the creek runs, and sometimes over streams. It was an overcast day and the soft light on the moss-draped oak trees and grey-green lichen-covered fences created an almost mystical effect. Eventually we reached a place where the canyon widened and we were in the valley called "Los Muertos" by the Spaniards.

We turned into the ranch headquarters, which are set against the hills. The entrance is marked by a giant oak. On hand to greet us were Martin Miller, manager, and his foreman, Bob Garner. Garner, who has been on the ranch for 28 years and lives in a little white house which is supposed to be the oldest building on the ranch, said that the name "Los Muertos" comes from a story about three men having been found hanging from a tree there. In those early days, when there was tension between the Californians and the Americans, this was not uncommon. Most of the old ranching people in San Benito County refer to this part of the ranch as Los Muertos and the upper part as Las Aguilas. The two ranches made up most of the Rancho Real de Las Aguilas grant. On an 1890 map Donnelly and Dunne and Mrs. Arques are listed as owners of part of the ranch.

Martin Miller is a young man still in his twenties whose family has ranched in the area for over 100 years. Like most of the present-day ranchers' sons, he studied at Cal Poly in San Luis Obispo. Martin said that John Irwin has a cow-calf operation on his 238,000-acre ranch near Prescott, that he is planning to bring the calves from the Arizona ranch here, and that the Aguilas has stockers which go to a feed lot from here. He said that normally they run about 7,000 head of cattle a year.

For many years in the early part of the century, Joaquin Ojeda, who came from Mexico, ran the ranch for its owner, Andrew McCreery. During this time he gradually accumulated 6,000 acres on the other side of the ranch for himself, and when he retired he worked that land. It was near the little community of Cleveland (a small school district), once a part of the Quien Sabe Ranch.

In 1933 Selby McCreery, grandson of Andrew McCreery, was married to Josephine Grant at the Grant Ranch. Both were from prominent old San Francisco families. Josephine's father was Joseph D. Grant, who owned the 9,482-acre ranch near Mount Hamilton where the wedding was held. It has been purchased since Josephine's death by Santa Clara County for a recreational area to be known as the Joseph D. Grant Park. Proceeds from the sale, according to the stipulations of her will, went to Save-the-Redwoods League, which her father founded in 1918.

The newly-married McCreerys moved into the main house, which was built in 1929. They always called it the Company House. It is H-shaped with a

View of McCreery ranch headquarters in Los Muertos Valley.

Oldest building on the Aguilas ranch, occupied by Mr. and Mrs. Garner. Garner has been on the ranch for 28 years.

Andrew McCreery was the owner of the Real de Aguilas Ranch from 1895 until his death in 1913, at which time it was incorporated into the McCreery Estate.

Martin Miller, manager, and Bob Garner, foreman of Rancho Real de Aguilas, formerly known as Los Muertas or Selby McCreery Ranch.

Above, Joaquin Ojeda, Jr. haying on the ranch above the Las Aguilas. Note 27 horses pulling equipment. Ojeda's father came from Mexico, worked for Andrew McCreery, and gradually accumulated 6,000 acres of land for his retirement.

146

living room in the middle, a bedroom wing on one side and a kitchen on the other. It originally had a walled garden, but the McCreerys had the wall removed so they could have an uninterrupted view of the valley. They also built a guest house. Mrs. Robert Law, who was a good friend of the Mc-Creerys, said that Josephine told her that one time when they decided to have the floors refinished they thought that they were redwood, but they turned out to be rosewood. For the last years of their lives Josephine and Selby lived apart, although they were never divorced. Before this break they used to entertain with Sunday luncheons at the ranch, and on the Sunday of the Bolado Park Horse Show they would always give a picnic in the park under the "McCreery Oak" in front of the stadium. One guest recalled attending the luncheon years ago and said that the butler was on hand to pour champagne. Josephine McCreery continued the picnic tradition in a less formal way, with bright-colored cushions, cloths and napkins, until her death in 1972.

The Aguilas ranch had been in the McCreery family since 1895. Selby's grandfather, who came from Ireland around the Horn to San Francisco in 1848, at the age of 17, purchased it from the estate of Jose Vicente De Laveaga. An auction was held at the courthouse in Hollister and McCreery offered $80,000. After the court refused to confirm the sale McCreery raised his bid to $90,000 and finally settled at $98,000. This was still considerably under the $180,000 amount paid by Jose Vicente De Laveaga to Frederick and Francesca MacDougall, Andrew and Mercedes Calderon, Joseph Estrem and Pablo Saca for 23,650 acres on June 10, 1875. This was one of several ranches MacDougall had acquired through his one-year marriage to Maria Antonia Castro de Anzar. Representing the Jose Vicente De Laveaga estate were Daniel Rogers, M. A. De Laveaga, and Thomas Magee. Around 1900 Andrew McCreery started purchasing parcels of the Guenoc Ranch in Lake County, including the Langtry Farms of Lily Langtry.

The ranch remained in Andrew's name until his death in 1913, at which time it was incorporated into the McCreery Estate Company. His eldest son, Richard, then took over until his grandson, Selby, bought one part of the ranch and Josephine the other. Selby's father, Walter McCreery, married an English woman and spent most of his time abroad, raising his two sons, Selby and Richard, as English citizens.

Andrew McCreery was an enterprising young fellow and foresaw the future in San Francisco real

Wedding of Josephine Grant and Selby McCreery at the Grant Ranch on Mount Hamilton. Mr. and Mrs. Grant, the parents of the bride, are at left.

estate. At that time the waterfront was at Kearny Street. The thing to do then was to buy waterfront lots, and he did. As the bay receded they became valuable. He had a number of houses and lots. He would build and then lease or sell. He also had land south of Market and upper Market. He built one of the first libraries in San Francisco, the McCreery Library, and among his many philanthropies he gave to Stanford Hospital a bed in perpetuity.

In the 1880s Andrew bought for his wife, Isabelle De Milt Swearingen McCreery, the historic villa, Castello di Urio on Lake Como. Isabelle liked the life in Europe; she also had a house in Paris and one at Bilton, England. Although Andrew visited her there, he preferred San Francisco where his business was. After her death the villa was left to her eldest son, Richard. He spent many summers there, with his wife and daughter Isobel (Mrs. Augustus Taylor, Jr. of Hillsborough). Their grandson, Lawrence McCreery, lives in Ireland with his family. His sister, Renee McCreery Moore, lives in Woodside.

Although Selby never bought a villa in Italy, he did on occasion lease one for the summer months and was visited there by the late Paul Hudner and his wife, Mary. During World War II McCreery returned to England and enlisted in the army, serving with the 12th Lancers with the rank of Captain. After the war he returned home to the ranch and became a naturalized United States

One of the old ranch buildings and troughs for watering horses.

citizen. He then requested that his friends not use his English army title. He was regarded as a brilliant polo player, playing in Pebble Beach as well as England. He was a member of the Pacific Union Club in San Francisco, the Cypress Point Club and the Burlingame Club, and in later years built a home in Pebble Beach. The simplicity of this western ranch at the far end of San Benito County, sprawling over 41,000 acres, bordered only by the Quien Sabe ranch, must have been quite a change of pace.

Many of his titled friends from England, however, came to the ranch. He entertained Prince William when he was at Stanford some years ago; his brother, General Sir Richard McCreery, who was knighted for bravery in the war and was head of the British delegation to the United Nations, used to come to the ranch frequently with his wife, the former Lettice St.Maur, second daughter of Lord and Lady Percy St. Maur. (Their wedding reception was held at the town house of her aunt, the Duchess of Somerset, in London.)

As unpretentious as the living quarters on the ranch were, the life-style of the McCreerys on the Aguilas was an improvement over its early days as a Mexican land grant, Real de Aguilas, when a daughter of Francisco Arias married a man named Hernandez and lived in an adobe here for many years.

Saturnino Carriaga, co-grantee of the rancho, apparently spent most of his time in his adobe townhouse in San Juan Bautista which had been the quarters on Mariposa Street that housed the soldiers of the King of Spain. He converted it into a saloon and the equivalent of a modern-day card club, a popular spot for residents of the pueblo to gather and the scene of more than one shootout. In 1867 he built an elegant two-story house with a balcony in San Juan.

After Selby McCreery's death in 1971, his share of the ranch, which was left to the Monterey Peninsula Hospital, was sold to Paul Green, brother of Lorne Green of "Bonanza" and other television shows. In 1976 it was resold to John Irwin II, a widower, who said he hopes to be able to spend time on the ranch with his children.

A CHAPTER XXVIII
Rancho Juristac

Rancho Juristac, located in the southernmost part of Santa Clara County, bounded by the Pajaro River, is unique. According to George Scovel, who has leased the ranch since 1956, it is the only rancho in the Gilroy area never to have been owned in any part by land and cattle baron Henry Miller. This is easily explained by the fact that it belonged to James P. Sargent of the Sargent Brothers, who were highly successful stock men themselves. They had started their partnership by purchasing large lands in the San Joaquin Valley and subsequently the 23,000-acre Rancho El Potrero San Carlos y San Francisquito and La Pestilencia rancho of 12,000 acres. Altogether they had about 80,000 acres in Central California.

Bradley Sargent, for whom the town of Bradley in Monterey County was named, had come to California in 1849 from New Hampshire, where his family had colonial ancestry—his mother was a Webster. He established a store at Weavertown in El Dorado County with his three brothers, Jacob L., Rosswell C., and James P. Sargent. They soon got out of that business, however, and into cattle raising. With a brother running each of the ranches, Scovel said, James P. Sargent took over the Juristac and lived there until his death shortly after the turn of the century. During this time he was Director of the Santa Clara County Agriculture Society for many years, and in 1877 was president. He was also elected to the State Legislature.

Always known as the Sargent Ranch, the Juristac (Castanoan for "At Juris") was acquired from the German brothers, Antonio and Faustino, who received the original Mexican Grant in 1835. They had a large adobe overlooking the Pajaro River. When Pedro Fages made his first inland expedition in 1770, he and his men noted features of the ranch.

An interesting sidelight to the Sargent brothers' operation is that they never kept books and that they never had any problems over business. J. P.

Sargent, as he was always known, ran 1,200 head of cattle. By 1862 he was importing Durham and Shorthorn cattle to improve his herds. A lover of fine horses, he also bred thoroughbreds. On the wall over the piano in the living room of the house the Sargents built in 1895 is a picture of "Green Mountain Maid," a standard bred horse with her history carefully recorded from 1862 to 1868. Frances Scovel said that J. P. favored trotting horses, that he kept them on the north side of town where St. Mary's Catholic Church is now located, and that he also had a race track there. The Scovels said that after Sargent's death Joe Ayer of Milpitas leased the property until his death in 1954. His father, Samuel F. Ayer, like Sargent, had been a Santa Clara County Supervisor. Joe Ayer also owned a part of the Rancho San Joaquin o Rosa Morada in San Benito County.

By his marriage in 1864 to Agnes Bowie of San Juan Bautista, J. P. Sargent had five children: two sons, Ross, who died while still a youth as a result of an accident, and James, who lived in Gilroy until the 1930s. The three daughters were Agnes, who never married, Ouida, who married a Fenwick, and Ida Sargent Blanding, who lived until 1956. At that time, the Scovels said, the estate passed on to the late Ed Rea who was the family attorney as well as a partner in some of the businesses (his heirs live in San Jose) and to Robin Anderson of Santa Cruz, a stepson of Ida. Frances said that although the Sargent sisters were the jet-setters of their time, having lived in New York and in Europe, after attending private schools in San Francisco, and were wealthy and very attractive, they came back to the ranch to spend their last years in this house.

At that time the Scovels were living in another house on the ranch. Frances said the sisters were gracious and charming and would stop by to see her every day. Ida, the last to die, had a summer house

James P. Sargent, owner of Juristac Ranch, always known as the Sargent Ranch. He was one of the Sargent brothers who came to California during the Gold Rush and became large property owners and prominent cattlemen.

One of the old workers' cabins on the Sargent Ranch.

Bradley Sargent, oldest of the Sargent brothers, who came to California in 1849 from New Hampshire.

The German adobe on Juristac Ranch. Antonio and Faustino German received the original Mexican grant in 1835.

Rea-Sargent party in camp on Sargent Ranch.

Sargent's Station. When the Southern Pacific line was put through in 1869 it ended here. A Mr. and Mrs. Stewart were in charge for years.

150

at Downieville, a ranch at Walnut Creek, and a winter house at Palm Springs.

On a wall in the living room was a picture taken in the 1880s of the original home built by the Sargents, with Mrs. Sargent, her sister, and three daughters on the porch. The house is of classic style architecture with dormer windows. The Sargent girls thought it was much prettier than the one they built later, which is rather square in shape. Another photograph shows the ranch house surrounded by a cluster of buildings, corrals and bunkhouses, with the old Monterey Road next to the house. Although these buildings have been torn down, through the kitchen window can be seen an umbrella-shaped oak tree that is in the picture.

George Scovel said that he has been ranching most of his life and that he had cut his teeth in the cattle business by helping the legendary Charlie Maggini break colts on the Easten Ranch. He had worked on the Sargent Ranch before he started leasing it. He said that the road leading back to the main house used to be the old Monterey Road and that the feed lots at the entrance are part of the Bloomfield Ranch of Joe Kerley, which borders the Sargent Ranch. It formerly belonged to Henry Miller.

Between the rolling hills covered with oak are Sycamore Creek and Tar Creek, where not only sycamore, cottonwood and willow trees grow, but a strange phenomenon can be seen—tar seeping up through the ground. Scovel said the only other place he knows where this happens is the La Brea Tar Pits in Los Angeles. Nearby are the remnants of capped oil and gas wells and the abandoned houses where the workers once lived when this was a going operation. These tar springs covered an area of 60 acres, and there were thousands of tons of asphalt in the vicinity of the main springs. Located about a mile from the railroad station by wagon road was a well that had been bored 700 feet in 1886. At this point the machinery broke and the well was abandoned. The remains of calves were found in several of the springs because they were unfenced, but as an early-day writer wrote, "What is a calf or two to a man who owns so many cattle he cannot himself tell except at the time of the annual rodeo when they are rounded up, branded, marked and counted?" The brea or asphaltum was shipped from Sargent's Station to San Jose for street paving.

Off the master bedroom upstairs in the old Sargent house is a sun porch. From here Frances Scovel pointed out the original location of this house near the overpass of Highway 101. It was

Frances Scovel in front of the Sargent house which she and her husband George, occupy on the ranch.

George Scovel, lessee of Juristac Ranch, known as the Sargent Ranch. The Old Monterey Highway used to run next to the house.

moved up on the hill in 1936. She also indicated where Sargent's Station was created when the railroad came through to this point in 1869. She said it was quite a recreational area, that people used to come from all over to swim in the creek and picnic in the early days.

Sargent's Station

As described in *Sunshine, Fruit and Flowers,* published in 1895 by the *San Jose Mercury,* "Sargent's is most beautifully located in a grove of oaks, upon the banks of the softly-flowing Pajaro." Continuing, the account told of the bank of the river covered with alders and willows, of the hotel surrounded by ornamental trees, and grounds

Cottages at Sargent's Station.

The Pajaro River, which divides Santa Clara and San Benito Counties. This was often the scene of boating parties, fishing and picnics.

provided with platforms and rural seats making it a popular picnic resort. The bridge spanning the river at Sargent's was the only bridge for miles. The river, overhanging with trees, could be navigated with rowboats a distance of two miles below the station. It was fed by Carnadero Creek (through Miller's Ranch), San Benito, Uvas, and Llagas Creeks, and emptied into the ocean.

Sargent's was described as a popular picnic resort with "merry parties" in the summer season. According to Celine Carrey of Gilroy, who was born at Sargent's Station in 1895, some of the parties were indeed quite merry and maybe a bit naughty for those times. She said there was a saloon and, to the right before you come to the bridge, an open air dance floor with torches on sticks all around it—that the cowboys used to dance all night with the girls who were brought down from San Francisco by train.

"Our house was on the other side of the bridge by a clump of trees. For the men, usually 12 or 14 milkers, they had a dormitory. My mother used to cook for all the workmen."

Celine's parents were Basque from the French side. Her father, Albert Carrey, made cheese. In 1880 J. P. Sargent wanted his son, James, who was considered a sort of a playboy, to do something constructive, and asked Albert Carrey to go into the cheese business with him. They had 40 or 50 cows (at times as many as 200). Celine said:

Father made huge wheels of cheese. To test it he would insert a gadget about the size of your pen, but hollow, and bring out a piece to taste. He could tell if it was aged or not. When it was ready they would ship the cheese by train to Goldberg and Bowen in San Francisco who, in turn, shipped back staples such as sugar, salt, and macaroni in 50-pound boxes. In back of the dance hall the stationmaster and his wife had a nice little place. The farmers would come with their flatbed trucks and horses to bring their produce or pick up a delivery.

May Day was always a big day at Sargent's, according to another Gilroy resident, Armand White. Hundreds of people came by train in their horse and buggies from Gilroy. "I was too young to go," Armand said, "but I remember my older sisters telling how much fun they were."

Yet another view of Sargent's Station was given by Mark Regan, who transported San Juan residents to the station to meet the trains:

Those were the days when an unregenerated railroad ran Sunday excursions from San Francisco to Sargent's. There were two bars at the clubhouse in the grove near the station and when the excursionists reached a certain stage they were carried in a box car on the siding and piled up like cordwood until it was time for the train to return. Today the old clubhouse is the center of an auto camp, where God-fearing people in Fords camp overnight and buy gasoline and lemon pop at the store.

CHAPTER XXIX
Æ Rancho San Ysidro

With El Camino Real running practically by its front door, Rancho San Ysidro of Don Ygnacio Ortega offered hospitality to many a weary wayfarer passing through in the early years of the 1800s. The oldest of the Spanish land grants in Southern Santa Clara County or Monterey County, it was located on the site of what is now called "Old Gilroy," three miles east of present-day Gilroy. Although most historians place the date of the San Ysidro grant around 1808 or 1809, according to research by J. Vincent Gallagher of Smartville, California, whose great-grandmother was Ygnacio's daughter, Maria Raimunda, Ygnacio was at San Ysidro by 1795, before the founding of Mission San Juan Bautista. One of his daughters was baptized at the mission in 1797, and Maria Merced de Ortega, who married Jose Antonio Castro, was born in San Juan Bautista in 1799.

Don Ygnacio was the son of Jose Francisco de Ortega, who came to California in 1769 as scout for the Gaspar Portola expedition and later led the first colony of settlers to San Diego in 1774. Jose Francisco is credited with discovering the Golden Gate. In fact, Fray Junipero Serra, presidente of the missions, wanted him appointed Military Commandante of Alta California. As a reward for his work, Jose Francisco Ortega received in 1795 the grant Nuestra Senora del Refugio near Santa Barbara which ran along the coast for 25 miles. Don Ygnacio is said to have left Santa Barbara with his family because of the menace of buccaneers along the coast. Although not named, Ortega's "son" was listed by Bancroft as receiving his grant a year or two later. This would be Ygnacio, in Gallagher's opinion, and he believes it indicates that Ygnacio received San Ysidro in 1796 or 1797, as it was the only other grant made at that time.

Don Ygnacio's adobe house was located a few hundred yards west of the present San Ysidro School. In the middle 1820s a frame addition was made to this house, probably by his friend, the Scotch carpenter named John Martin, who later married his granddaughter, Maria Basilisa Encarnacion Bernal y Ortega. In the list of his possessions at the time of his death in 1829 is a "frame" house so it may have been the first in California. Also listed was the soap kettle into which some elk and grizzly bears from the ranch found their way, as well as cattle. He raised some tobacco—a forerunner of J. D. Culp, who later had a successful tobacco plantation in this same area. This apparently had no connection with the concoction of wild tobacco and other plants which the Indians would take and which made them very drunk.

In addition to running his rancho, Ygnacio was the father of a large family by his wife, Maria Gertrudis de Arce; was the *mayordomo* of Mission San Carlos (Carmel), 1805–06, and a judge until his death. Among his other activities he discovered the first silver mine in California in 1802.

His friend, John Martin, seemed to live two lives successfully. He first married a Cantua girl who lived on the San Ysidro, in 1826 at San Carlos. In 1835 he married Maria Basilisa Encarnacion Bernal y Ortega, daughter of Maria Raimunda Ortega de Bernal and granddaughter of Ygnacio, at San Jose. He then continued to live with both wives, with the first wife in Marin County, where he was the grantee of Corte Madera de Novato, and Santa Clara County with Basilisa, grantee of the Embarcadero de Santa Clara (now the site of Alviso).

J. Vincent Gallagher said that a cousin told him that when the family would go to Monterey to spend the summer with the Castro and Soberanes families, they would stop over at San Ysidro—and this would be the occasion for the usual fiesta with music and dancing. The women and children would

Catarino Gilroy, son of John Gilroy and Maria Clara Ortega Gilroy, born at Rancho San Ysidro in 1840.

Jose Quintin de Ortega y Arce with two of his daughters, Magdalena and Arabia Lucrecia. Jose Quintin was granted one square league of his father's Rancho San Ysidro by Mexico.

Left: Eliseo Gilroy, son of John Gilroy.

Above: Soledad Ortega, an Indian girl who was raised by Jose Ortega, son of Quintin Ortega. Soledad had a prepossessing personality and is remembered by her grandchildren as being strict.

Descendants of John Gilroy at Gilroy family picnic in Christmas Tree Park, Benny Gilroy, George Gilroy, and Ernest Salazar.

travel by carreta and the men by horseback. As has been noted by all the early California visitors, the men were always on horseback—they never walked. One of the men, probably an Indian, would walk along with a container filled with tallow to apply to the squeaky carreta axles.

After Don Ygnacio's death, three of his children, Jose Quintin, Maria Clara and Ysabel, received grants from Mexico of one league each from the San Ysidro. Maria Clara and her husband, John Gilroy, had their adobe at the "Y" on the Pacheco Pass and Frazier Lake Roads. Jose Quintin's was across the road about 50 yards away. Ysabel, who married Julian Cantua, sold their part of the ranch in the northern section to Bernard Murphy, son of Martin Murphy. He renamed it La Polka. A little community called San Ysidro, now known as Old Gilroy, grew up around the ranch. An 1833 census of San Ysidro shows 16 families living there with a total of 115 persons.

The resident of San Ysidro remembered best is the Scotsman, John Gilroy, for whom the town was named. Born John Cameron at Inverness-shire, North Scotland in 1794, of a distinguished clan, he ran off to sea when still a boy. Arriving at the port of Monterey in 1813 on the *Isaac Todd*, sick with the scurvy and having had an altercation with his superior officer, he jumped ship with one of his mates known only as Deaf Jimmy. Taking his mother's name, Gilroy, he was baptized Juan Bautista Gilroy at the Carmel Mission and given permission by the Viceroy at Mexico City to remain in California permanently and to marry.

John Gilroy and Deaf Jimmy walked to Mission San Juan Bautista and then on to San Ysidro. Deaf Jimmy continued on north, but Gilroy stayed to become the first non-Hispanic citizen of Santa Clara County. He rented a little land from Ygnacio Ortega and bought a few cows, and with hard work he prospered. In 1821 Gilroy was married to Don Ygnacio's daughter, Maria Clara Ortega, at Mission San Juan Bautista. Of the 17 children born to the couple, nine survived. Described as six-feet tall, a well-built and intelligent Scotsman, Gilroy served many years as alcalde of San Ysidro by appointment of Commodore Stockton and was appointed *juez de paz* (justice of the peace) by H. C. Smith in 1851.

In 1824 Gilroy was asked to join Captain Arguello on an expedition up the Columbia River as interpreter because of the many American trappers, and during the Mexican War he was sent by General Castro to Gabilan Peak to deliver a mes-

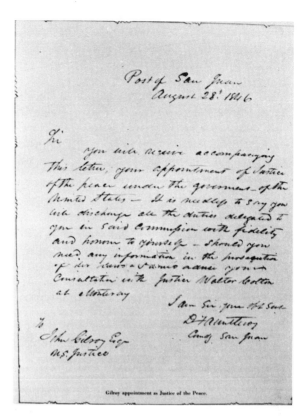

Letter to John Gilroy notifying him of his appointment as Justice of the Peace. The letter is dated August 28, 1846, and suggests consultation with Walter Colton, justice at Monterey, if necessary.

sage to Fremont, only to find his camp deserted. The Americans had already retreated. In 1855 Gilroy received a letter from his brother, Alexander Cameron. He told of having written before and of receiving no answer, and said that all the rest of the family were gone. This letter is in the Bancroft Library.

There have been many references to Gilroy's gambling away a "princely estate." A gambler he was, but the one square league (4,460 acres) which he and Maria Clara received could hardly be called princely at the time when grants of eleven square leagues were not uncommon. There was also the severe drought of 1864—whatever land he had left at that time he would not have been able to keep.

In Monterey County in the 1860s there was a man named John Swan who called himself the "Pioneer of 1843." From time to time he wrote letters to the newspapers about his reminiscences. When he read of John Gilroy's death, he was prompted to write a letter to the *Monterey Democrat* describing San Ysidro. He said that it was a lively village in the early days and as was the common custom, relatives would spend a week or a fortnight at each other's houses. He wrote:

I have seen a bullock killed at Gilroy's in the morning and nothing left of the meat for supper the next day; for in addition to his wife's relations from other parts of the country over forty in number, his own family and the Indians were numerous. The women would be at work on their knees from daylight until ten o'clock making tortillas for breakfast for such a crowd. Certainly the women of Upper California in early days were entitled to do less penance in church after doing so much on their knees while making tortillas.

He also told of the fandango-dancing and card playing:

One Sunday afternoon I went out from the village for a walk with Gilroy and his brother-in-law Cantin [Quintin] Ortega, but no sooner had they got a short distance from the houses when down went the serapes on the ground, out came the cards and they commenced playing monte for money.

In writing of Gilroy's wife, Dona Maria Clara, Swan said that she must have been beautiful when a young girl. He wrote, "She was a fine looking woman when I saw her first in 1846, with beautiful eyes which when young must have been jewels of the first water."

He also wrote about the wheat grown on the San Ysidro Ranch and surrounding area. He said that Gilroy had a grist mill propelled by mule power. "The grain was trodden out on the ground by horses, after which it had to be washed and dried before it could be ground."

In his final years Gilroy received help from the British Benevolent Society, and he died in 1869 with what he had when he arrived at Monterey some 50 years earlier—nothing.

Gilroy's descendants are many and a hundred or so of them gather every year at Christmas Tree Park in Gilroy to pay tribute to their ancestor. Most of them seem to be descendants of Gilroy's son Catarino, who was born on the ranch in 1840 and died in 1911. He married Soledad Ortega, an Indian girl who had been raised by Jose Ortega, son of Quintin and Maria Ignacia Ortega. According to the stories told by her grandchildren, she was a colorful personality. Although they all knew she was pure-blooded Indian, she would never admit it. "She and my mother used to roll their own cigarettes from a box of Bull Durham tobacco," said Sarah Jensen of San Jose, adding that Soledad used to smoke cigars and sometimes a pipe, too.

Telling of the parties they used to have at her house in Old Gilroy, George Gilroy said they would sometimes roast a young pig in the ground overnight, that his father Eliseo played the guitar,

Alfred the violin, and a cousin the cedar box. "Everyone would sing and dance and sometimes the party would go on for three days," he added.

Ernest Salazar of Hollister particularly remembered how strict Soledad was, that she had a buggy whip she would use if they didn't do what she said. Salazar said his grandmother was very angry when his mother, Macrima, married Frank Salazar, who was 30 or 40 years her senior. He was deputy sheriff of Santa Clara County in 1906, had been a vaquero, and during his career drove a Wells Fargo stagecoach.

When asked about the stories that his father had known the famous bandit, Tiburcio Vasquez, Ernie said, "I don't know if he ever rode with Vasquez, but he used to speak of him quite a lot."

Also attending the picnic were the Bill Aceves family of San Jose, descendants of Nicodemus Gilroy, eldest son of John Gilroy. Three generations of John Gilroys were on hand, the eldest of which was a grandson of Catarino and Soledad. Only one family of Gilroys (or Ortegas for that matter) is still living on the original San Ysidro land—Ben Gilroy, Jr. and his family.

△ La Polka

Maria Ysabel Ortega, who married Julian Cantua, sold her portion of San Ysidro, later called "La Polka," to Bernard Murphy in 1849. It consisted of one league. Murphy had crossed the plains with his father, Martin Murphy, and family, in 1844 as part of the first wagon train to cross the Sierras. The family settled on the Rancho Ojo de Agua de la Coche some 20 miles south of San Jose, where Martin built an adobe home. He later extended his holdings to 40,000 acres.

In 1851 he sent Bernard back to Frampton near Quebec, where they had lived after leaving Ireland, to bring his sister, Johanna, to California. He brought back not only his sister but also a bride—while in Frampton, Bernard married Catherine O'Toole, also of County Wexford. They came by way of the Isthmus of Panama and moved into the pre-fabricated tin house which had been shipped around the Horn in 1844 and assembled on his La Polka rancho, where he started farming and ranching. A piece of the tin from the house is in the Gilroy Museum.

In 1853 Bernard was on the *Jenny Lind*, a little side-wheel steamboat that plied the waters from San Francisco to Alviso, when the boilers exploded, and he, along with 30 others, was killed.

Martin Murphy, according to Gilroy historian Armand White, whose grandmother was a sister of Catherine O'Toole Murphy, wanted to take over the running of Rancho La Polka and Catherine's business affairs. In those days, he said, women were supposed to be seen and not heard, but Catherine put her foot down. She said that she could handle her own business, and she did. Tragedy was to strike again for Catherine when her only son, Martin J. C. Murphy, was stricken with a fever and died while away at school at Georgetown. There was a tremendous funeral for young Martin. Yet another sad incident was to occur when the train bearing mourners from San Francisco was passing under the tunnel at Coyote and crashed head-on with a train heading north. Someone had made a wrong signal. Fortunately no one was killed, but Michael Cullen, a nephew of Catherine, was injured and spent the rest of his life in a wheelchair.

Catherine O'Toole Murphy was to become a large landowner and a wealthy woman. Not only did she inherit her son's share of Martin Murphy's estate, including Rancho La Polka and parts of La Coche, Las Uvas and Las Llagas ranchos, but in 1862 she married James Dunne, who owned the San Felipe or Dunne Ranch and a part of the Topo Ranch. Dunne died in 1874, 12 years after their marriage. Three children were born to the couple: Peter Dunne; Mary Phileta, who married Joseph Rucker of the Rucker area; and Bridget Catherine, who became the wife of R. W. Hersey.

In the *San Jose Mercury*'s 1895 edition of *Sunshine, Fruit and Flowers,* there is a story on progress in the valley. It tells of the "great Catherine Dunne Ranch of 18,000 acres" being sold in lots of five, ten, twenty and forty acres "by Burbank and Devendorf of San Jose. Prices range from $25 to $125 per acre."

Catherine's sister, Johanna, and her husband, Thomas Cullen, both natives of County Wexford, who came to Santa Clara County by way of Frampton, Canada, farmed La Polka starting in 1868. Thomas died in 1895 and Johanna in 1904, at which time William, youngest of their 12 children took over. According to Rev. Leo Cullen, S.J., his father, William Cullen, ran the ranch until 1907, when he was married. Father Cullen said James Murphy was next to take over. He was followed by Catherine Dunne's daughter, Bridget Catherine, and her husband, Ralph Hersey. La Polka is now owned by Lawrence Abruzzini, who bought it in the 1940s.

Catherine Dunne always said she would live to be a hundred. She didn't quite make it. She passed away in 1925 at the age of 97, in the Santa Barbara home of her daughter, Catherine Hersey.

Mathew Fellom

One of the early settlers at San Ysidro was Mathew Fellom, a Dane born in 1801 who, having decided on a seafaring career, shipped out on a merchant vessel. Arriving on the California coast in the 1830s he apparently decided it was the place for him because he left ship at Sonoma and set off by foot. Reaching the Santa Clara Valley, he continued down to San Ysidro where he found employment as a soapmaker for John Gilroy.

With his energy and skill as a soapmaker, he accumulated a little money and bought some acreage on the San Ysidro Ranch east of the Llagas Creek running to the foothills. He also acquired a wife, a California girl named Manuela Briones, of Santa Clara County. Later his sons, Semfriano and John, also bought parcels of the San Ysidro. His daughter, Adele, married a Martin and lived in San Juan Bautista. The Felloms prospered—Mathew was known for years as the most extensive stock raiser in the area, and in 1861 they built a beautiful place on the Leavesly Road. Apparently they enjoyed living, as their everyday life was described as a continuation of the wedding feast, with the traditional California fiestas—feasting, dancing, horse races and horse events that went on for two days. After the American occupation Mathew Fellom was appointed *alcalde* of San Juan.

One of his sons, Semfriano, who was sent to Santa Clara College, was said to have a striking personality and an adventurous life. Handsome and educated, he is said to have had no trouble establishing himself as a dashing cavalier and beau brummel, as he appeared at dances in Gilroy wearing a Prince Albert coat. He had the Californian's talent for horsemanship and the finest horses with which to display it. "His Satanic Majesty," as he was called by his friends, would think nothing of riding into a saloon on his black steed, ordering drinks for the house, and riding out with a few shots in the air from his revolver. If light fixtures or glasses were shattered, he always footed the bills.

He had many women and many adventures—women were attracted to him, and he was attracted to adventure. He went to Southern California and then into Mexico where he was hired by the Mexican government. After wandering in Texas for a while (Guinn's *Biographies of Santa*

John Fellom, his wife, Blandina, and Willam, who had just returned home from World War I. William ranched on the San Ysidro until two years ago.

Blandina Ortega.

Catherine Dunne, whose husband, Bernard Murphy, purchased Maria Ysabel Ortega's portion of Rancho San Ysidro and renamed it La Polka in 1849.

John Fellom Ranch on Leavesly Road just before the turn to Gilroy Hot Springs. Note the old-fashioned feed bins.

158

Clara County lists him as being in El Paso, Texas in 1904), he returned to California and married a cousin. From this marriage there were three sons, State Senator Roy Fellom of San Francisco, Landon, and James Fellom of San Jose, the latter a writer. Like their father, the boys were educated at Santa Clara College. Semfriano later married again in Mexico and had three more sons by his second wife: Roger, an attorney in Washington, D.C.; Mario, who is in Louisiana; and William, who is said to be in Los Angeles.

On a trip to Baja California (a mining boom trip to Sierra Pintada), Semfriano was believed to have perished. The mystery of his death has never been solved.

His older brother, John, born in 1840 at San Ysidro on their parents' ranch, was a quiet, highly respected rancher who was a knowledgable stock raiser. Unlike Semifriano, John received no formal education. According to his son, William, he could barely sign his name. In 1874 he married Blandina Ortega, great-granddaughter of Don Ygnacio Ortega, who received the original Spanish grant for Rancho San Ysidro. The house they built on Leavesly Road is still standing. Of their large family only two children survive: Lauretta Fellom Jones of Gilroy, and William Fellom, who until two years ago lived on a part of the Fellom ranch facing Crews Road, where he had orchards and vineyards. Now a resident of Gilroy, he was the last of the Felloms to live on the family ranch, and probably the last of the Ortegas to live on the San Ysidro, with the exception of Ben Gilroy, Jr. and his family.

Julius Martin

The first American to settle at San Ysidro was Julius Martin. When a courier named Charles Bennett from Sutter's Fort stopped at Rancho San Ysidro on his way to Monterey with the news of the discovery of gold, Martin was among the first of the local residents to drop everything and head for the gold fields. He had come to San Ysidro in 1843 after crossing by wagon train from Missouri with his wife and daughters. In the war with Mexico he was a Captain of the American scouts under Fremont and was at Sonoma when the Bear Flag was raised.

Julius Martin returned to San Ysidro with enough gold dust to purchase 1,220 acres of Rancho San Ysidro from John Gilroy. He built a flour mill and became a cattleman. One of the three homes that he built on the property still stands

Ranch buildings at old Horace Willson home on Pacheco Pass.

beside Freeway 101 in the vicinity of Leavesly Road, now looking sad and neglected.

Horace Willson

An 1853 arrival in San Ysidro was Horace Willson, with his wife, Eunice Eliza, and his mother, Levina Willson. They had come from Swansey, New Hampshire by way of the Isthmus of Panama. Horace lost no time in buying land. In his account book, which also served as a diary and is now in the possession of his brother Albert's great-grandson, George White, he told of buying 42 acres from John Gilroy in 1855. The house he built in 1859, in the sturdy New England tradition, is still standing, hidden from Pacheco Pass by tall trees, but in good condition. The present owners are the Robert A. Dunn family.

Horace Willson's diary is almost a history of the little community which was renamed "Old Gilroy" after the town of Gilroy was founded. One notation in it tells of his making brick for his house in a kiln on the property. Also recorded is the hauling of the first lumber from Bodfish in the Santa Cruz Mountains. Another item indicates that he held a mortgage on John Gilroy's rancho, and among the names of those paying poll tax (which he collected) was Hanna. The Walter Hanna family of Gilroy are descendants of this pioneer family.

Horace Willson continued to buy land in the hilly area above George Milias' ranch until he had accumulated 20,000 acres. Almost 3,000 acres of this ranch are still owned by his great-granddaughters, Hazel Jones and Eddys Thomas, who until recently ran cattle on it. The house on the Pacheco Pass in which the sisters were raised, built by their grandfather, Edwin Willson (son of Horace), is still in excellent condition and well-kept by its present owners, the Anthony Schmidts.

Until a few years ago the brick house that Horace

159

The house Horace Willson built in 1859 of bricks made on the property and lumber hauled from Bodfish.

Horace Willson, who came to California in 1852 from New Hampshire and started buying property, eventually owning 20,000 acres, mostly in the hills above George Milias' ranch.

Old Gilroy, a little community that grew up on the San Ysidro Ranch.

Below: View of Pacheco Pass from behind and above Willson house.

Willson had built remained in his family. His son, Lyman, died shortly after purchasing the house in 1915, but his widow, Nettie, stayed on for many years. The next owner was a niece, Leola, and her husband, Dr. Harry Brownell.

Close by was the site of Quintin Ortega's adobe, which was 50 yards or less from that of John Gilroy. This particular piece of the ranch is now owned by George White, who was born less than a half mile away on Frazier Lake Road, which shoots off from the Pacheco Pass Road. In working the ground for planting, George has uncovered many pieces of old dishes and household articles that belonged to the Ortega family. For a time Willson leased some land across the highway where Julius Martin had had his flour mill. It had long been planted in prunes and when he uprooted the trees to prepare for planting, he discovered two millstones that had been used in Martin's mill.

CHAPTER XXX

Gilroy

Pleasant Valley was the original name for what is now the city of Gilroy when it was but a stagecoach stop on the route between San Jose and Monterey. In 1850 a man named James Houck built a roadside inn and stable and even though he could neither read nor write, in 1851 he became the first postmaster. In front of his inn he placed a cigar box on a post to handle incoming and outgoing mail.

Although there seemed to be a gradual movement westward from the little village of San Ysidro in the 1850s and '60s, it was not until the railroad came in 1869 that the town named for John Gilroy, picturesquely set in the valley between the Coast Range on the east and the Santa Cruz Mountains rising up in the west, began to move forward. Lots were laid out and sold by the firm of Zuck, Rogers and Hoover. Zuck was the town's first lawyer and Rogers the town's first dentist. San Ysidro, which had grown up around the Ortega Rancho, following the pattern for so many of the early-day communities, is now known as Old Gilroy.

Massey Thomas

Although there are no members of the family living on the Old Homestead, as the family place on Thomas Lane southwest of Gilroy was always called, and the land has been pared down to a minimal amount compared to the original holding of Massey Thomas, it is still owned by the Thomas family.

With visions of gold dancing through his head, Thomas came to California with a wagon train. After a year or two of working in the Mother Lode country, however, he decided that farming was what he knew best and what he wanted to do after all. Consequently, he returned to Missouri, organized a party, and in 1851 drove 300 head of cattle to Gilroy—the first such drive. He settled on

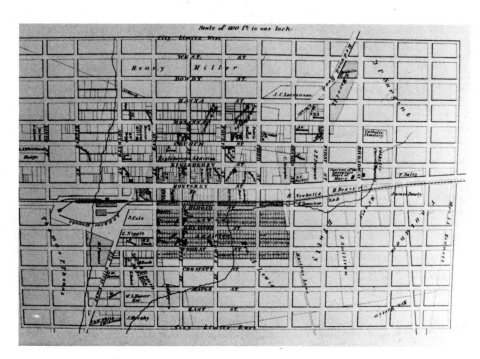

Early map of city of Gilroy.

161

Whitehurst and Hodges lumber mill in mountains adjoining Mount Madonna.

Charles Sanders homesteaded land outside Gilroy in the 1850s. In 1870 he built a resort and also farmed.

Charles Sanders house at Redwood Retreat, now the summer home of his grandson, Charles Pond.

Left to right: Mrs. Irville Sanders; her baby, Leslie, in carriage; Irville Sanders; Charles E. Sanders, who homesteaded the property; Annis Sanders, mother of Charles Pond, who now owns Redwood Retreat; Mrs. Charles E. Sanders; Mrs. Wilburn Sanders; and Wilburn Sanders. Picture taken beside the old tank house in the grove at Redwood Retreat.

GILROY and LOS ANGELES.
COAST STAGE LINE.

W. G. Roberts, Agent, office 208 Montgomery street, San Francisco.
General Agent, W. Buckley, San Jose, California.
Local Agents: Jos. Knowlton, Jr., Gilroy; Wm. Balch, San Juan; Chris. Hamel, Natividad; L. C. Boctick, Plato Ranch; Chas. Knowlton, Paso Robles Springs; J. C. Ortega, San Luis Obispo; Eli Rundell, Santa Barbara; J. Woolfson, San Buenaventura; Geo. M. Fall, Los Angeles.
Stage leaves Gilroy daily at 12 M. Stage leaves Los Angeles daily at 6 A. M.

From Gilroy To Los Angeles.			TOWNS	See	From Los Angeles To Gilroy.		
Fare.	Hours	Miles	May 18th, 1871.	Page.	Miles.	Hours	Fare.
0.00	0	0	Dep.........Gilroy.........Arr.	161	366	58	
1.50	2	12	.............San Juan.............		354		
2.50	4	24	...........Natividad...........		342		
4.00	6	38	...........Uttz Station...........		328		
5.50	8	52	........Salinas River........		314		
8.50	11	76	.........Last Chance.........		290		
9.00	13	92	.........San Antonio.........		274		
2.00	15	107	........Plato Ranch........		259		
4.00	17	121	..........Nacimento..........		245		
5.00	19	136	...Paso Robles Hot Springs......		230		
6.00	22	150	.......San Margarita.......		216		
6.00	25	164	......San Luis Obispo......	174	202	36	
7.50	28	180	.......Arroyo Grande.......		186		
7.50	31	196	.........Zury Station.........		170		
7.50	33	214	............Foxens............		152		
7.50	35	228	...........Ballard's...........		138		
7.50	37	243	.........San Marcus.........		123		
7.20	40	257	.........McCaffey's.........		109		
7.50	41	265	......Santa Barbara......	174	101	15	
8.00	44	280	............Rincon............		86		
8.00	47	293	......San Buenaventura......		73	11	
0.00	49	306	.......Santa Clara Valley.......		60		
0.00	51	320	.............Sime.............		46		
0.00	53	333	.......Mountain Station.......		33	5	
0.00	56	350	............El Cino............		16	2	
0.00	58	366	Arr.........Los Angeles.....Dep.	164	0	0	

Connections.
At Gilroy, connects with cars of S. F. & S. J. R. R. for San Francisco.
At San Juan, connects with stages for Watsonville and Santa Cruz, New Idria, Castroville, Salinas City, and Monterey.
At San Luis Obispo, connects with stage for San Simeon.
At Los Angeles, connects with stages for San Diego, Fort Yuma and Tucson, San Bernardino, La Paz and Clear Creek.

Schedule for Coast Line Stage between Gilroy and Los Angeles. It connected with trains for San Francisco.

162

Massey Thomas. He drove 300 head of cattle to Gilroy in 1851, settled on a squatter's claim, and later added additional land.

a squatter's claim of 475 acres, which he subsequently purchased, along with 900 additional acres. Besides breeding prize cattle, he became a prominent orchardist and a substantial citizen.

His son, Massey Thomas, Jr., who also came overland, settled first in the Panoche Valley of San Benito County where he raised sheep. Hugo Horlein, whose sister was married to Judge Leon Thomas, said that a favorite story in the family was about a bear getting into the sheep on that ranch. The younger Massey eventually moved to Gilroy.

One of the sons of Massey Thomas, Jr., Leon Thomas, was a foreman for Henry Miller at the Bloomfield ranch. After Miller's death Massey Thomas assisted Miller's son-in-law, Leroy Nickel, in dividing up the land and selling it in small parcels. He later served for many years as a municipal judge. After Judge Thomas's death ten years ago his widow, Hazel Thomas, stayed at the Old Homestead a year or two and then moved to Ventura to be with her daughter, Phyllis Gormley. Another daughter, Jewell DeWitt, lives in the Sierras.

James Thomas, son of Charles Edward Thomas, who came to Gilroy about the same time as his brother, Massey, bought the beautiful 475-acre Glenn Ranch from Miller and Lux in the early 1920s, according to his son, Jack Thomas of Gilroy. He also managed the Mount Madonna estate for the Nickels. During the depression he lost the Glenn Ranch, but managed it for Miller and Lux heirs. Another son of James Thomas lives in Gilroy, and a daughter, Peggy Thomas Lytle, in San Jose.

The Redwood Retreat

Nine miles out of Gilroy, at the base of the Santa Cruz Mountains, is a wooded piece of property homesteaded by Charles E. Sanders in the 1850s. It borders Rancho El Solis, one of the early Mexican land grants, and close by is Mount Madonna where Henry Miller had his summer home. Along Arthur Creek, which runs through the property, Sanders had a thriving summer resort called Redwood Retreat. In those days families would come down from San Francisco with their trunks to spend the summer. One of the Sanders would meet them with the wagon at the train in Gilroy. The visitors were housed in primitive little cabins with kerosene lamps or candles, water pitchers and bowls. Many of these buildings are still standing.

Charles Pond, grandson of Charles Sanders, now owns the property, and he and his wife Elsie have redecorated Charles Sanders' original house by the creek. There are two 100-year-old fig trees between the house and the lodge that replaced the original 20-room hotel which burned in 1908. Meals were served there to 60 or more people. Pond said his grandfather didn't move down to the property until 1870. A native of Nova Scotia, he had come to California by way of the Isthmus and headed straight for the gold fields. He returned to his home in 1861 to marry Annis Hilton, but was soon back in California digging for gold. His wife joined him a year or two later. In her diary was a touching story of her trip by way of the Isthmus and of her dismay when no one met her in San Francisco. She told of going to the wharf every day. Finally her husband arrived—he had overestimated the date of arrival of the ship. Their trip by stage to Susanville, where they were to make their first home, was long and arduous. Their son Wilburn was born in Susanville, and Jamesville was the birthplace of a second son, Irville, who later ran the Redwood Retreat with his wife and six children.

Eventually, reluctantly acknowledging that he was unable to make a living from the mines and that his wife's health was declining from this hard life, Sanders moved his family to his homestead land. A daughter named Annis, for her mother, was born in the little house in 1870. Charles Pond told a sad story:

My grandmother died in childbirth, and Grandfather, not knowing how to care for a newborn babe, wrapped her up and took her by horseback to his friend Henry Miller's place on Mount Madonna. The Indian women wet-nursed my mother until she was big enough to be taken back to the ranch and to have someone take care of her.

163

Cabin of Frank Norris in Murphy's Canyon. He was not able to enjoy it for long because of his sudden death in 1902.

Vanumanutangi, which means "Vale of the Singing Birds," was built by Mrs. Robert Louis Stevenson in Murphy's Canyon, adjoining Redwood Retreat.

Charles Sanders, who gave up digging for gold to settle down on homestead property outside Gilroy. He also developed Redwood Retreat resort.

Gazebo at Gilroy Hot Springs. This picture was taken in 1892, at the peak of its popularity.

Below, Albert Allemand, who lived in Gilroy for 94 of his 96 years.

George Milias, a native of Gilroy. The Milias Hotel in Gilroy was long a landmark. Milias is a former city councilman and mayor of Gilroy.

His grandmother, Annis Sanders, was buried in the little family cemetery on a knoll under a grove of oak trees.

Charles told an ironic story about his grandfather. He said he had chosen this particular piece of hilly land with the creek running through in preference to another piece of land, which would have been much more suitable for agriculture, because, in truth, he had never recovered from the gold fever, even though he stayed at Redwood Retreat the rest of his life. "One time, after his death, one of the Chinese cooks found a gold nugget in a chicken's craw while cleaning the chickens for Sunday dinner," Charles said, adding, "Of course, it didn't take long for word to get down to Gilroy and we were beset by men from town with their picks and shovels."

Fannie Vandegrift Osborne Stevenson

Mrs. Robert Louis Stevenson became a neighbor of the Sanders in Murphy Canyon in the early nineties. She bought the property from a nephew of Charles Sanders and built a house in a setting of bay, sycamore, madrone and oak trees. Fannie Stevenson hoped to bring her husband there. There was much that reminded her of Samoa—the tranquility, the rich greenery, the trickling brook and the many birds. The poetic name she chose for her place was "Vanumanutagi," which means "Vale of the the Singing Birds." Unfortunately Stevenson was never to see it. He died in 1894.

The present house, owned by Leonard Ware and John Bartlett of Palo Alto, is a two-story New England colonial, remodeled by Fannie's son, Lloyd Osborne and his wife, the former Ethel Head of Gilroy, who had been Fannie Stevenson's nurse. They moved into the house after her death in 1914. Osborne and Ethel had a house in Paris and brought their butler from Paris to Vanumanutagi. Osborne was also a writer and drafted the map for *Treasure Island.* His sister, Isobel Osborne, who was married to Edward Salisbury Field, also a well-known writer, would frequently come to spend weekends.

Yet another member of the literati was to move up Murphy's Canyon—the noted Frank Norris, a friend of Fannie Stevenson. Fannie gave him 20 acres on which he built a log cabin. He had big plans for novels he hoped to write there, including *The Wolfe,* which would complete the trilogy of *The Octopus* and *The Pit.* All of his plans came to an abrupt end when he died suddenly in 1902 in San Francisco at the age of 32. The cabin was designated a national landmark in 1963. A monument believed to have been built and inscribed by Fannie Stevenson reads: "Frank Norris— 1870-1902 — Simpleness and Gentleness and Humor and Clean Mirth."

Albert Allemand

Albert Allemand died on August 2, 1976, and there is no one who remembers Gilroy as he did. He spent all but two of his 96 years in this town and his memory was sharp until almost the end of his life. He lived on the old Fitzgerald ranch on the old Monterey Highway in the Rucker area. His wife, Nellie Fitzgerald, had belonged to the family that had a 500-acre ranch there. Indicating the area along the Monterey Road, he said, "This was all timber—oak trees. There were wildcats, mountain lions and deer all through here. At Day Avenue there was an oak tree that stood above all the rest. You could see it from anywhere in the valley. It was a landmark." He added that he worked for Ferry Morse, ranched for himself with a few head of cattle, and farmed.

Recalling the Henry Miller cattle drives down the dusty, dirt Monterey Road, he said they would continue for hours. Not one of Miller's admirers, he said that one of Miller's vaqueros told him that when they were driving cattle down from Oregon they would pick up strays along the way. If they were branded they would be abandoned.

In talking about his family, Albert said that his father, Isadore Allemand, ran away from home in Grenoble, France at the age of 16 to come to California to dig for gold. Like so many others, he soon decided there was more money to be made supplying meat or grain to the miners. In the 1880s he brought his French wife and children to Gilroy while he spent most of his time with his brothers in the San Joaquin Valley running 10,000 head of sheep. Albert said he knew only Spanish and French when he started school The first day of school he came home early. His mother asked him why—had he learned everything already? Albert said, "I told her I talked French to them and I talked Spanish to them, and they didn't understand me."

His memories of the Chinese who came to build the railroad and stayed on afterwards were many. He said the Chinese raised row crops on land leased along the east side of Monterey Street. They would put their vegetables in baskets suspended at either end of poles balanced on their shoulders and sell them to the people of Gilroy. They also cut lumber to make charcoal to sell to the Chinese laundries and foundries. He recalled the Chinese girls in the hand laundries with their little six-sided corner stoves on which they heated their irons.

There was a Chinese doctor in town who actually used rattlesnake medicine and, for a while, Albert said, he and his brothers had a good thing going, catching these deadly snakes and selling them to the doctor for a dollar each. One boy would pin the snake to the ground with a two-pronged stick while the other would catch the head in a wire noose and drop the snake in a sack. When their uncle found out what they were doing, that was the end of that. The Chinese section was the south end of town. Some found work as cooks on the ranches and others at homes in town. A curious thing, Allemand said, was how Three-Fingered Jack, the noted outlaw, hated Chinese and, it was said, would ride ten miles out of his way to shoot a Chinaman.

One form of recreation in Gilroy was horse racing at Safstrom's one-mile dirt track off Old Gilroy Street. The children weren't allowed in, but they would peek through the fence. One time one of the horse owners galloped up and told one of the boys to hold his cart. Apparently he had heard that his jockey was going to throw the race, because he pulled out his gun and shot over his head, yelling, "Go!" The racing men, among them Henry Miller, Jr., used to congregate at the San Francisco Saloon on Monterey Street between Seventh and Eighth Streets. Albert described it as the "biggest and best" in town, with gambling tables, 40 to 50 girls, and a busy bar.

In those days gunfights were not uncommon. Allemand told of a gunfight between Lucas Padrone, a lawman, and a man he was about to arrest. Each took refuge behind a telephone pole. Padrone, a heavy man, had a disadvantage and was winged in the hip. He, however, tricked his opponent into firing by holding out his hat, and as Padrone was an excellent shot, he won the fight. Contrary to what we see on television and in the movies, he said that lawmen didn't shoot to kill. In telling about the gunfights in those days he said, "You had to be tough. You had to know where to look and what to see."

Albert's father died when the eldest child was 11 years old, and Albert quit school to go to work when he was 13. His mother had been raising hay, ploughing the fields with a single plough behind a horse. "She pitched hay like a man," he said. Later he and his brothers rented horses to make up the six-horse teams for farming 1,200 acres of hay and grain, which were the important agricultural products at that time. There were six threshing outfits in the area. The train stops in Gilroy were marked by poles at spaces 75 to 80 yards apart so the four or six-horse teams and wagons would have room to turn around while loading bales on the trains.

Looking back on his 96 years, Albert Allemand felt that he had been very fortunate. The best thing in his life, he said sadly, was his wife, Ellen Fitzgerald. He still missed her, even though he was surrounded by children, grandchildren and great-grandchildren.

GM *George C. Milias*

Although George Milias didn't arrive in Gilroy until 1881, his name is a part of the Gilroy story. The hotel and restaurant bearing his name was an institution for over 85 years. His son, George C. Milias, carried on the family business until 1975. During this time he served as councilman for eight years and as mayor of Gilroy. The restaurant and hotel was a popular stopping-off place for travelers from San Francisco on their way to Monterey. The Sargent sisters used to come from their ranch. Many a big cattle deal was said to have been made in the restaurant, and one of its most famous patrons, whom George came to know and admire, was Henry Miller. The portrait of Miller that used to hang in the hotel now hangs in the Milias home. Retired, Milias and his wife live on their ranch in the eastern hills.

In addition to his hotel and restaurant business, early in the century the senior George Milias went into ranching. The first property he bought was the 800-acre Rahl Ranch. He continued to add on parcels until he had extensive holdings. George C. and Rachel live on what was the old Daniel Regan part of the ranch on Canada Road. "The Regans had a beautiful two-story frame house on it when my father bought the property about 1906," said George, "but it burned down in 1929." Some of the old barns and bunkhouses are still standing and the tack room was hauled over from the Rahl Ranch. Adjoining the Regan Ranch was the Kickham Ranch which Milias, Sr. bought from the heirs. Then in 1913, when the state water people said the Spring Valley Water Company couldn't take water to San Francisco, he said his father walked up and bought 22,000 acres of the House Ranch from Hunt and Hollow (the name of the water district). One of the Houses' sons worked for the Miliases until

1930. His mother called him "Son" and he was never known by any name other than Son House.

The Miliases said that they refer to this ranch where they live as the Mountain Ranch and the other part of their ranch as the Valley Ranch. It is part of Ygnacio Ortega's San Ysidro Ranch off Pacheco Pass Road on Bloomfield Road, surrounded by former Henry Miller properties. Since he retired from active ranching, Milias' daughter and son-in-law, Carol and Don Silacci, run the ranch as a cow-calf operation. They have an attractive modern ranch house on a knoll above George and Rachel, with a beautiful view. Milias' son, George W. Milias is in Washington, serving in the Department of the Interior as deputy director of the Fish and Game Commission.

The ranch property extends up into the Diablo Range. Sometime around 1913 Milias bought the 658-acre Flagpole Ranch adjoining Gilroy Hot Springs from William Cullen. The flagpole was a landmark for guests at the Hot Springs, who used to hike over to it. There was a book there which they

Don and Carol Silacci, who manage the Milias Ranches. The Mountain Ranch is made up of a collection of homestead ranches, and the Valley Ranch is part of the old San Ysidro off Pacheco Pass Road on Bloomfield.

would sign. The Gilroy Hot Springs was a popular resort in its day. People would come down from San Francisco on the train and then transfer to the stage. Milias said that about all that is left of the resort now are the hot springs.

Hugo Horlein, who grew up in Gilroy, is one who has memories of the Hot Springs. At the age of 16, he said, he would sometimes drive the stage when they needed a driver. Some of the ladies were a little afraid of such a young fellow driving a four-horse stage up into the hills, but he assured them that the horses knew the way. Horlein talked about the mineral baths—he said people went there for rheumatism, and some to "dry out"—that there were cabins, a swimming tank, a dance floor, music and gambling. According to Horlein and other old-timers, they had some really big poker games there.

167

Las Animas

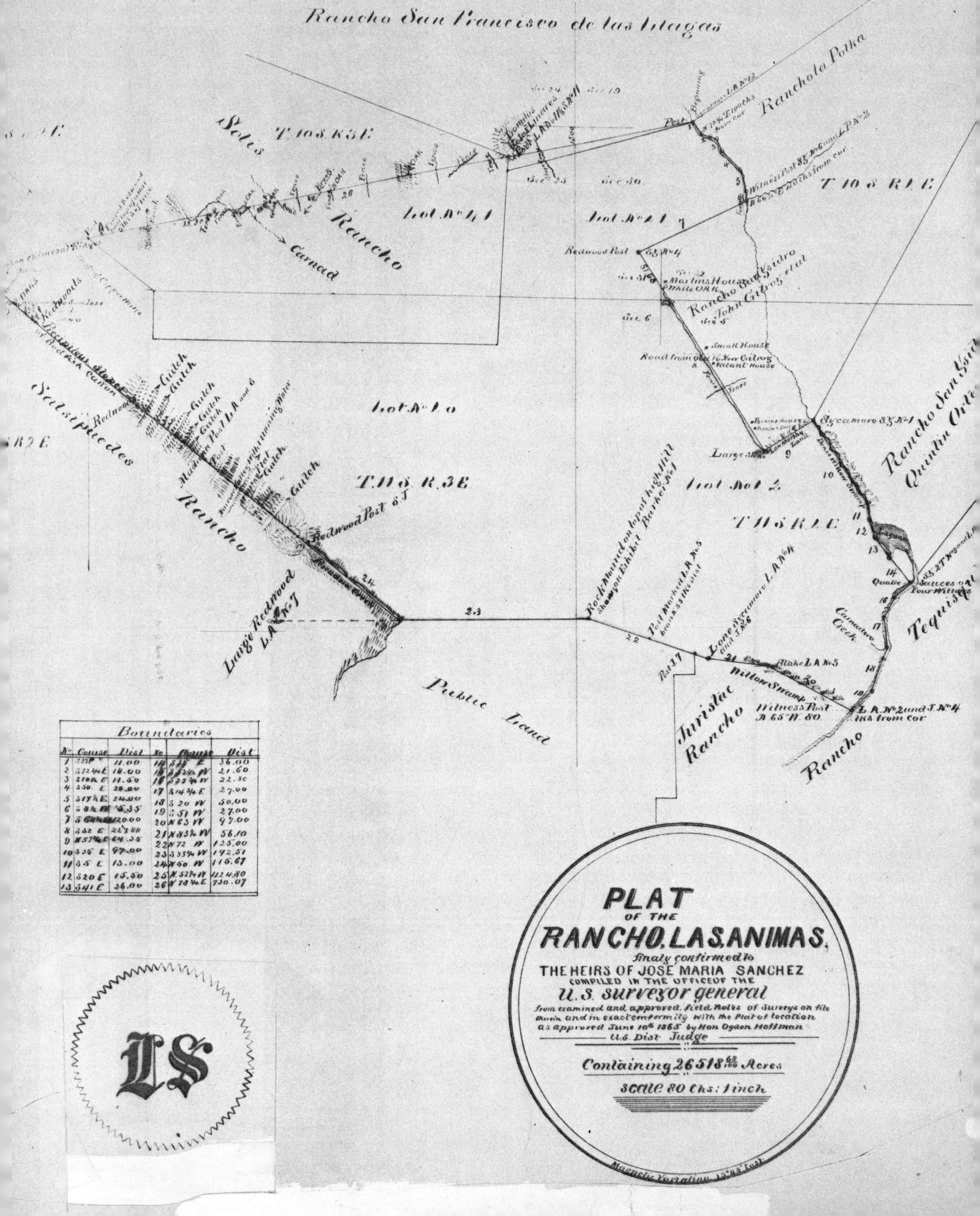

Rancho San Francisco de las Llagas
Rancho la Polka
T. 10 S. R. 3 E.
T. 10 S. R. 1 E.
Lot No. 41
Lot No. 41
Lot No. 40
T. 11 S. R. 3 E.
Lot No. 2
T. 11 S. R. 1 E.
Rancho
Canad
Solis
Sausipuedes
Rancho
Redwood Post
Rancho San Ysidro
John Gilroy et al
Small House
Road from old to New Gilroy
Vacant House
Sycamore S.T. No. 1
Large Stone
Rancho San Ysidro
Quintin Ortega
Redwood Post S.T.
Large Redwood
Public Land
Juristac
Rancho
Rancho
Willow Swamp
Witness Post
Tequisquita
Gulch
Gulch
Gulch
Gulch
Gulch
Gulch
PLAT
OF THE
RANCHO LAS ANIMAS
finaly confirmed to
THE HEIRS OF JOSE MARIA SANCHEZ
COMPILED IN THE OFFICE OF THE
U.S. surveyor general
from examined and approved field notes of Surveys on file therein and in exact conformity with the Plat of location as approved June 10th 1865 by Hon Ogden Hoffman
U.S. Dist Judge
Containing 26518 63/100 Acres
SCALE 80 Chs: 1 inch
Magnetic Variation 15°45' East
LS

Boundaries

No.	Course	Dist	No.	Course	Dist
1	S 57 E	11.00	14	S 35 E	36.00
2	S 72¾ E	18.00	15	S 52½ W	21.60
3	S 10½ E	11.50	16	S 23¾ W	22.80
4	S 50 E	28.00	17	S 14¾ E	27.00
5	S 17½ E	24.00	18	S 20 W	50.00
6	S 8½ W	5.35	19	S 51 W	27.00
7	S [illegible]	20.00	20	N 63 W	97.00
8	S 82 E	227.88	21	N 83½ W	56.10
9	N 57¾ E	64.35	22	N 72 W	125.00
10	S 35 E	97.00	23	S 33¾ W	192.51
11	S 5 E	13.00	24	N 50 W	116.67
12	S 20 E	15.50	25	N 52¼ W	124.80
13	S 41 E	36.00	26	N 78¾ E	730.07

CHAPTER XXXI
Rancho Las Animas

From its beginnings as a Spanish land grant to Mariano Castro in 1802, the only direct grant by a Viceroy in California, according to the historian Hittell, Rancho de Las Animas (the Spirits) has never been classified with the commonplace. The original grant of 25,518 acres—later surveys showed it was closer to 40,000—ran from Mount Madonna in the Santa Cruz Mountains down to the Pajaro River, bordered by the San Ysidro on the east, on the northeast by the Llagas and La Polka, and on the northwest by El Solis. The latter was owned by a distant relative also named Mariano Castro.

In 1835 Mariano Castro's widow sold the rancho to Don Jose Maria Sanchez. The complexities of this sale were later to be the basis for a gigantic lawsuit involving more than 1,000 persons, counting plaintiffs and defendants. Before that the sudden death by drowning of the wealthy Don Jose Maria Sanchez touched off the famous search for the Sanchez treasure in which a dozen or more men lost their lives.

Las Animas reached its peak, however, after it was purchased by the incomparable cattleman Henry Miller and he chose it for his ranch headquarters. He owned 25 square miles of land around it and had his beautiful summer home at Mount Madonna.

Part of the ranch, known since Miller's time as the Castro Valley Ranch, was taken over during Prohibition by a gang of rum runners (it is only 15 miles from the coast). This same part was purchased in the twenties, when Miller properties were being dispersed to pay off bonds, for $15 an acre by Will Tevis and Lewis Carpenter. They used it to run their polo ponies. Carpenter's wife, Ernestine McNear Nickel Carpenter, was formerly married to Henry Miller's grandson, George Nickel. Will Rogers, an avid polo player, often visited the ranch

in those days. It was later purchased by H. L. Chase of Santa Barbara.

Today the lower portion of the Castro Valley Ranch is owned by the three daughters of Fenton O'Connell, Barbara Munson, Madelyn Bourdet, and Karene Vernor. On a contemporary note, almost as far removed as possible from the slow-paced early California of Mariano Castro, the upper portion of the ranch is owned by Arab interests who were reported to be putting in a helicopter pad. What their plans actually are, no one seems to know for sure.

Joining the Castro Valley Ranch is the 1,300-acre ranch, called "Bloomfield," of the Joe Kerleys. It is across from the original headquarters of Henry Miller. Some of the old ranch buildings can still be seen, including the silos built by Miller's son-in-law, J. Leroy Nickel. The Kerleys' well-designed Spanish style house never fails to catch the eye of travelers down Highway 101 south of Gilroy. It is in a setting of oak trees well back from the road, with cattle grazing in front, the hills rising up in back, and a long drive bordered with sycamore trees that meet overhead to form an archway.

The Kerleys' house was built by Dickie Calhoun, a Philadelphia mainliner who came out in 1927 to raise thoroughbred horses which she rode sidesaddle at shows throughout California. While at the ranch she married her chauffeur, Harry Lane, who became a polo player. After she returned to the East, the ranch was sold to Harry Rianda of Gilroy and subsequently to Eugene Shumaker of Denver, Colorado. Not far from the Kerley house is the little cypress cemetery with iron picket fence, where Miller's first wife, baby son, and his beloved daughter, Sarah Alice, were buried. The bodies were later moved to Mount Madonna.

Mariano Castro, the original owner of Rancho Las Animas, came to California from Mexico as a

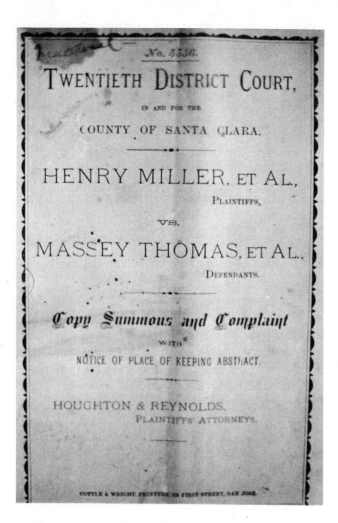

Complaint filed by Henry Miller, et al (Johanna Fitzgerald, Thomas Rea and the Castro heirs) vs. Massey Thomas, et al (the Sanchez heirs). Altogether 1,000 persons were involved. The outcome was the clearing of title to their land for the people of Gilroy.

young boy with his parents, Joaquin Ysidro Castro and Maria Botilliere, as part of the De Anza colonists in 1776. Under orders from Governor Felipe de Neve they were among the soldiers sent to start the Pueblo of San Jose along the Guadalupe River near Mission Santa Clara.

After his marriage to Josefa Romero in 1801, Mariano made a trip to Mexico where he obtained the Rancho La Brea (later changed to Las Animas) grant of 25,518 acres from Spanish Viceroy Marquinas, dated August 17, 1802. In 1810 it was re-granted with an additional piece of land, by Viceroy Lizano y Beaumont. One of the Castros' daughters married a whaler, Thomas Doak, who arrived on an American ship in Monterey in 1816, was baptized Felipe Santiago, and made his way over to the Santa Clara Valley. He and his wife settled down at the Castro headquarters on Carnadero Creek near what became Bloomfield Ranch. In con-

trast to so many ambitious Americans, Doak (Santiago) became a Californian in spirit and adapted their easy-going ways.

Don Jose Maria Sanchez

After Don Jose Maria Sanchez took over Las Animas, there was a drastic change in operation. Unlike his fellow rancheros, he was a businessman all the way. Sanchez had bought the James Stokes adobe in Monterey in 1834. That same year he was appointed alcalde of Mission San Juan Bautista under the secularization act when the mission lands were taken away from the church, and also served as magistrate of San Juan. This no doubt helped him to get the Rancho Llano del Tequesquite grant. He also owned a two-story adobe building on the plaza that had been the guard house, as well as a one-and-a-half-story frame building on the Alameda in San Juan. The guard house was later combined with the Juan Anzar house next door and turned into the Plaza Hotel. Sanchez also had a thriving soap business with the ships stopping in Monterey.

A young man from New Hampshire named Dan Willson, who came to California in 1849, wrote in his diary of stopping in 1852 to make camp on the road running past the Sanchez Ranch house. Sanchez came out to the road and told Willson no one stopped on his ranch but guests, and then invited Willson to be a guest. This was his introduction to the Sanchez family.

Willson said that Sanchez drove a hard bargain, that he was shrewder than the owners of the surrounding ranchos, and that there was no *manana* in his makeup. Whenever there was something to be done, such as a rodeo or a trip to Monterey with cartloads of hides and tallow to be shipped in Yankee Clippers, everybody was up early and Sanchez was always there.

Sanchez never carried a gun in public, but was known to be an expert at throwing a hunting knife. In 1838, at the age of 30, he wooed and won the beautiful Maria Encarnacion Ortega (always called Chona), 16-year-old daughter of his neighbor, Quintin Ortega on the San Ysidro Rancho. They were married at Mission San Juan Bautista. He built for her a two-story adobe home near the confluence of the Pajaro and San Benito Rivers.

The couple had five children before he met his death by drowning, on Christmas Eve of 1852. He had been to the gold fields where he had sold a large herd of cattle. Returning home with pouches

170

full of gold dust, he stopped during a storm at the Gilroy Rancho of his wife's relative, who pleaded with him not to proceed because the storm was getting worse. But Don Jose Maria wanted to get home to his family. As he started to cross the rising Pajaro his horse went down in the quicksand and he was swept off the horse and drowned. The sacks of gold he was carrying were never found.

Also never found was the $85,000 in gold dust which he had stored in the house, the returns from his profitable trade at the mines. When the gold rush hit, Sanchez had bands of horses, cattle and hogs, more than anyone in the state, and he capitalized by getting them to the gold country. Because of his business acumen he was nicknamed "El Judio." Unfortunately the land and the fortune he had amassed was to bring tragedy to his widow and death to a dozen men. One of the key protagonists was William Roach, who came to Monterey with Stevenson's Regiment to fight in the war with Mexico. These renegades stayed on to loot the estates of the Californians. A helpless widow such as Dona Encarnacion de Ortega y Sanchez, the wealthiest woman in California, with five minor children and no one trustworthy to advise her, was an easy prey. Roach persuaded Dona Encarnacion to have him appointed administrator.

The gold was said to have been hidden under the floor of Roach's adobe, and when opposing forces headed by his arch-enemy Lewis Belcher were closing in, his brother-in-law, Jerry McMahon, re-hid it. McMahon later fought a duel with Encarnacion's third husband, Dr. Henry L. Sanford, in the Washington Hotel in Monterey. Both of them were killed, and dying with McMahon was the secret of the hiding place of the gold.

Other stories were told about the gold being buried on the Sanchez ranch, and for years people would be seen digging for it. There were many conflicting accounts about the mismanagement of the estate and the dissipation of the Widow Sanchez's wealth. According to a series that appeared in the *Salinas Daily Post,* the fight over the handling of the estate caused a feud between William Roach and Lewis Belcher. Roach tried to escape into Mexico with three notes totaling $9,100, but was captured in a church in Ventura. He was brought to Stockton for trial; the politics of Monterey were so biased that a fair trial there was impossible. On the other hand, Belcher's attorney was David Terry, who had things pretty much his way in Stockton. Roach was found guilty of taking $84,650 from the estate.

Cemetery on the Bloomfield Ranch where Henry Miller's first wife and infant son were buried, and later his daughter Sarah Alice.

Belcher, known as the Black Eagle of Monterey, like McMahon and Sanford, was killed in the Washington Hotel. The curse of the Sanchez gold brought death to many others also. Two innocent victims, State Senator Isaac Wall and Thomas Williamson, who were friends of Roach and were mistakenly believed to be carrying the gold, were shot in the back while leaving Monterey on a camping trip. David Terry, who had been Belcher's attorney and later became Supreme Court Justice, met a violent death when he was shot by a sheriff's deputy in the San Joaquin Valley. After nine years of hiding out, William Roach was drowned in a well.

There were others, too, including Anastacio Garcia, a noted horse thief who is said to have been the one to start Tiburcio Vasquez on the road to lawlessness. He is believed to have been the killer of Wall and Williamson, and met death by hanging in his jail cell at the old Colton jail in Monterey, after killing three members of a sheriff's posse who had gone to arrest him at his house.

Although she was the only person involved in the Sanchez treasure not to lose her life, Dona Encarnacion was the victim of these fortune-seeking,

Joe Kerley residence on Las Animas Ranch across the highway from former headquarters of Henry Miller's operations at Bloomfield. The house was built in 1927 by Dickie Calhoun of Philadelphia.

ruthless men. Three times widowed, the unfortunate woman married George Crane, her attorney, at the mission in 1855. Crane, a Virginian, had been sent by the U.S. government to join Fremont's regiment as an intelligence agent disguised as a supply officer. Known to have been a heavy drinker and a gambler, he is said to have dissipated most of what was left of her fortune. He died during the smallpox epidemic of 1868.

Encarnacion's fifth and last husband, Anastacio Alviso, who had worked on the ranch, was killed in a hunting accident the year after they were married. To add further to the tragedies of her life, her son Gregorio Sanchez killed two men in San Juan in self defense. Her remaining days were spent in the little house in San Juan which became known as the Crane house. It was across the street from the convent.

Dan Willson

Dan Willson, the young man invited by Don Jose Maria Sanchez to be a guest at the ranch, stayed on and married the oldest Sanchez daughter, Vicenta. He had gotten the urge to come to California from New Hampshire in 1848, from a picture he had seen of a spreading oak tree with a man beneath it shoveling gold nuggets. He went to Boston and with 60 others who had the same idea, purchased the

bark *Emma Isadora,* a discarded "ex-slaver" which had taken missionaries and rum to Africa and brought back cargoes of slaves. They put in $300 apiece to purchase the ship, reconditioned it, and came to California around the Horn.

In his diary Willson told of the Stevenson Regiment, which had come to California in 1846 to fight in the Mexican War with the understanding that when the war was over the regiment would be disbanded in Monterey. Some members of the regiment took control of Monterey politics, practicing what they had learned from Tammany Hall in New York. Willson told of his and Vicenta's efforts to have him appointed Vicenta's guardian, as they felt it was the only way to save her property and to help her sisters and brother to be freed from the stranglehold of the Stevenson gang. They finally succeeded in getting a change of venue to Stockton and the change in guardianship, which prevented Roach from selling $70,000 worth of additional cattle.

Vicenta received the patent to the Tequesquite and the Lomerias Muertas ranchos for herself, her sisters and brother, Refugio, Candelario, Guadalupe, and Gregorio. Willson also took action against "squatting," the custom of occupying land and then applying for title to it. With the exception of some town lots, the Stevenson gang was stopped before they got the ranch property.

A sad notation appears in Dan Willson's diary of July 9, 1866: "Dave Hilderbrand went away and took my wife with him." On July 10: "Vicenta and Mr. Crane came to my house and took away her things and wanted a settlement."

HH CHAPTER XXXII
Henry Miller

A butcher boy from Germany, who never lost his accent but amassed a fortune of $50,000,000, became owner of Rancho Las Animas in the 1860s.

As a boy tending cows on the Brackenheim hillsides, young Heinrich Alfred Kreiser could not possibly have dreamed he would one day own more cattle than anyone could count, that he would possess over a million acres of land, the largest privately-owned domain in the country, head two banks and their branches, and be known by the name of Henry Miller.

In the latter years of this Henry Miller's life he used to like to stop by the carriage painting shop of Otto Horlein in Gilroy and talk with him in German. The blacksmith who shared the shop was a friend of Miller's. After school, when Otto's son, Hugo, would come in to help his father, Miller would tell the boy stories about his early days, and of coming to California at the age of 23 from New York by ship via the Isthmus of Panama. He said he used the ticket and passport of an acquaintance named Henry Miller, a shoe salesman. At first he didn't know what to do about this new name, but then he decided he liked it and would keep it. Some years later the California State Legislature passed a specific act formally changing the name of Heinrich Alfred Kreiser to Henry Miller.

When Miller arrived in San Francisco in 1850, wild cattle still roamed the hills. In fact, they could be seen from the boats entering the Golden Gate. Hides were still an important item for trade. Having worked in a butcher shop in New York, Miller decided to put that experience to work. He told Hugo he would follow the fellows who were stripping hides and salvage the good meat, which he would then peddle from door to door. Within two years, as American cattle began to arrive in San Francisco, young Henry opened his own butcher shop. He was able to purchase from Livingston and

Kincaid 300 prime oxen — supposed to be the first band of American cattle driven to San Francisco. This was the beginning of boom times — the price of beef cattle had risen from two dollars to $30 or $40 a head. The American ranchers were having a heyday, and the Californians, with their longhorn cattle, were crowded out of business.

Knowing his beef and that the way to control the local market was through raising his own cattle, Miller decided to go to the source. Although he had had only six dollars in his pocket when he arrived in San Francisco, by this time he had bought a horse and managed to save some money. After seeing the HH brand on especially good hides from the San Joaquin Valley, Miller decided to go there to see the

Henry Miller, the German immigrant who arrived in San Francisco with $6 in his pocket. When he died in 1916 he left an estate of $50,000,000. He amassed more land than any other man—one million acres.

Mr. and Mrs. Charles Lux. Mr. Lux, Henry Miller's partner, took care of the office work in their huge enterprise.

owner of this brand, a man named Hildreth, about buying some land.

On his way by horseback he rode down the El Camino Real through the oak-covered Santa Clara Valley, passing through Rancho Las Animas, where he would eventually make his headquarters at the Bloomfield Ranch and own 65,000 acres of surrounding land. Heading east on El Camino Real he passed the small settlement which had built up at San Ysidro (Old Gilroy) where the John Gilroys and the Quintin Ortegas lived with their families in their adobe homes. This was the beginning of the Pacheco Pass and the only route to the San Joaquin Valley through the Coast Range and the San Luis Gonzaga Rancho of Francisco Pacheco. Not much more than a path, and a tortuous one at that, it had been made by the Indians and was used by Spanish officers looking for runaway soldiers less than 65 years before.

As he began to rise into the hills he paused at a point where he could look out on the panoramic view of the Santa Clara Valley. Directly below him was Soap Lake (San Felipe) on the Rancho Tequesquite. He could see the Tequesquite Creek and the San Benito River which join the Pajaro River and eventually empty into the Pacific Ocean. He looked across the valley to the Santa Cruz Mountains and saw Mount Madonna standing out. Impressed as he was, he could not have imagined that he would someday own a magnificent summer estate in those mountains and 25 square miles of that valley.

His mind was on cattle and the land in the San Joaquin Valley. When he reached the summit he looked out on the immense valley 50 miles wide and 200 miles long, with the San Joaquin River running down through the middle. After descending into the Valley he found his man, Hildreth. Fortunately for Miller, at this point Hildreth wanted to go to the mines. Miller purchased from him 8,885 acres, or one-quarter interest in Rancho Sanjon de Santa Rita, at $1.15 an acre, and 7,500 head of cattle at five dollars a head. Included in the deal was the HH brand which he so dearly coveted. This brand, which had its origins on the Mississippi River, where it was used for identifying logs, had been brought across the plains from Missouri by Tom Hildreth and his older brother, John.

The famous Double "H" brand left its mark on the left hip of hundreds of thousands of cattle and horses, more than any other brand in the West. Ironically, after some 65 years, at the Canal Farms Ranch in Los Banos, the brand was sold to H. Moffatt and Co., along with 10,000 head of cattle, to help pay off debts incurred against Miller's estate. His grandson, George W. Nickel, and his family were living at Canal Farms at the time. George's daughter, Sally Nickel Mein (Mrs. William Wallace), of Woodside, recalled that she and her two brothers, George, Jr. and Beverly, and her sister, Mary Nickel Lombardi James, helped the vaqueros with the roundup. It went on for several days, she said, and every night they would have a barbecue. When the family lived at Canal Farms, Sally remembered, they could ride to the Delta Ranch without meeting any fences, and instead of going to school, they were tutored.

In 1858 Henry Miller formed a partnership with Charles Lux of San Francisco, also a native of Germany. This marked the beginning of the Miller and Lux empire. Lux was the office man, and Miller was the overseer of the ranches and the dominating force. From their original holding they embarked on a land- and cattle-buying spree that spread out into Nevada and Oregon and continued for 50 years. In one of his talks with his young friend, Hugo Horlein, Miller said that his plan was to have ranches a day's distance apart so that the cattle and the men would have a place to rest for the night—that he would start out by horseback and ride all day to determine where he wanted to buy his next ranch.

174

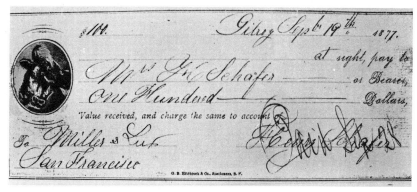

Henry Miller's Bull's Head check, referred to as "good as gold." So respected were they that they were accepted as cash at a government auction.

A receipt written on foolscap paper bearing the signature of Henry Miller. Dated August 31, 1883, it states that the amount of $146.25 was received from W. A. Robertson and others as payment in full for a caboose for Orofino Mining Company.

Miller and Lux bought up land that belonged to the government, land from squatters and from homesteaders, from railroads, from bankers who found themselves in a bind, and from Californians who couldn't wait for their patents. Miller would buy out one heir of a Mexican grant and would graze his cattle on all the land without sharing the profits. In most cases he would buy up the rest of the ranch, but if the heirs wouldn't sell, he would force a partition. Never in his career, however, was he accused of fraud, and he was known for taking care of his employees. Hugo Horlein gives an example of this in his story about the foreman of the Castro Valley Ranch, who was a descendant of the Castro family which had held the original Las Animas grant. Miller kept Castro on the ranch, even when he became too old to work.

There was a steady run of Miller's cattle in the San Joaquin Valley and from the Santa Rita over the Pacheco Pass to Gilroy and along the El Camino Real. Gradually he added to his growing domain part or all of Ranchos Salsipuedes, La Laguna, Bolsa de San Felipe (now Hudners'), San Justo (formerly of Flint and Bixby), the Aromitas y Agua Caliente of Guadalupe Anzar, the San Antonio at San Juan Bautista of Manuel Larios and, among others, the Tequesquite and Lomerias Muertas which, like Las Animas, had belonged to the heirs of Jose Maria Sanchez.

Miller was the least showy of the tycoons the West produced. He scorned the nabobs of the Bonanza rich such as the Fairs, Hopkinses, Hunt-

The Mexican longhorn which thrived on California lands and multiplied profusely.

ingtons and Stanfords. Always moving from ranch to ranch, checking on water, employing vaqueros, and otherwise keeping the ranches working, his trademark was a broad-brimmed black hat, black coat and trousers, white shirt with black shoestring tie, and black congress gaiters. Neatness was an obsession and frugality his ruling passion. "Fortunes are made by taking care of small things" was one of Miller's favorite sayings. His generous side, however, was not limited to small things. During

175

Left, Joe Rodriguez, head vaquero for Henry Miller. Right, Joe's son Andrew.

Cabin and corrals on Pacheco Pass, a stopover for feeding cattle which were being taken from San Joaquin ranches to San Francisco. The land was leased from San Luis Gonzaga Ranch.

the depression years of the 1890s he is said to have wiped off his books $350,000 in mortgages, notes and debts owed him by San Joaquin Valley settlers. A Los Banos resident of that period said that he carried everyone in town on his books at the store and didn't even send out bills. When he stopped at the Adobe Inn, three miles east of the Pacheco Pass, the daughters of the owner used to fight over which one of them could polish Henry Miller's boots, because there was always a $20 gold piece left in one of the boots as a tip.

An inveterate letter-writer, he carried pen and paper everywhere and was constantly writing missives directing the operations of the ranches. One of his most frequent topics was cats. One day he would write to a foreman, "You should have some cats to destroy the mice in the granary." The next day he would write, "I have directed that two cats be sent for the granary." He would follow up the next day with, "Have the cats arrived for the granary?"

This would continue until he received word from the foreman that the mice were destroyed. The foreman would then receive a letter from Miller, "You don't need more than one cat now, so send the other to the Midway Ranch."

Other letters would contain such minutiae as advice on the advantages of boiling potatoes in their jackets, the importance of opening haystacks at the south end, how to use willow limbs for fences to save freight on fence posts, how to make use of cow chips as fuel to run farm machinery, and the importance of rubbing salt all over a hide to keep it from shriveling before hanging it up.

Always Miller was on the lookout for more land. Edward F. Treadwell, who was one of the cattle baron's attorneys and whose comprehensive book *The Cattle King* is a great source of information on Miller, wrote that Miller was "...a man who knew dirt" and had an amazing ability to evaluate it. He told of a San Francisco real estate man who wanted Miller to sell a lot on Jackson Street and said to him, "Why not sell it?"

Miller's reply was, "Land in California is cheap

The Henry Miller mansion at the headquarters of Miller and Lux below Gilroy. The 44 rooms were elaborately decorated.

now. It will be valuable. Wise men buy land, fools sell. I will keep it." This was his ruling principle, to buy and not to sell.

Not only did Miller know dirt; he also knew water, and he knew that in California water was like gold. Along the San Joaquin River he had 120 miles of land. Whenever possible he arranged to have lands that bordered rivers. During the rainy season, to take advantage of the flood waters, he built thousands of miles of levees and irrigation ditches in the surrounding plains. Fields watered in this way supplied natural grasses for nine months of the year and grew feed that sustained cattle during the dry months.

Among his innovations was the planting of alfalfa with seeds he had ordered from Chile. This led to the development of the dairy industry in the state. He also initiated the growing of rice and cotton. When he decided to go into sheep raising in the Valley he became the biggest sheep rancher in the West and owner of one of the largest shearing plants in the country. With his amazing foresight he stored up great quantities of hay, always keeping on hand a year's supply of feed. As a result, during the drought years of 1887–89 he was able to acquire the vast Nevada interests of N. Y. A. Mason, who was unable to feed his cattle.

He was involved in a gigantic lawsuit with Haggin and Tevis over riparian water rights — a suit known as Lux vs. Haggin which he finally won in a Supreme Court decision. As a result he was for a time one of the most unpopular men in the state.

For 50 years or more Miller spent most of his time traveling either by horseback, buggies or trains, and eventually automobiles, from San Luis

Sarah Wilmarth Sheldon Miller, second wife of Henry Miller and niece of his first wife, who died in childbirth.

Obispo and Kern Counties to Oregon and Nevada. The ranch headquarters were at Bloomfield, three miles south of Gilroy on the Las Animas ranch where the Bolsa Road meets Highway 101. Here he had a self-contained community: warehouses, blacksmith shop, machine shops, a tannery, granaries, livery stables, hay barns, a milking barn, slaughterhouse, poultry houses, a general store and a railroad shipping station. Some of

Bloomfield, the headquarters of the vast Henry Miller empire, four miles south of Gilroy. Almost completely self-sustaining, there was a general store, poultry houses, slaughterhouses, milking barn, blacksmith and machine shops, and a railroad shipping station.

One of the old ranch buildings still standing at the old Henry Miller headquarters where Bolsa Road meets Highway 101.

these buildings can still be seen. Dominating the whole scene was the 44-room Miller mansion with a palatial tower and ornate trimmings. Some of the furnishings, such as the hangings and handiwork, were quite beautiful. Others were unusual, such as highly polished horns from the bulls used as legs and arms for chairs.

This house was built for his second wife, Sarah Wilmarth Sheldon. The courtship of Sarah, niece of his first wife, Nancy, who died in childbirth, is said to have been done in typical Henry Miller fashion. After proposing to her one morning, stating the advantages of the proposition, he said he was going out to look over some cattle and she would have time to think it over. He would be back that evening for her answer. When she accepted he was pleased, but he felt that it was a reasonable proposition.

Henry Miller, Jr. and his wife, the former Sarah Onyon of Gilroy, later lived in the house, and after young Henry's death Sarah stayed on and was there when it burned in the mid-1920s. Henry was said to be an attractive-looking young man. Indulged by his father, he was the prodigal son who squandered a fortune. Sarah is remembered by the family as a lovely girl, much loved by her nieces and nephews.

Many anecdotes which reveal the character of the man are told about Henry Miller. He had a driver named Federico Romero. One time Federico drove his boss down to the Buena Vista Ranch in the San Joaquin Valley. As they got to a gate a fellow

driving a team, stock and plows, was passing by. Miller called to him, "Young man, open that gate."

"Open it yourself," was the reply. So Miller got out and opened the gate. When he arrived at the house he asked, "Who was that young fellow driving that cow team?"

The answer was, "He's a new man. Only been here about two weeks."

"He's a good man," said Miller. "Raise his wages." He obviously realized that if the man had gotten off the horse he might have lost the cattle.

Another story told by Federico was that when they were going to the Peach Tree Ranch, coming out of Priest Valley through Coalinga, along the road they saw a hide. Miller said, "Fritzie, stop, stop!" (To the German Miller, Federico was always Fritz.) He got out, looked at the hide and saw his HH brand on it. They continued on to the house on the ranch. The lady of the house said, "Mr. Miller, we're going to have dinner."

Miller said that was all right and sat down and had dinner. Afterwards he said, "That was the finest roast beef I ever had. Where did you get it?" Without waiting for an answer he said that it was all right for them to eat the beef, "but that hide belongs to me."

Although Miller knew that some of his neighbors stole beef, he didn't do anything about it. Just as with the hobos, he was afraid of retaliation by fire, which could have been disastrous.

Miller himself told Hugo Horlein a story about a time when he was riding out from one of his ranches and saw some men barbecuing meat. They invited him to have a little bite. Miller said he sat down and ate with them. "When we were through I told them who I was. I said, 'I know what you have done. Now, I want you to take what is left to one of my ranches.'" Henry Miller couldn't stand to see food wasted, but he would never stop a man from eating.

Although he could be parsimonious, Miller was also generous. He was concerned about the young Hugo working so much in his father's shop and he asked him one day, "Don't you ever have time to play? Would you like to go fishing on my Castro Valley ranch?" Hugo agreed that he would, so Miller made arrangements at Bloomfield that the boy could take a cart and horse and go fishing and hunting.

Clarence Fagalde of Aptos was born on the Miller ranch at Bloomfield. Before his father, Joseph Fagalde, married his mother, Louise Gilroy, granddaughter of John Gilroy, at San Juan Bautista Mission, Joseph was a driver for Miller. He used to take a big team of stallions pulling a dray truck to get food to bring back to the ranch stores. Food was dispersed from there to the ranches.

"My father always drove Miller in a surrey drawn by two horses. On their way from Gilroy to his big place at Mount Madonna they would pass a swale. One time the water was so deep there that they got stuck in the mud. The shaft broke loose and left them stranded. They got out and rode horseback the rest of the way to Mount Madonna."

Another story Fagalde's father told him was of driving Miller to San Juan Bautista. On the way they were stopped by a bandit who took all of Miller's money. Miller said to the bandit, "You left me broke. How about giving me a loan of $20. We have to eat." The surprised bandit handed him back $20. He was even more surprised about two years later when Miller, again being driven by Fagalde, spotted him and said, "Fagalde, stop! I owe that man some money."

Miller had a rule that he wouldn't let a married man drive carriage. When Fagalde went to see him to tell him of his plans to be married, Miller said, "You know my rules. Married men can't drive. Your place is at home with your family. You take a horse and go away for a month." Although Miller had this policy for his employees he didn't practice what he preached. According to family members he was seldom home. How could he be when he was always traveling? When Fagalde came back Miller

had a nice little house built for him. "Now, you are foreman of Bloomfield," he said.

Still another story about Miller was told by well-known cattleman Carroll Hayes of San Martin, who still lives on part of the old Rancho San Francisco de Llagas. He and his father, Frank Hayes, bought the ranch from the Lazard Lion estate in 1921. The senior Hayes, together with a group of men from San Jose, subsequently subdivided the lower portion. Carroll Hayes kept the mountain and valley part to run cattle.

One time Frank Hayes was moving horses from Livermore to Visalia. He ran out of hay and went into Henry Miller's store to see about credit. Henry Miller, who was in the store at the time, overheard the conversation. He talked to Hayes himself, decided he was all right and then instructed the storekeeper to give Hayes unlimited credit.

There were apparently many facets to Miller's personality. Henry Coe of Rancho San Felipe near Evergreen said:

My father knew him well. He used to rent the Morrow (now Hewlett and Packard) ranch next door. I only saw him once. George Carey was foreman of the ranch for Miller. In those days he was paid $75 a month. Miller would send him 20 gallons of lard, sacks of red beans, coffee, flour, a side of bacon and two brooms.

A man named Doc Arena was superintendent of all of Miller and Lux's livestock. The story they used to tell was that when Miller hired an Irishman to be foreman he only paid him half the usual wage because he said the Irish like to be boss.

Charlie Maggini, foreman on Coe's ranch, who became a champion team roper and steer roper in his youth, worked for Miller on the Fatjo family land on the Pacheco Pass in California and in Utah and Nevada. He told the story about how Miller gave orders that hobos were to be allowed to spend one night at a ranch and be fed. The Chinese cooks, who knew that the hobos went from ranch to ranch, resented this and got satisfaction from making them eat off the same plates the hired men had just used for their dinners.

Another opinion expressed which is contrary to popular belief was that Miller didn't like Gilroy because he couldn't own it as he did Los Banos. He is reputed to have said he was going to make a sheep corral out of Gilroy. It is true that Miller did own practically every building in Los Banos, where Canal farm was located, and regarded it as his town. It is also true that he had an interest in Gilroy. He was credited with the planting of the elm and palm trees on Miller Avenue bordering Christ-

Mount Madonna, the place Henry Miller called home. No business was conducted here. It is located among the redwoods west of Gilroy in the Santa Cruz mountains.

Henry Miller liked to entertain relatives at Mount Madonna with barbecues. He is in the center of the second row, wearing a hat. Nancy Place is seated at his left and Mr. Sheldon is directly behind him.

Tents with deluxe appointments were used to house guests at Henry Miller's Mount Madonna spread. Dr. Weaver, a Gilroy dentist, is seen standing between two ladies.

mas Hill Park, and the rock for the Gilroy City Hall built in 1904 was quarried at his Glenn Ranch.

In the 1870s he showed his concern for the people of Gilroy. There was uncertainty among the landowners as to whether they held clear title to their property, which was originally part of Rancho de Las Animas, and business was at a standstill. Miller resolved this by initiating a lawsuit in which he was the principal plaintiff with Johanna Fitzgerald and Thomas Rea and all the Castro heirs. Massey Thomas and the Sanchez heirs were the defendants. Altogether there were more than a thousand plaintiffs and defendants. The result of this suit, which cost over $101,000, cleared the land titles for the people of Gilroy once and for all. In his will Miller left $300,000 for a hospital to be built in Gilroy and to be named "Las Animas." He also left a $15,000 fund to be distributed to the poor of Gilroy.

The biggest day of the year for Henry Miller was May Day at Los Banos. In fact, according to Ernestine Carpenter, who was married to his grandson, George Nickel, "May Day was the only holiday Mr. Miller recognized." The holiday began as a picnic for the ranch hands — eventually it became a big event with a parade, horse shows, barbecues and rodeos and has been carried on since his death at the fairgrounds in Los Banos. Miller was known as the "Father of the Barbecue." Ernestine and George Nickel raised their family in the valley, first at Ortigalita, then they built on Delta Ranch, and finally at Canal Farm, which had been a favorite of his grandfather.

Henry Miller called Mount Madonna home, however, because it was not connected with business. He enjoyed giving barbecues to which all were invited. including his relatives from Germany, to whom Miller had given the opportunity to come to the United States. Also included were the superintendents of ranches and their families who might be there at the time. They were invited to come to Mount Madonna from time to time to enjoy a change of climate and the cool breezes from the Pacific side. After dinner Miller liked to take his guests for a walk and show them where they could look down on the Santa Clara Valley on one side and the Pacific Ocean on the other. The tables were set under the trees, and there would often be 30 or 40 guests.

Mount Madonna is well remembered by Anna Sturla of Gilroy, who went there to live in 1888, when she was three years old, and stayed until 1905. The family lived in a house where the Ranger's Station is now. Her father, Frank Schmitt, a native of Germany, was ranch foreman and a jack-of-all-trades. Besides taking care of the vineyards, prune and apple orchards, and some sheep, he installed a water system. One time, she said, Mr. Miller came over to their house and said some men were at Mount Madonna for dinner and the cook was gone. Anna's mother had formerly cooked for the workmen, but by this time she had died, so it fell upon young Anna to do the cooking. She said she was very frightened because if Mr. Miller were unhappy about something, he could be quite a tyrant. However, she said, everything turned out all right.

One of Anna's jobs was to ride horseback down to Gilroy every other day to get the mail — a trip that took about an hour or an hour and a half each way. Just as she rounded a curve on the return trip one day, she saw about 20 feet in front of her two cougars who had killed a calf. Her horse snorted but, to her relief, kept right on going. In those days there were still some bear in those mountains. A man named Shell, who was at Mount Madonna before Miller, was supposed to have been chased by a bear right to the door of his cabin.

Sarah Miller's style of entertaining was quite different from her husband's. To satisfy his wife's wishes, Miller built an elaborate summer home with 15 or 20 rooms to replace the five- or six-room redwood cabin he had built in the 1890s. The huge mansion spread out almost 250 feet and had a separate 3,600-square-foot ballroom. There were five houses altogether, one for each member of the family, and tents for overnight guests. Miller's granddaughter, Beatrice Nickel Bowles Morse, was quoted as saying her grandfather could be quite strict and would inspect their tents to see that all was in place. Heaven help any child whose tent was not in apple-pie order! Inasmuch as there were no kitchens in the bungalows, everyone ate in the communal dining room, which had at one end a large fireplace with an enormous moose head over it.

Anna Sturla said that as a young girl she was impressed with the tents; they were of brightly-colored stripes such as red and white and were set on platforms with carpeting, closets and washstands. Even though they were quite plush, they didn't have inside plumbing. For those who had to get up during the night the way was lighted by Japanese lanterns strung from the trees. In the morning the servants would put out the candles.

Nellie Nickel, as Anna remembered, was not a favorite with the help at Mount Madonna. She could be quite difficult, but kind and generous to those she liked. One of the maids told Anna a story about Nellie, who preferred to stay in the big house and had a room there. Apparently she liked limburger cheese but didn't want anybody to see her eating it in the dining room, so she would have it sent up to her room. Nellie usually gave one big ball a year, Anna said, and invited those who were considered to be the social people of Gilroy. She remembered in particular one party of Nellie's when there were so many horses that they were tied to every available tree on the hillside.

A cotillion party given by Mrs. Henry Miller in the ballroom in 1900 was described at length in the Gilroy press:

...the first of a series of social functions which are planned for this summer under the skillful direction of her daughter, Mrs. J. Leroy Nickel....a cotillion was to be a feature of the affair — a marked innovation in the local dancing curriculum...has been the means of setting society agog with delirious expectancy ever since the invitations have been issued....Thirty couples from Gilroy accepted the charming hospitality of the beautiful mountain home of the Millers. Clad in dust-proof outer garments they left town in happy spirits at six o'clock and after a delightful, cool and invigorating ride, arrived some two hours later at the crest of the hill where hundreds of lights among the stately trees shed out a cordial welcome and drew into bold relief the graceful outlines of the handsome cottages with their broad verandas and sloping southern roofs.

The story went on to describe the dinner, the orchestra, the party decorations and the dresses of each lady. The long guest list included, of course, family members, Mr. and Mrs. Henry Miller, Jr., George Nickel (Nellie's son), and Mrs. S. W. Sheldon, a sister-in-law of Mrs. Miller. Familiar names among those present were Messrs. and Mmes. R. G. Einfalt (publisher of the Gilroy Telegram and father of Mrs. Duncan Oneal of San Jose), Henry Hecker, G. E. Rea, P. W. Robinson, F. C. Staniford and C. R. Weaver. Also there were Misses Nancy Place of San Francisco (a niece), Mary, Evelyn and Josie Casey, Nettie Whitehurst, Grace and Minnie Willey, Grace Holsclaw, Pearl Whittington and Kate Onyon.

After Henry Miller's death the buildings at Mount Madonna fell into disrepair. During the twenties they were a cache for rum-runners due to their proximity to the coast, and in the thirties they provided a "haunted" house for the high school students from Gilroy and Watsonville. In 1927 Nellie Nickel turned the property over to the county for a park, with 100 acres reserved for the family. George (Corky) Bowles, one of the heirs, has built a home there.

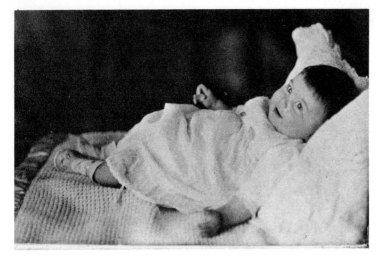

Sally Nickel, a 50 million dollar heiress. The first great-grandchild of Henry Miller, when she was six months old she was the sole heir to his fortune. As six other great-grandchildren were born, the estate in trust was shared with them.

J. Leroy Nickel, a handsome man 20 years his wife's senior, had come out from Philadelphia and lived at the Palace Hotel for two years before he married Nellie. He never liked Mount Madonna. In fact, one family member said he hated it. Anna Sturla remembered his being there only once or twice. Certainly he preferred Menlo Park, where they had a beautiful mansion on Middlefield Road called "Oakley," one of the grand estates on the San Francisco Peninsula.

Nellie is remembered by some of the old-time Gilroy residents as a plain-looking woman, and a story was told that she went into a bank in Gilroy one time to cash a check and was refused because nobody recognized her. Sally Mein (Mrs. William Wallace of Woodside), her first and favorite grandchild, did not completely agree with this description. She said that her grandmother had large, beautiful eyes and that although she could be arbitrary, the servants at the Menlo Park home were devoted to her.

Unfortunately, Henry Miller never really knew his children or grandchildren very well because he was always preoccupied with building and maintaining his empire and traveling from ranch to ranch. He did, however, live to see his first great-grandchild, Sally, daughter of his grandson, George Nickel. Her mother, Ernestine McNear Nickel Carpenter, told a story of Miller's holding the baby in his lap as he sat in his wheelchair. He put a twenty-dollar gold piece in the palm of her hand and pressed her little fingers around it. Her mother took it from Sally and said, "I'm going to keep this for you until you are 21 years old, and then you can do what you wish with it." She did just that, even though she said there were times when she was tempted to spend it, adding that Miller's grandchildren did not receive any inheritance. Sally

Mein now wears the gold piece on her charm bracelet.

When Henry Miller died in 1916 at the age of 89, six-month-old Sally, said her mother, was a "fifty-million-dollar baby." Miller left his estate in trust to the third generation, and she was the only heir at that time. Before long, however, little Sally had two brothers and a sister and three cousins who shared this large sum with her. Her younger brother, Beverly, died in a plane crash in 1954; her sister, Mary Lombardi James (Mrs. Ted) lives in Honolulu, and her brother, George Nickel, Jr. lives in the San Joaquin Valley with his wife, the former Adele Selfridge of Santa Barbara. George has developed the posh Rio Bravo Tennis Ranch and

Four generations of Henry Miller descendants. His daughter, Nellie Miller Nickel, third from left, is seen with her face in profile because she would never face a camera. At left is her son, George Wilmarth Nickel, and his grandson, William Wallace Mein III, and to the right is Nellie's granddaughter, Sally Nickel Mein (Mrs. William Wallace Mein, Jr.) holding her son, Thomas Tucker Mein.

Lodge along the Kern River in the Bakersfield area. In recognition of his great-grandfather, he has used framed Henry Miller brands in the decor.

Beatrice Nickel, daughter of Nellie and Leroy, married George McNear Bowles and later, after his death, Philip Cotting Morse. She had three children: Henry, who married Constance Crowley and has Bowles Farming Company at Los Banos on old Henry Miller property; Amy Beatrice, now deceased, who was married to Dr. John Lawrence and lived at the Delta Ranch (her share has been sold); and George (Corky) Bowles, a bachelor of San Francisco.

Henry Miller spent 55 years building his estate, and its magnitude will probably never again be equalled. The way the estate was handled, at least by the first and second generations, would certainly have displeased him. When his son-in-law, J. Leroy Nickel, assumed control of Miller and Lux, neither he nor anyone else possessed Miller's vast knowledge of the properties and their administration. Nickel experimented with new and unproved farming practices that were for the most part unsuccessful and, because of that and the depression of the early 1920s, he found it necessary to borrow money by issuing bonds. In 1926, unable to meet the $28 million in bonds, Nickel was removed as president and a bondholders' company was formed. Through the Bank of California, with James Fickett appointed its representative, the properties were sold to pay off the outstanding bonds. It was the largest private land sale in American history and at depression prices.

In 1940 the Bank of California turned the management of Miller and Lux back to the trustees of the Henry Miller Trust and J. Leroy Nickel, Jr., who had acted as vice president, became president. At this time, according to George W. Nickel, Jr., over 100,000 acres of land were still held by Miller and Lux. George, who had worked on the properties during summer vacations, said he was aware of the potential of the remaining lands and urged that their sale be curtailed. He became a full-time employee of the company in 1939 and entered into a successful land development program on the lands remaining in Merced and Fresno counties. He said he was never satisfied, however, with Leroy Nickel's continuing to sell land after the bonds had been retired. What is more, he became concerned when he heard rumors of irregular real estate transactions on Miller and Lux lands in Kern County, particularly in relation to mineral rights, namely oil.

After investigation he and his brother, Beverly, acquired the services of an aggressive Merced lawyer, C. Ray Robinson. Representing all the heirs of Henry Miller's estate, Robinson filed suit. The *Call Bulletin* of June 6, 1959 described the action as follows:

The sum and substance of the complaint was...James Leroy Nickel, Jr., Fickett, Olsen, Wooley and Houchin conspired to sell and lease through Houchin money-making oil land with "dummy" organizations obtaining the land from Miller and Lux, conveying it to oil companies and other buyers or lessors with Houchin taking his cut and then kicking back to Nickel and Fickett.

George Nickel said the Superior Court dismissed the three trustees of the Henry Miller trust, including Leroy Nickel, Jr., and replaced them with three San Francisco attorneys.

As a result of the litigation there was an out-of-court settlement of $10,000,000 with the estate of C. E. Houchin, who had died in the meantime, and the return of certain former Miller and Lux assets from J. Leroy Nickel, Jr., who took his own life before the suit came to trial.

George W. Nickel, Jr. was re-employed by the trustees to head up the development and preservation of Miller and Lux land holdings remaining in Merced, Fresno and Kern Counties. Together with the trustees he was successful in the reclamation of the 30,000-acre Buena Vista Lake property in Kern County as well as development and reclamation on other Miller lands. Consequently, there was still substantial property to distribute to the Miller heirs.

The Summing Up

For all his triumphs and material successes, Miller had great sadness during his life. He lost his first wife, Nancy Sheldon Miller, in childbirth in 1859, and his first son died at the same time. His 12-year-old daughter, Sarah Alice, riding horseback with her sister Nellie on the Bloomfield Ranch in Gilroy, was thrown when her horse stumbled and was killed instantly. This was the great tragedy of Miller's life, and he grieved so that he suffered a nervous breakdown. His second wife preceded him in death by ten years. His only son, Henry Miller, Jr., died of syphilis when in his early forties. There were still more tragedies: his grandson, Henry Nickel, died in a snowstorm in Oregon. He was already an alcoholic at the age of 21. Miller's nephew, Albert Long, was crushed to death between freight cars while shipping cattle, and a young foreman died after drinking poisoned water on an isolated ranch.

In the latter part of 1910, suffering from arthritis and rheumatism, Miller paid his last visit to his offices at Bloomfield. He visited with old friends and then drove up to Mount Madonna, where he had chosen the site for his mausoleum, looking down on the Pajaro Valley which he loved on one side and the Santa Clara Valley on the other. He was to be denied his wish to be buried there, however, because Nellie decided he should be cremated.

On October 4, 1916, death came to Henry Miller, the German immigrant born Heinrich Alfred Kreiser, who amassed more land than any other person in the United States. His vast estate was larger than the King Ranch in Texas and twice the size of Belgium. Sitting in his wheelchair in the Menlo Park home of his daughter, Nellie Nickel, he passed away quietly in his sleep.

Appendix

Land Grants and Patents

SAN BENITO COUNTY

RANCH	GRANT	PATENT
LAS AROMITAS Y AGUA CALIENTE (Part in Santa Cruz County) 8,659 acres	JUAN M. ANZAR January 10, 1853	FREDERICK A. MACDOUGALL et al March 17, 1862
AUSAYMAS Y SAN FELIPE (Part in Santa Clara County) 35,504.34 acres	FRANCISCO PACHECO February 24, 1852	FRANCISCO PACHECO April 18, 1859
BOLSA DE SAN FELIPE 6,794.76 acres	FRANCISCO PACHECO 1852, 1867, and 1861 (2 square leagues each)	FRANCISCO PACHECO January 14, 1871
CIENEGA DEL GABILAN (Part in Monterey County) 48,780.72 acres	ANTONIO CHAVEZ October 26, 1843	JESSE D. CARR October 15, 1867
CIENEGA DE LOS PAICINES 8,917.52 acres	ANGEL CASTRO et al October 17, 1854	ANGEL CASTRO et al September 23, 1869
LLANO DEL TEQUESQUITE (Part in Santa Clara County) 16,016.30 acres	JOSE MARIA SANCHEZ March 14, 1854	VICENTA SANCHEZ et al December 29, 1871
LOMERIAS MUERTAS 6,659.91 acres	JOSE A. CASTRO August 16, 1842	VICENTA SANCHEZ et al August 9, 1866
REAL DE AGUILAS 31,052.18 acres	FRANCISCO ARIA and SATURNINO CARRIAGA January 17, 1844	FREDERICK MACDOUGALL et al September 23, 1869
SAN JOAQUIN O ROSA MORADA 7,424.69 acres	CRUZ CERVANTES September 24, 1853	CRUZ CERVANTES January 6, 1874
SAN JUSTO 34,615.65 acres	RAFAEL GONZALES 1835 JOSE CASTRO April 15, 1839	FRANCISCO PACHECO December 6, 1865
SAN LORENZO (TOPO) (Part in Monterey County) 48,285.95 acres	RAFAEL SANCHEZ July 27, 1846	RAFAEL SANCHEZ November 22, 1870

Land Grants and Patents

RANCH	GRANT	PATENT
SANTA ANA Y QUIEN SABE 48,822.60 acres	MANUEL LARIOS and JUAN M. ANZAR April 8, 1839	MANUEL LARIOS et al May 1, 1860
SAN ANTONIO 4,493 acres	MANUEL LARIOS May 4, 1839	MANUEL LARIOS August 8, 1870
LOS VERGELES (Part in Monterey County) 8,759.12 acres	JOAQUIN GOMEZ August 28, 1835	JAMES STOKES April 3, 1875

SANTA CLARA COUNTY

LAS ANIMAS 25,518.68 acres	MARIANO CASTRO By Viceroy 1802 JOSEFA ROMERO Mexico - 1835	HEIRS OF JOSE MARIA SANCHEZ 1873
SAN YSIDRO 13,066.10 acres	YGNACIO ORTEGA Dates vary between 1797 and 1810	QUENTIN ORTEGA et al October 23, 1868 (John Gilroy)
LA POLKA (part of San Ysidro) 4,166.78 acres	YSABEL ORTEGA DE CANTUA 1833	MARTIN J. C. MURPHY 1860
SAN LUIS GONZAGA (Part in Merced County) 48,827.43 acres	JUAN PEREZ PACHECO JOSE MARIA MEJIA 1843	FRANCISCO PACHECO 1871
JURISTAC 4,540.44 acres	ANTONIO and FAUSTINO GERMAN 1835	J. L. SARGENT 1871

Glossary

agua	water
aguaje	water hole
alameda	avenue of trees
alcalde	mayor
arroba	25 pounds
arroyo	creek
ayuntamiento	council of representatives of an area
bolsa	pocket
bota	leather bag used for transporting tallow or wine
brea	tar
buena vista	nice view
caballata	a group of horses led by mare with bell around neck
caballero	gentleman
capilla	chapel
camino	road
carreta	two-wheel cart made entirely of wood
casa	house
casita	little house
chili colorado	red pepper
cienega	marsh or swamp
diseno	map drawn by freehand method
don	title of respect used in front of given name; in California for large landholders
dona	title of respect used with given name of Latin lady
embarcadero	wharf
fandango	a Spanish dance popular in California
fiesta	party or celebration
flaco	thin
gente de razon	civilized person or person with some education
grande	large
gringo	slang term for American
hacienda	estate or farm
jarabe	Spanish dance
jota	Spanish dance

juez	judge
juez de paz	justice of peace
league	2.6 miles
llagas	wounds
llano	flat or plain
manana	tomorrow
matanza	the killing of cattle for hides
manteca	fat for cooking
mas o menos	more or less
mayordomo	manager
monjerio	nunnery
padres	Catholic priests
pealadores	strippers of hides
plaza	square in center of town
pozo	pool
presidio	garrison; military station
primo	cousin
pueblo	town
¿quien sabe?	who knows?
rancherias	Indian villages
ranchero	rancher
real	royal
respuesta	answer; report of mission priest to superior
riata	rope made of horsehair
rodeo	roundup
sala	living room
sombrero	hat
temescal	Indian sweat house made of mud
vaquero	cowboy
vara	unit of measurement, a little over 33 inches
zanja	ditch or trench

Bibliography

PRINTED WORKS

Abbott, Carlisle S., *Recollections of a California Pioneer,* Neale Publishing Co., New York, 1917.

Atherton, F. D., *The California Diary of Faxon D. Atherton - 1836–1839,* ed. Doyce B. Nunis, Jr., Special Publication 29, California Historical Society, San Francisco, 1964.

Arbuckle, Clyde, *Santa Clara County Ranchos,* The Rosicrucian Press, Ltd., San Jose, California, 1968.

Bancroft, H. H., *History of California,* 7 vols., History Co., San Francisco, 1886–1890.

Brewer, Wm. H., *Up and Down California - 1860–1864: The Journal of William H. Brewer,* ed. Francis P. Farquhar, Yale University Press, 1930.

Browne, J. Ross, *Crusoe's Island,* Harpers, New York, 1864.

Bryant, Edwin, *What I Saw in California...Being the Journal of a Tour...Across the Continent of North America...In the Years 1846–1849,* New York, 1849.

The California Missions, A Pictorial History, Lane Book Co., Menlo Park, 1964.

Colton, Walter, *Three Years in California,* Barnes, New York, 1850.

Dana, Richard Henry, Jr., *Two Years Before the Mast, A Personal Narrative of Life at Sea,* New York, 1840, ed. John Haskell Kemble, 2 vols., Ward Ritchie Press, Los Angeles, 1964.

Fink, Augusta, *Monterey, The Presence of the Past,* Chronicle Books, San Francisco, 1972.

Flint, Dr. Thomas, *Diary: California to Maine and Return,* reprinted from the annual publication of the Historical Society of Southern California, Los Angeles, 1923, reprint, *Evening Free Lance,* Hollister, 1926.

Engelhardt, Zephryn, *Mission San Juan Bautista, A School of Church Music,* Mission Santa Barbara, Santa Barbara, 1931.

Gudde, Erwin G., *California Place Names,* University of California Press, 1969.

Guinn, J. M., *History of the State of California and Biographical Record of Coast Counties, California,* Chapman Publishing Co., Chicago, 1904.

Guinn, J. M., *History and Biographical Record of Monterey and San Benito Counties, Volume l,* Historic Record Co., Los Angeles, 1910.

Harte, Bret, *The Story of a Mine and Other Tales,* Houghton-Mifflin, Boston, 1877.

Hawkins, Thomas S., *Some Recollections of a Busy Life,* privately published by author by Paul Elder and Co., San Francisco, 1913.

Hittell, Theodore H., *History of California,* 4 vols., N. J. Stone and Co., San Francisco, 1897.

Historic San Juan Bautista, San Juan Bautista Historical Society, 1967.

Hoover, Mildred Brooke, Hero Eugene Rensch and Ethel Grace Rensch, *Historical Spots in California,* 3rd ed., revised by William Abeloe, Stanford University Press, Stanford, 1966.

Hotchkis, Katharine Bixby, *Story of a Trip from Piedmont to Los Angeles,* privately published.

Jackson, Helen Hunt, *Glimpses of California and the Missions,* Little-Brown, Boston, 1903.

Johnston, Robert B., *Monterey County, A Pictorial History,* Monterey Savings and Loan Association, 1970.

Milliken, Ralph LeRoy, *California Dons,* Valley Publishers, Fresno, 1967.

Mylar, Isaac L., *Early Days at the Mission San Juan Bautista,* Valley Publishers, Fresno, in cooperation with San Juan Bautista Historical Society, 1970.

Older, Mrs. Fremont, *California Missions and Their Romances,* Coward-McCann, New York, 1938.

Outland, Charles, *Stagecoaching On El Camino Real - 1861–1901,* A. H. Clark, Glendale, Ca., 1973.

Rambo, Ralph, *Tiburcio Vasquez,* The Rosicrucian Press Ltd., San Jose, 1968.

Robinson, W. W., *Land in California,* University of California Press, Berkeley and Los Angeles, 1948.

Sawyer, Eugene T., *History of Santa Clara County with Biographic Sketches,* Historic Record Co., Los Angeles.

Smith, Sarah Bixby, *Adobe Days,* Jake Zeitlin, Los Angeles, 1931, currently published by Valley Publishers, Fresno.

Starr, Kevin, *Americans and the California Dream, 1850–1914,* Oxford University Press, New York, 1973.

Sunshine, Fruit and Flowers, San Jose Mercury, 1895.

Taylor, Bayard, *Eldorado or Adventures in the Path of Empire,* G. H. Bohn, London, 1850; G. P. Putnam, New York, 1850, 1864.

Thompson-West, *Historical Atlas of Santa Clara County - 1876,* Smith and McKay, San Jose, 1973.

Tompkins, Walter A., *Santa Barbara's Royal Rancho,* Howell-North, Berkeley, 1960.

Treadwell, Edward F., *Cattle King,* Macmillan Co., New York, 1931, currently published by Valley Publishers, Fresno.

Wood, Dr. William Maxwell, *Wandering Sketches of People and Things...During a Cruise on the U. S. Ships* Levant, Portsmouth *and* Savannah, Philadelphia, 1849.

PERIODICALS

Acheson, Thomas J., "Pony Express Riders Had Their Day—And So Did Bicyclists Back in 1894," *The San Francisco Examiner,* May 3, 1959.

Busch, Niven, "They Rode to the Fair," *California Today,* the Sunday magazine of the *San Jose Mercury-News,* June 21, 1970.

California Cattleman, "Santa Clara County's Livestock History," March, 1966.

The Evening Free Lance, daily, Hollister, California.

The Gilroy Dispatch, daily, Gilroy, California.

Johnston, Robert B., "The Early Days of the Cattle Industry," *California Cattleman,* November 1965.

Rogers, Col. Fred B., "The Battle of Natividad," *The Salinas Californian,* November 15, 1958.

San Benito County Centennial Edition, *Hollister Free Lance,* June 14, 1974.

The San Jose Mercury-News, daily, San Jose, California.

Shumate, Dr. Albert, "Rancho San Luis Gonzaga," *The Pony Express,* October, 1960.

192

193

194

Rodeo on the San Felipe Ranch by Andrew Hill, 1909. The locale of the painting is one mile east and north of Casa de Fruta on property owned by Fenton O'Connell on the Pacheco Pass.